Stop Medicating, Start Parenting

STOP
START

REAL SOLUTIONS for you
"PROBLEM" TEENAGE

MEDICATING, PARENTING

AVID B. STEIN, PH.D.

AYLOR TRADE PUBLISHING

nham • New York • Dallas • Boulder • Toronto • Oxford

Published by Taylor Trade Publishing
An imprint of The Rowman & Littlefield Publishing Group, Inc.
4501 Forbes Boulevard, Suite 200
Lanham, Maryland 20706

Distributed by National Book Network

Library of Congress Cataloging-in-Publication Data

Stein, David B.
    Stop medicating, start parenting : real solutions for your "problem" teenager / David
B. Stein.
       p.   cm.
    Includes index.
    ISBN 1-58979-133-9 (alk. paper)
       1. Behavior therapy for teenagers.   2. Problem youth—Behavior modification.
3. Adolescent psychotherapy—Parent participation.   4. Attention-deficit disorder in
adolescence—Alternative treatment.   5. Adolescent psychopathology.   6. Parenting.
7. Parent and teenager.   I. Title.
RJ506.C65S743   2004
616.89′00835—dc22   2004007011

∞ ™ The paper used in this publication meets the minimum requirements of American
National Standard for Information Sciences—Permanence of Paper for Printed Library
Materials, ANSI/NISO Z39.48-1992. Manufactured in the United States of America.

To my wonderful children
Alex, Kevin, and Heidi
Thank you for being the greatest blessings in my life.

To Professor Ed Smith
Deceased, 2003
Your support and friendship never wavered.
I miss you.

To Professor Steve Baldwin
Deceased, 2001
You traveled across the globe, from England to the United States,
just to meet me and let me know
how important you thought my work was.
I miss you.

Contents

Acknowledgments

Writing is one of the most difficult of things to do. It is a seven-day-a-week job. The birth of a book requires thinking and rethinking, and then rethinking some more. It never goes away, but when one is passionate about what one has to say then the end product is worth it. It is especially worth it when one believes that it adds something productive and worthwhile to humanity. It is worth even more when the future bedrock of our world, our children, benefit.

I could not have done this were it not for some wonderful people in my life. Joyce Trent, who is always there to help, and whose respect means so much to me. Laura Birdsong, whose friendship sustains me when the going gets rough. Becky Anderson, Dr. Baldwin's doctoral student, who has endured much, but who bravely stood her ground to fight the good fight. She has graduated, and is now one of us. I look forward to years of friendship.

The support and friendship of John Rosemond and Dr. DuBose Ravenel has kept me centered. They are two of the most honest and clear thinking people I know. I salute their bravery, morals, and steadfast courage.

Special thanks to Cris Rucci, executive director and partner, for our Child Resource and Information Services center (www.theparentacademy.com). Her support and encouragement are invaluable. Her enthusiasm is contagious.

There are two very special people at the Virginia State Police who deserve a ton of appreciation. I regularly work as a consultant to the state police, and these folks work tirelessly and quietly, behind the scenes, to protect and serve this country. They rarely get the appreciation they so very much deserve. My heartfelt thanks to my supervising officer, Special Agent Jon Perry, and to my partner Special Agent Ken Morris, both with the Virginia Bureau of Criminal Investigations profiling unit.

I could not keep fighting this fight were it not for the love and support of those who mean so much to me: Ruth McGrath, Debbie Wilson, Charlotte Lomax, Lois Rakoff, Ira Rakoff, Seth Rakoff, Ross Rakoff, and Donna Briggs.

Preface

Numerous writers and theologians of the Christian church have traditionally written about the seven deadly sins that they claim deserve eternal punishment: pride, greed, lust, envy, gluttony, anger, and sloth. However, when one is familiar with the New Testament, it is evident that the greatest abomination to Jesus is hypocrisy. His grace was readily extended to thieves and prostitutes, but not to hypocrites:

> Woe to you, teachers of the law and Pharisees, you hypocrites! You are like white-washed tombs, which look beautiful on the outside but on the inside are full of dead men's bones and everything unclean. (Matthew: 23: 27)

I feel deeply that there is yet another sin which should be at the top of the list: stupidity. Stupidity is related to the sin of sloth, because it is the lazy person who fails to search and dig for information. Stupidity involves not thinking for oneself, but instead relying on others. Stupidity involves acting without first learning. Sometimes I will have a student who asks, "What is the difference between knowledge and wisdom?" I reply, "Knowledge is the gathering of information, and wisdom is applying that information in our behaviors and our decisions."

How does this introduction relate to what is in this book? It relates because several sins are simultaneously being committed within the practices of medicine, education, psychology, and psychiatry, and, even worse, with our children being the victims. Greed, sloth, hypocrisy, and stupidity now permeate, and more importantly, attack the practices within these professions. Physicians, psychiatrists, psychologists, and educators are now freely dispensing dangerously unhealthy psychiatric drugs into the developing brains and bodies of our children and teenagers. A handful of charlatan researchers and writers are producing massive amounts of research about mysterious and nonexistent psychiatric diseases and about the safety of psychiatric drugs that any textbook on psychopharmacology clearly states are toxic, that is, poisonous. Are they liars and hypocrites, or merely stupid fools? I can't say which one for certain. But I can say that they are growing rich off their works. Add to this mixture the pharmaceutical company executives, their salesmen, and their lawyers, and sadly, what emerges is one of the most sinful pictures I have ever witnessed in my thirty years of teaching and practicing.

The philosopher Pirsig once said, "If one fools with science, then science will make a fool of him." Ergo, emerge the practices of modern psychiatry and psychology. A handful of pharmaceutical company executives, along with their lawyers and sales force, have hired the guns of unethical scientists to promote their psychiatric products. They have discovered that falsifying research, and camouflaging it with great skill and deceit, and presenting it as science is serving as one of the most powerful advertising tools ever devised. Billions upon billions of dollars are being made. And what bothers me most are the countless hoards of practicing physicians, psychiatrists, psychologists, and educators who are stupidly accepting this bilk as gospel, and, as I said, at the expense of the health of our young. We are supposed to protect our young. It is our most important job in life, and we are not!

Very few professionals seem to be taking the time to examine this research closely. Instead, they accept it mostly on faith. I don't know which concerns me more, the few who lie, the many who rely on the lies within their practices, or those who know what is going on and do nothing.

> The only thing necessary for the triumph of evil is for good men to do nothing.
> (*Letter to William Smith* [January 9, 1795])

I was recently asked, while testifying before a state legislative subcommittee, whether or not I believed that certain childhood psychiatric disorders were diseases and that the drugs are mostly safe. I replied, "It is impossible for me to answer that question, because I can no longer trust any of the research that is massively being produced in psychiatry and psychology. The only thing I know for certain is that I treat children and teenagers without drugs, and mysteriously their supposed diseases disappear by the last session."

I have treated the children of pharmaceutical company executives who pointedly said to me within the sanctity of my office, "There is no way I'm going to put this crap into the body of my child. Can you help me doc?" Most of these executives attend church regularly!

Few psychiatrists, or physicians for that matter, have ever been trained in behavioral treatment methods. They therefore rely on psychiatry drugs to control, subdue, and constrain behaviors of the young. In addition, I've witnessed the decay over the last few decades in the effectiveness of the behavioral techniques practiced by psychologists. I once called one of my former professors, one whose work and ethics I admire. I asked him what the hell was happening within our profession, and why are we going backward instead of forward. He said simply, "They ran out of ideas." He was telling me that they are pressured to publish, and with no new ideas, they'll publish anything. It is because currently popular behavioral methods don't work that there is a heavy reliance on psychiatric drugs.

I ask the parents, psychologists, psychiatrists, educators, and physicians to reflect for a moment. How would you react if you discovered that your teen was smoking pot? You'd go ballistic, wouldn't you? How would you react if you discovered they were taking amphetamines? You'd go ballistic, wouldn't you? But it is amphetamines that most practitioners are relying on to control the behaviors of our young. The only thing we are really doing is switching pushers. We are circumventing the South American drug cartels, and, instead, we are readily buying the wares of the pharmaceutical company cartels, with the physicians and psychiatrists being the modern-day pushers. While the main thrust of the prescription drug movement is the amphetamines, other drugs are also used, just not as much. In this book, you will learn what they are and why you, as a parent, should be concerned.

It is for the sake of our youth that we must do better. And we can. My books are devoted to behavioral/cognitive treatments that work. That is what you, the parent, will find in this book. I am not offering a miracle, because in order for what I present to work, you are going to have to make changes and you are going to have to work hard. If you are willing to do this, then not only will you get the behaviors of your teen under control, you will restore communications, and you will once again have a close, loving relationship.

I offer to any practicing mental health professional my help in using the techniques presented in this book, or any of my books, free of charge.

God bless,
Dr. David B. Stein—Dr. Dave

Struggling with Teenagers Isn't New

Each generation probably sees its teenagers as worse than at any previous time in history. There are countless times in my thirty years as a practicing psychologist and teacher that I've heard parents say something such as, "When I was a kid we showed respect for adults. If we behaved the way kids do today my daddy would take a switch to my backside, and I damn well better have shaped up!"

It may surprise you how far back adults have complained about the behavior of teens. In 500 b.c.e., the government of China banned the use of marijuana, called "ma," by their youth claiming that "they would become wild and disrespectful and would not listen to their elders." In the 1950s concern for teens focused on their wearing black leather motorcycle jackets and being gang members. The idea was to look like Marlon Brando. Perhaps some of you recall the 1950s movies *Blackboard Jungle*, *The Wild Ones*, or *Rebel without a Cause*. The late 1960s and early 1970s saw the emergence of a counterculture where it seemed that every behavior of the young was designed to irritate their parents. For example, historian Patrick Anderson (1981), in his book *High in America*, writes of the popular use of pot during that time, "It was illegal, it produced a nice high, and it drove parents up a wall! Who could ask for more?"

THINGS ARE DIFFERENT

Unfortunately, I do see things as far more problematic for teens today than at any other time in history. Many statistical indicators are scary. There is a 300 percent increase since the 1970s in teen suicides, drug use, and delinquency. We're witnessing teens committing crimes of horror, where they senselessly

1

shoot and kill fellow students. Gangs today are not like in the 1950s when, as Billy Joel says, it was important to look tough; now they *are* tough—frighteningly tough. Now gang members carry guns and indeed they use them. Today gangs use, transport, and sell drugs and they protect their turf with death.

Teachers have become afraid of their own students. Even elementary school teachers tell me that they fear for their safety if they discipline a child or give a failing grade. In many locales a police officer has to be assigned to *every* school.

THE ESCALATING MISBEHAVIORS OF TEENS

Teen disrespect, rudeness, anger, aggression, drug use, and emotional problems are escalating at an alarming pace. Let's explore some of the things *you*, as a parent, may be dealing with.

The Oppositional-Defiant Teen

Some degree of teenage rebellious behavior has always been a parental concern. The teen years are a transition from compliant childhood to independent adulthood; some rebellion in the breaking away process is to be expected. However, the cases I've been seeing in the last fifteen years have been growing worse, with teenagers being outrageously rude, disrespectful, and sometimes even violent. Teenagers that demonstrate excessive patterns of rebellion are diagnosed or labeled by psychologists and psychiatrists as having oppositional defiant disorder (ODD). This term is in the diagnostic manual for psychology and psychiatry, the *Diagnostic and Statistical Manual*, fourth edition or *DSM-IV*, which was published in 1994. ODD cases are now the most frequent referrals for therapists who treat adolescents. Let's take a look at a case example.

Ruth

Ruth was fifteen when I first saw her. Her parents came in for the first interview without her. I initially see the parents and the teen separately in order for them to speak more freely.

Ruth's parents were very upset. They said she had been such a great child, but, during the latter part of her twelfth year, she began changing. Up to then, she had been a good student with grades mostly consisting of Bs and a smattering of As and Cs. The next year her grades dropped to mostly Ds. She began to no longer care about school. She became belligerent and argumentative. If her parents said "No!" to any of her demands she would scream and curse at them. "F——k you!" was not an uncommon sentence. Actually, most of the time when at home, she would not talk. She would either watch television or she would stay in her room isolated from the family while talking to her friends on the phone or listening to heavy rock music. She smoked. She wore heavy makeup. She wore either skintight jeans or very short dresses.

If her parents asked her for help with housework, she would respond with well-mastered hate stares and eye rolls. A sarcastic tone of voice was routine. Her room was a disaster with books, underwear, clothing, and a variety of junk typically lying all over the floor. The bed usually remained unmade. The room reeked from stale cigarettes. Ruth constantly fought with her younger sister and brother.

Ruth's parents reported that she would go out with her friends every day after school and would not come home until after 9:00 p.m. On weekends, she never came in on time for curfew, which was midnight. Sometimes she would get in around 2:00 a.m. They discovered that during the week she was occasionally sneaking out of the house in the middle of the night and not returning home until about 5:00 a.m. I later found out from Ruth that she would meet her boyfriend someplace (I never found out where), and they would have sex. She even told me that sometimes her boyfriend would sneak into her house at night to have sex.

Ruth appeared for the second appointment. She was extremely pretty. It was a difficult session because she was very reluctant to answer questions. Most of the time she kept her eyes on her fingernails and answered my questions with "Yeah!," "No!," or "So!" The little information I could get from her had the general theme that she hated her parents, her sister, her brother, and school. She had no career aspirations and frankly told me that she'd worry about the future when it got here. She also told me that she neither wanted to get married nor to ever have children.

Since the oppositional-defiant teen is the most commonly presented adolescent case (which is probably why most readers picked up this book), years ago I developed very powerful, but nonconfrontational, behavioral techniques for getting cases like Ruth under control, called the REST (real economy system for teens) program. With the REST program Ruth's case was a complete success. Later in the book, in chapter 5, you will learn how to accomplish this, but many of you are dealing with other types of problems with your teens and you, too, want answers.

ADD/ADHD

In the last few years, a new and very frightening trend has emerged, labeling teenagers as diseased with disorders such as attention deficit disorder/attention deficit hyperactive disorder (ADD/ADHD), bipolar disorder, and even autism. There are two reasons for this recent disease trend: first, most psychiatrists and psychologists are clueless about how to behaviorally treat teens, and, second, disease labeling justifies the use of powerful psychiatric drugs. If I weren't concerned about these drugs I wouldn't be writing this book, but as you can see in chapter 3, psychiatric drugs are very risky in the developing bodies and brains of teenagers. Later in this chapter, and in the following chapters, I'll address this issue in more detail.

Right now I want to focus on the most popular disease labels, ADD and ADHD. As you'll soon see, use of this disease label has been growing at a frightening rate. Behavioral treatments for younger children have failed, and, therefore, there has been a heavy reliance on psychiatric drugs. When these drugs fail to control behavior in teens, the diagnoses are changed to such diseases as bipolar disorder or even autism, in order to justify switching to other categories of drugs in the hope of constraining difficult behaviors. For example, children once placed on amphetamine drugs, as treatment for ADD/ADHD, can't stop taking them as teens. When they try, any improvements they may have experienced collapse. Previously, ADD/ADHD was rarely diagnosed for teens. Now there is an escalating trend to continue both the diagnosis and the use of drugs into the teen years. Furthermore, many teens now have to continue the drugs, or change the diagnosis and the drugs, into early adulthood.

The apparent problem is not only possible addiction to the drugs but also being unable to function academically without them. Teenagers who were started on these drugs as children are discovering that they have learned nothing. They haven't learned the requisite educational skills of organization, deep concentration, and memorization. Without the drugs they fall to pieces, and can't do their schoolwork. If you have read my three books on childhood ADD/ADHD, you can't say I didn't warn you. I saw this coming, and I said so. Those parents who used my program for the younger children, called the Caregiver's Skills Program (CSP), don't have to deal with this problem. From the thousands of letters I've received, their kids were able to get off the drugs and therefore don't need them as teens. But, those parents who relied on the drugs now can't get their children off of them. I'm not blaming parents, who were innocently led to believe this wouldn't happen, but sadly it has!

To make matters worse, there is a growing trend to impose this label on any, and almost all, teenagers who aren't performing well at school. The fact that almost all of these so-called ADD/ADHD teens "hate schoolwork" seems to elude the professional community, and instead they're now saying that somehow when they were younger the diagnosis was overlooked. This growing trend must be making the pharmaceutical companies happy, because the market for their drugs is continually expanding.

I hope that the chapters on ADD/ADHD, ODD, bipolar disorder, and autism will open the eyes of parents and professionals alike. When you read what is going on to perpetuate the ADD/ADHD and other diagnoses into the teen years just to justify the use of the drugs, I believe you will be shocked. But the most important thing is that you will learn in this book that there is a real, drug-free solution to the problem.

In chapters 5, 6, and 7, I'll introduce the REST program, which will get your teenager behaving properly at home and performing well in school. The REST program is designed to control difficult teens, no matter what the diagnosis, and is just as effective without the use of drugs as the CSP has proved to be for hundreds of thousands of younger children. As you learn the REST program, I think you'll agree that for the first time you're being instructed in something that makes sense, and, as you use it, you'll quickly see that it really works! It is easy to implement, produces almost immediate results, and works without drugs.

Thomas

Thomas was fifteen when I first saw him and his parents. His parents reported that Thomas was always a difficult child. He was diagnosed as having ADHD at the age of eight. Reports of misbehavior at school were common, which usually included not doing his work, talking to other children and interfering with their work, leaving his seat to walk aimlessly around the classroom, rarely completing assignments, and turning in sloppy work. He was held back in the fifth grade, but continued to perform poorly academically. His parents desperately sought help, but were only advised to implement ineffective behavioral programs, and he was also started on stimulant drugs. Several medications were tried until after being placed on a combination of Desoxyn (methamphetamine) and Mellaril (thioridazine), a powerful antipsychotic tranquilizer, he seemed to calm down in the classroom and at home. His parents stated that while the drugs calmed his behavior, his grades and academic work did not improve.

The drugs seemed to contribute to his losing his spiritedness and humanness. He became lifeless, like a drugged-out zombie. They tried repeatedly to stop the drugs, but each time he seemed to go "crazy." He'd cry constantly, he couldn't sleep, he'd have severe headaches and stomachaches, and he'd pace the floor wringing his hands. These symptoms are common when suddenly stopping psychiatric drugs, and are known as a rebound affect, but Thomas's parents were never told this. After each attempt to stop the drugs the parents would cave in to the doctor's and school's incessant pressure, and would wind up putting him back on the drugs.

At thirteen, he started becoming defiant. When at home, he stayed in his room, refusing to interact with his parents. When he did interact he was defiant and belligerent toward them, often yelling, cursing, and slamming doors. School continued to be a problem. During the week, he stayed with his friends, not returning home until about 11:00 p.m., and on weekends he rarely got home before 2:00 a.m. He wore black clothing and dyed his hair black, appearing as "goth" in the teen subculture. The doctors wanted to put him on other drugs, but the parents refused and continued to maintain him on the Desoxyn and Mellaril.

When I saw Thomas for his first appointment, he answered questions with sarcastic "Yeahs!" and "Nos!" He constantly looked at the ceiling, clearly conveying the message that I was an annoyance to him. After three sessions with no responsiveness, I told him that I would not need to see him for a while and that I would be working only with his parents.

In the following session with his parents, I briefly sketched the REST program and requested that they take a week to discuss with each other whether or not they wished to go forward. They agreed, and the following week, I trained them in a two-hour session but told them to hold off using it until his system was cleared of drugs. I requested that a psychiatrist I often worked with help wean Thomas off the medications. It took four weeks for him to be completely taken off the drugs, and three more months until most of his rebound, or immediate withdrawal symptoms, subsided. In addition, Thomas was unused to feeling, having his emotions blunted by the drugs for so many years. For the first time in many years he was dealing with a host of human emotions. It was a difficult time for both him and his parents.

Finally, after several months, the REST program was begun. The details will be discussed later in chapters 5, 6, 7, and 8. Within a month, his behavior at home started changing. He was no longer permitted to go out during the week. While at home he was permitted to stay in his room only with the door open, in order to do homework. The rest of the time he was required to interact with the family.

Interactions at home improved considerably. After two more months a Weekly Report Card program was added to the REST program in order to get academic problems under control. A special education teacher, at school, taught him study and organizational skills. For the first time in his life he began doing homework in earnest. His grades improved to passing, and he became respectful toward his teachers. All ADD/ADHD symptoms were gone. I began seeing him individually, and this time he was cooperative and friendly. Eventually, he graduated high school and chose to attend a technical college to learn computer repairs. I no longer see him, but at his last session, he reported enjoying his new school.

His parents recently contacted me to let me know he graduated from the technical school and quickly found an excellent paying job. He was still living at home, but his plan was to accumulate enough savings to buy a townhouse and a new car. He seemed to be happy.

Drugs and Alcohol

The third most frequent teen problem involves the use and abuse of drugs and alcohol. The pervasiveness of the drug problem in this country frightens me. Many teenagers tell me how extensive and readily available drugs are. My teen patients report to me that they "get hit on" at least five times a day with coded messages from fellow students such as, "You need?" "You want?" or "Are you low?"

I live in a large city, where drug problems are quite obviously extensive, but I teach and practice in a small rural town fifty miles away. One would think a drug problem would be minimal in a rural town, but it's not. It's equally as bad.

Gregory

Gregory was fifteen when I first saw him. He was living with his single mother in the small town in which I practice. He had two older brothers. The oldest, twenty, had dropped out of school and was living in an apartment, supporting himself by working in a grocery store. The second brother was a year older. The mother reported that he too was a difficult teen, but Gregory was the most difficult of the three.

Her main concern was Gregory's involvement with alcohol and pot, which began when he was twelve. Recently the problem was getting extremely severe. Gregory had been kicked off the football team for failing to show up at practice sessions. He was failing all of his subjects. In fact, he was truant most of the time. Her main concern was that he was staying in bed almost every day. She indicated that he was increasingly losing control of his substance abuse.

Behaviorally, he would go from one extreme of being both isolated and nonresponsive to being angry, belligerent, and verbally abusive. His room was a mess, and he refused to help with any household chores.

Gregory's mother seemed to care about him deeply. She felt guilty about her divorce five years earlier and about her inability to control the boys. I found her to be very depressed and in need of therapy herself, to which she consented. She was overwhelmed with her job, the responsibilities of housework, and the degeneration of the boy's behaviors. She had little social life, only two friends, and very little support from her family.

When I met Gregory for his initial session, he was polite and cooperative. It became clear that he was depressed. He knew he was losing control over his use of pot and alcohol and that his life was taking a nosedive. He wanted to perform better in school, quit smoking pot, not treat his mother so badly, and get back into athletics. Gregory admitted his life was out of control. I judged his concern to be sincere, but his repeated attempts at self-control kept failing miserably.

It later came to my attention through another patient that Gregory had gotten into pushing drugs. He did this to support his habit, a not uncommon avenue for users. I must admit that when I heard this I felt my heart sink. Gregory joined Alcoholics Anonymous (AA), and began individual therapy with me. It took three years, with repeated slips, until he was drug free. He finished high school and then joined the U.S. Army, which is where he is today.

In this book we're going to explore why drug and alcohol use has been escalating. We'll explore alternative ways to prevent your teen from getting into drugs in the first place. But, if they are already involved, we'll explore how to help them.

One of the ironies of psychotherapy is that young people's abuse of drugs is viewed as a diseased addiction and then treated with more drugs. This makes no sense to me whatsoever!

Emotional Pain

Oppositional-defiant teens, ADD/ADHD teens, and drug users typically don't voluntarily come to therapy. Generally they are dragged to the therapist's office by irate parents urgently seeking to get the problems fixed. However, the fourth most frequently presented case is the teen who is in emotional pain and desperately wants the pain to stop. He wants help. Depression and anxiety are fairly common with teens and comprise a significant part of a psychologist's caseload. Let's take a look at a case example.

Shelly

Shelly, age sixteen, had asked her parents to take her to see a therapist. At our first session, she reported feeling depressed most of the time. Generally she got along with her parents. Arguments were rare. Her main concern was her ongoing feeling of emptiness.

While her grades were fairly good, mostly Bs, she indicated that she saw no purpose to her studies. She said her courses had little to do with "the real world." She said she planned to go to college but saw it as a continuation of studying meaningless and empty trivia. Going to college for her meant merely satisfying her parent's expectations. Shelly had no interests or hobbies. Her family attended church, which she hated. Most of her free time was spent watching television.

After several sessions, having gained her trust, she admitted to me that she had become pregnant a year earlier and had an abortion. When I asked how this affected her emotionally, she indicated that having the abortion didn't bother her and that I shouldn't search for any emotional trauma.

Diagnostically Shelly is a dysthymic, which means she has an ongoing, mild state of depression. Shelly represents a number of teenagers who are confused about life. They have no direction, no meaning, no purpose, and little interest in anything. Life to these teens is merely a confusing and painful existence.

I worked vigorously with Shelly and her parents for several months. All three had to make many changes, most of which we will cover in this book, and eventually Shelly did change. It took a long time, but finally Shelly developed a joy and passion for life and a purpose. She announced at one of her last sessions that she wanted to become a psychologist, which is exactly what happened. Shelly is now a practicing, doctoral clinical psychologist.

I want you to notice that Shelly was treated without drugs. Her depression was the result of a meaningless and empty lifestyle. However, there is a growing trend to label depression as a disease; recall, if you will, presidential candidate Al Gore's wife, Tipper, trying to convince the public that her depression was a disease. If Shelly had seen a therapist who saw her as diseased, he would probably have placed her on antidepressant drugs. She would have viewed herself, perhaps for the rest of her life, as having an incurable disease and needing to always stay on drugs, in which case she may never have learned to conquer her life problems in healthy and constructive ways.

Anger and Hate

Teens who are filled with rage compose a fairly significant part of most therapists' caseloads. The level of anger in these teens covers a wide range. Some teens do not overtly express their feelings of anger. They keep them inside and desperately try to contain these powerful feelings. On rare occasions, the rage in one of these youngsters explodes and something terrible happens, such as shooting fellow students. Anger, however, is more commonly and regularly manifested in behaviors such as severe temper tantrums or even in periodic acts of aggression such as hitting other kids or engaging in fistfights. Although I have not personally witnessed a fistfight at the college, the campus police tell me that in the past few years these are becoming more and more common.

Periodically, I receive referrals from the local police for highly aggressive teens, such as Tina, who broke her mother's arm with a hammer; Joanne, who frequently kicked her sister, her mother, her dad, and the walls; or Allen, who hid behind a wall at the bottom of the stairs, and then swung a golf club into his father's face as his father reached the bottom of the steps. Teens who have severe temper tantrums make up a large percentage of my caseload, and of this group, 19 percent are also aggressive. Later in the book we'll cover behavioral techniques for controlling severe temper outburst and aggressive behaviors.

Danny

Danny was a very unusual case. He was seventeen when I received his phone call requesting to be seen. Danny's remarkable intelligence was immediately apparent. His red hair was shaved close to his head, and he sported tattoos of swastikas and skulls and crossbones. He admitted being a member of a white supremacist group, and he desperately wanted help to get out.

Danny had a history of a violent temper. He had dropped out of school, where he had numerous fistfights, a year earlier. He had joined the supremacist group two years earlier, and at first he liked it, but for the last several months he began to view the group as ludicrous. All they did, he stated, was sit around, drink beer, and talk about all "the niggers they were going to kill." He felt himself becoming increasingly disgusted with his comrades. Most of all, he did not like himself anymore. He wanted help to find a better way of life.

His father was an alcoholic who had recently joined AA to overcome his drinking problem. When I saw the father, he reported that for many years when drunk he had frequently beaten Danny. His guilt was enormous, and he very much wanted for Danny to get help. I sensed in Danny a caring, nurturing, and gentle side. He had never hit his younger brother and actually was very protective of him. Some of his fistfights occurred when Danny had come to the aid of a helpless kid being taunted by some of the school bullies.

Oddly, Danny's membership in the hate group was so he could be in an environment where he felt love. I know this sounds somewhat convoluted, but often these groups form a family unit composed of lonely misfits who ban together under the guise of having a common enemy. Hitler recognized the sociology of group cohesiveness and comradeship through targeting a mythological hated enemy. At first Danny enjoyed the supportive environment. But eventually his caring side gained dominance and he wanted out.

I helped Danny get into a teen church group. I worked with him in cultivating a more spiritual meaningfulness within. Over time I began to see a calm settle over him. He began to develop a profound joy in nature and in being out of doors and a passion for fishing.

One week I had been out of town and I bought a small Christian cross lapel pin for Danny. When I gave it to him he said nothing, lowered his head, and cried.

Danny is currently a welder; he's attending a junior college to learn automotive skills, and his dad helped pay to get all the tattoos removed.

THE NORMAL TEEN

Ruth, Thomas, Gregory, Shelly, and Danny are teens who manifested some of the more severe behavioral and emotional problems. These are the teens whom therapists mostly encounter in the course of practice. In reality they only compose a minority of teens throughout the population. No reliable statistics are available that accurately reveal the demographics, that is, percentages, of teens with severe problems compared to the so-called more normal teens. Fortunately, I teach at a college; therefore, I stay in constant communication with teens who do not ordinarily require the services of a therapist.

I find a powerful thread of commonality between the normal teens and the teens with severe problems—*confusion*. Too many teens are confused over their values, beliefs, thoughts, and behaviors. They aren't diseased; they are confused. In my class discussions, in my private advising with students, and with my patients I find a pervasive and overwhelming confusion over many issues. Many of these teenagers indicate their disillusionment with marriage—they see too many divorces. Many don't know if they ever want to have children. They are confused over the recreational use of drugs and alcohol. Issues of sex, sexually transmitted diseases, and abortions perplex many of the young. Choosing a career while still a child is difficult and burdensome for many teens. Many come to school only because their parents expect them to. Sadly, many tell me they hate school and their only joy is their social life. They see their future jobs as entry into a potentially meaningless "rat race" merely to earn money for paying bills. In general, they see life as a void. Today, existential meaningfulness and purpose are absent for too many of our teens.

Medical and Psychiatric Treatment: More about a New and Very Dangerous Trend

As you can see, teen problems can take many different forms and can be quite complex. Parents, out of deep concern, frequently seek "professional" help, but what they often get is anything but professional. Most psychiatrists and psychologists are clueless about how to properly and effectively treat teenagers. It may shock you to learn that many psychiatry residency programs have either no course work in how to perform psychotherapy with children, adults, *or* teens, and if they do have any course work, it is usually in the old Freudian psychoanalytic methods. H. J. Eysenck (1952) long ago proved that these older methods not only do not work, but actually make patients worse. The vast majority of psychology graduate programs have no courses or hands-on training for working with teenagers. Thus, psychiatrists and psychologists are frequently frustrated or completely lost about how to work with complex and difficult teen cases. They literally do not know what to say or what to do with a teenager, and this is especially made worse when the teenager does not want to see a therapist and adopts an uncooperative attitude with the "shrinks."

What do those psychiatrists and psychologists do when faced with teenagers who refuse to talk with them? They resort to drugging them! Constraining and subduing the rebellious and uncooperative behaviors of teenagers is increasingly being viewed as the proper course of treatment. And, to make matters even worse, the shrinks often impose unsubstantiated diagnoses in order to justify the prescribing of powerful psychiatric drugs. When one class of drugs doesn't work, they change the diagnosis and try a different category of drugs. The teen who is labeled as ADHD and continues to be belligerent and perform poorly in school, may be rediagnosed as ODD, and put on powerful tranquilizers. If he still acts defiantly and continues to fail in school the "doctor" may switch and tell the parents that their child has bipolar disorder, and then even more dangerous and risky mood-stabilizing drugs may be prescribed. If after a while that doesn't prove to "shut the damn kid up" and "make him cooperative," he may even be diagnosed as having some form of psychosis, and then even more powerful and more dangerous drugs will be prescribed. Many, many teens are now receiving multiple diagnoses and being placed on several psychiatric drugs, all at the same time, and worse, they are rarely, if ever, taken off of them. With enough drugs in any system, even an elephant will become constrained. The sad part is that this is called treatment, when all it really is is "zombieifcation" (my terminology).

Neither the diagnoses nor the drugs in the overwhelming majority of cases are justified, but it is the only answer poorly trained shrinks have when they are simply clueless about what to do. The teen and the parents wind up the victims when they put their trust in this ill-begotten system.

Angela

Angela is a pretty and petite sixteen-year-old. She is an A student. She is somewhat shy and presents a quiet, reserved demeanor. During the first session she spoke softly, and seemed reluctant to share personal information. Everything was presented as "good." Her parents were "good," her school was "good," her friends were "good," and her life was "good." When I met her parents, I immediately suspected that little was actually "good" in her life, but that because of their excessive domination she was terrified to really speak her mind. It only took me a few minutes to figure out that her very wealthy parents were control freaks, and quite narcissistic. Angela couldn't breathe without their consent. She had to be their perfect little girl.

The town's most eminent psychiatrist and psychologist had treated Angela. She had been diagnosed as having ADD, and bipolar disorder, and was prescribed Adderall, a powerful drug containing a cocktail of four stimulants; Wellbutrin, a powerful antidepressant; and Depokate, a powerful antiseizure drug recently being prescribed as a mood stabilizer for bipolar patients. Neither she nor her parents wanted her to see me. She stated that she very much liked the female psychologist she had been seeing for the last five years. However, her boyfriend had previously been successfully treated by me, read some of my books on treatments without drugs, and had expressed concern to her that she was on too many medications. She had agreed to try seeing me, even though it meant confronting her parents.

I educated Angela about the risks of each of the drugs she was on, especially over so many years, and I expressed concern that she had been seeing a psychologist for so many years without any significant improvements. I asked her if her relationship with the therapist was therapeutic or whether it was too comfortable and only fulfilling some type of dependency need in her. I pointed out to her that if she saw me there would be two major changes made in therapy: first, there would be times when she might not feel comfortable with me because I would probably challenge her in a variety of ways to help her make real improvements, and, second, I felt she would need, under a doctor's supervision, to discontinue some, and perhaps all, of the drugs. She said she'd have to think about what I presented, and that her parents would call if she wanted to come back. Two weeks later her mother called to make another appointment.

I requested a session with the parents. I presented to them the risks of being on the drugs for so many years; they were surprised because the psychiatrist had assured them the drugs were quite safe. I suggested several books for them to read, which over the next several weeks they did. They became angry about the misinformation they had been given.

Angela slowly warmed up and began trusting me. She reported having problems with depression for many years, and she also confided that she was bulimic, an eating disorder.

The doctor I sent her to slowly took her off all the medications, and she gradually learned to overcome her depressions by learning how she made herself depressed and how she and her parents had to learn to relate differently. Both she and her parents increasingly cooperated with me, and made numerous changes. Today Angela is free of all psychiatric drugs and has only occasional bouts of sadness, which she now understands is normal for everyone. Her eating disorder is no longer a problem; instead she uses a sensible diet and exercise to control her weight. She now knows she is neither ADD nor bipolar, and never was.

What a Terrible Thing

What a terrible thing it is to tell a child that she has incurable psychiatric diseases, and that she will have them for the rest of her life, when it is completely false. Think of all the implications such a pronouncement has on a youngster for her entire life. Almost all of her major life decisions will be made believing that she is an incurably sick psychiatric patient. What will happen to her choices about continuing her education, her choices about marriage, her choices about having children, and her overall attitude about herself?

Throughout this book you will learn about the falsehood of the renewed movement to convince parents about the existence and prevalence of childhood and teenage psychiatric diseases, and the increased use of dangerous and powerful psychiatric drugs to handle them. But you will also learn real alternative solutions. You will learn how to parent your child not only to control difficult and sometimes obnoxious behaviors, but you will also learn how to grow close with them in order to teach them important values and give them a healthy shot at productive and glorious lives! You will learn what too many shrinks don't know!

How We Can Really Help

This book deals with the wide variety of problems teens face today. We're going to learn about what underlies these problems, and what concrete steps can be taken to change things. We'll learn not only how to get teen abusive behaviors under control, but more importantly, we'll explore how to change the confusion and purposeless feelings that have become too common in our young. However, it is crucial that you understand that if you desire these changes for your teenager, then you, too, will have to make changes. Hopefully, as you read along you'll like the ideas presented and put them into use for the expressed purpose of developing a closer and more loving relationship between you and your teen.

UNDERSTANDING HOW TEENS FUNCTION

I think it is important to set goals and objectives in order to know where we are heading and what exactly needs to be done to get there. In order to accomplish this in this book we need to look at what makes people in general function and how this applies to teens. When we know how we function then we know what we can change. This will help clarify the direction this book will take.

Cognitions—What We Think and Believe

It has taken psychology two thousand years to rediscover what several ancient philosophers knew; that *what we are is what we think*. This fact was reflected long ago in the writings of Epicurus, Epictetus, Zeno, and Plato. Psychiatrist Aaron Beck (1988) states that psychology and psychiatry are undergoing what he calls "a Cognitive Revolution." Cognition consists of basically two elements, our thoughts and our beliefs. Our cognition determines our behavior and emotional patterns. Psychology is now focusing on cognition in order to understand what underlies how people behave and feel. To change the way we behave and feel we must first alter or restructure our cognitions, our thoughts and beliefs. Faulty or irrational cognitions produce inappropriate behaviors and painful feelings. Rational cognitions produce more positive behaviors and better feelings.

For example, if I believe that I can be happy only if I have lots of money and that to live without money would be terrible and awful, then as a rather poor college professor I will guarantee that I'll indeed be unhappy and have a rather miserable life. But, if I change my belief to "money is not of crucial importance to me," I make enough to live comfortably, and my true riches and rewards lie in my love of teaching and learning, I can justify for myself why I'm a professor and feel more content with my life. Thus, a healthy belief leads to practicing a healthy behavior, that is, teaching, and to a more satisfying feeling of joy in my life.

This whole concept was redeveloped in modern times by three pioneers, Albert Ellis, Aaron Beck, and Norman Vincent Peale (the latter in his book *The Power of Positive Thinking*). Psychotherapy that is aimed at helping people change self-defeating thought patterns and beliefs is called *cognitive restructuring*. When cognitive methods of therapy are combined with behavior modification, the term then used is *cognitive/behavioral therapy*. This is the foundation of what you will be learning in this book. Thus the intent of this book is to learn how to change the defeating thoughts, beliefs, and behaviors of teenagers into healthy ones. This is more difficult to accomplish than labeling a teen as diseased and giving her pills.

If we look at thoughts and beliefs in terms of increasing levels of depth, we see the following profile, where we descend from our surface behaviors to our thoughts just below the surface to our deepest beliefs in the deep recesses of our minds:

Behaviors are what we observe.

Thoughts are at the surface of our minds, and are easily retrievable. If I ask you what you are thinking right now, you can probably readily tell me.

Beliefs begin to go to the next level. You can probably readily tell me some of your beliefs such as what you believe about hard work and earning money. But then there are some beliefs you may not have sorted out or perhaps even been aware you had, such as "What is your overall view of life? Do you see life as fundamentally good or as fundamentally bad?"

Values are deeper beliefs. These go into your beliefs about what you consider right or wrong, morality, what is important in life, and what kind of person you aspire to be. Again, some of your values you can readily recite, while others you can't because you are either confused about them, unaware of them, or have not decided them.

Attitudes are your deepest beliefs. These involve in general how you view yourself, that is, your self-worth, and how you view other people. They are formed in the first few years of life and they form much of the foundation for personality.

How Cognitive/Behavioral Psychology Applies to Teens

Now we can see where we are headed with teens. As I stated earlier, teens are very confused. The teen years are a period of transition. Teens are moving from being compliant children to independent adults. They are going through the battle of sorting out their thoughts, beliefs, values, and attitudes. The fundamental problem is that the normal social-familial mechanisms that traditionally helped teens in this figuring out process have been eroding over the last twenty years. The structure of the family has changed from one where values and beliefs were taught by the traditional extended family of grandma and grandpa, and other family members, to one where single-parent families comprise over 50 percent of all households. Daily routines have changed drastically. Our lives often seem harried and out of control with little time for parents to teach values and beliefs or to help teens sort out their thoughts. What children are exposed to in the media has changed. The media strongly influence teens' values and beliefs, but sadly what they are teaching is often pure trash. We're going to look at all of this in more depth. But my central point is that teens today are very confused about what to think, what to believe, what is right or wrong, what are healthy values, and where to find joy, passion, and meaning in life. It will be the task of this book, or rather the goal, to help you sort out your teen's thinking and beliefs. I will endeavor to help you better communicate with your teen in order to facilitate your teaching them more positive and healthy thought patterns.

If your teen is abusive and out of control, you will learn some very powerful methods to get her under control in order to reestablish a more close and loving relationship. In this way, the doors between you and your child can reopen in order for you to once again reach her and therefore help her restructure her faulty thoughts, beliefs, and values.

It is impossible to affect teen cognition without meaningful communication. It is impossible to communicate if a teen is behaviorally out of control. Therefore, our first task is to gain control over their behaviors. We'll then learn effective communication skills. Finally, we'll learn how to change their cognitions.

Succinctly we have two goals: first, to control teen behaviors, and, second, to restructure their cognitions, or rather their thoughts, beliefs, values, and attitudes. We want them to succeed in life and to feel peace, serenity, and joy most of the time. Our ultimate goal is to reestablish a close, loving relationship, where you, as a parent, can strongly influence the behavioral and emotional development of your teen. In other words, we're going on a thorough exploration of what makes your teenagers tick, and therefore how to improve their behaviors, how to help them change confused cognitions, and how once again to grow closer to them. My hope is that you will learn how to win back your teenager.

I believe that when you finish this book you will have a happier, more focused, and better-behaved teenager. I also believe you, too, will be challenged and find clarification and meaning for your own well-being.

If you accept the false notion that your teen is diseased and only needs pills then you deny her growth. You will deny her mental, emotional, and spiritual growth because there is no way pills can do that. Personal growth requires learning; pills teach nothing.

In the next chapter we'll look at the chicanery that underlies the disease theories, and then, in chapter 3, we'll look at why psychiatric drugs should be viewed with caution and skepticism.

2

ADD/ADHD, ODD, Autism, Bipolar Disorder, and Other Mysterious Teen Diseases

Is your teen a pain in the neck to live with? Have you taken him to a psychologist, perhaps several, only to be told that he has several varieties of disorders? I'll bet many of you reading this have been told that you child has attention deficit disorder/attention deficit hyperactive disorder (ADD/ADHD), along with the "comorbid" disorders of oppositional defiant disorder (ODD), bipolar disorder, perhaps cyclothmia (mild episodes of manic-like behaviors, followed by mild depressive periods), and finally the latest addition, autism. Are you snowed, baffled, and befuddled by all this psychological jargon? Cheer up, your teen is not sick with a host of mysterious diseases. As you read this chapter you'll learn how arbitrary these labels are, and how loosely they are used. Your teen may be moody, irrational at times, difficult to live with, and doing poorly in school, but he's not sick.

Was it suggested that you put him on a drug, or a variety of drugs, to normalize his nervous system? This too is often inaccurate, and unnecessary. As you read this book, you'll learn how to get his behaviors, habits, and more negative moods under control without any need for powerful chemicals.

It is not just you who is confused; so is the professional community. I ask parents and professionals to read with great care to help unravel much of this confusion and hopefully learn new and more accurate ways of looking at teen problems and know how to effectively fix them.

Let's review the current criteria used for making these diagnoses. Then, I'll help you make sense of it all.

THREE CONFUSED DIAGNOSES: ADD/ ADHD, ODD, AND CD

The source for diagnoses in psychology and psychiatry is a manual called the *DSM-IV, Diagnostic and Statistical Manual*, fourth edition. Boxes 2.1, 2.2, and 2.3 list the specific criteria for these three diagnoses: box 2.1 lists the criteria for ADD and ADHD, box 2.2 lists the criteria for ODD, and box 2.3 lists the criteria for conduct disorder (CD). Being listed as a diagnosis does not qualify any disorder as a disease. These are labels, which are assigned as descriptors for clusters of

---

BOX 2.1
DSM-IV ADD/ADHD Criteria

ADD
1. Often fails to give close attention to details or makes careless mistakes in schoolwork, work, or other activities
2. Often has difficulty sustaining attention in tasks or play activities
3. Often does not listen when spoken to directly
4. Often does not follow through on instructions and fails to finish schoolwork, chores, or duties
5. Often has difficulty organizing tasks and activities
6. Often avoids, dislikes, or is reluctant to engage in tasks that require sustained mental effort
7. Often loses things necessary for tasks or activities
8. Is often easily distracted by external stimuli
9. Is often forgetful in daily activities

ADHD-Hyperactivity and Impulsivity
1. Often fidgets with hands or feet or squirms in seat
2. Often leaves seat in classroom
3. Often runs or climbs excessively
4. Often has difficulty playing or in leisure activities quietly
5. Is often 'on the go'
6. Often talks excessively
7. Often blurts out answers
8. Often interrupts or intrudes

BOX 2.2
Oppositional Defiant Disorder

I. Symptoms—a pattern of negative, hostile, and defiant behavior with 4 of the following:
  A. Often loses temper
  B. Often argues with adults
  C. Often actively defies or refuses to comply with adults' requests or rules
  D. Often deliberately annoys people
  E. Often blames others for mistakes or misbehaviors
  F. Is often touchy or easily annoyed by others
  G. Is often angry and resentful
  H. Is often spiteful and vindictive

---

behaviors. The labels are included in the *DSM-IV* after being voted on by a committee of experts. Therefore, diagnosis is nothing more than a label of consensus, made by a committee; it is not considered as a disease.

ADD/ADHD

If you carefully study box 2.1, you'll soon discover that the ADD/ADHD criteria reads as if one was describing a normal, rambunctious six-year-old, which is what numerous authorities have stated (Weiner, 1982). Note, in particular, the criteria for hyperactivity. I was the first writer to point out that this list describes behaviors that occur mostly in school.

In the last twenty years there has been a massive campaign within psychiatry and psychology to prove that ADD and ADHD are diseases. The influx of new computerized medical devices that measure a variety of functions, such as positron-emission tomography (PET scans), to measure metabolism; computerized axial tomography (CT scans) and magnetic resonance imaging (MRIs), serving as sophisticated X-rays to measure anatomy; and single photon emission computed tomography (SPECT scans), to measure blood flow, are being used more and more to study the brain. Researchers, intent on proving that ADD/ADHD are diseases, have produced hundreds of studies making all types of claims about children's brains. Some claim that they've found abnormal anatomy in several

---

BOX 2.3
Conduct Disorder

Aggression to people or animals
1. Often bullies, threatens, or intimidates others
2. Often initiates physical fights
3. Has used a weapon that can cause serious physical harm to others
4. Has been physically cruel to people
5. Has been physically cruel to animals
6. Has stolen while confronting a victim
7. Has forced someone into sexual activity or destruction of property
8. Has deliberately engaged in fire setting with the intention of causing serious damage
9. Has deliberately destroyed property
10. Has broken into someone's else's house, building, or car
11. Often lies
12. Has stolen without confronting victims
13. Often stays out late despite prohibitions
14. Has run away
15. Is often truant from school

---

different parts of the brain, that children's brains' metabolism is below normal, and that a variety of things are wrong with the chemistries of their nervous systems (see table 2.1). Not one single study has produced findings that can regularly be replicated or used for diagnosis at the clinical level. Succinctly, these studies are poor science (DeGrandpre, 1999), and worthless for proving the existence of an underlying disease causing ADD/ADHD. If one single study was definitive, then its technique would readily be used as a diagnostic screening test for your child, but no such test exists. And yet, just about every book advising parents on how to treat these children, with a few exceptions (Breggin, 1998; Stein, 1999; DeGranpre, 1999), opens by making definitive claims that ADD/ADHD are diseases, or biological disorders, or neurobiological disorders, and so forth. No such proof exists. In the last fifteen years hundreds of studies making claims of disease discoveries have yielded nothing definitive and reliable, which lends credence that no such disease exists. Flick (2000) falsely states that the

TABLE 2.1
ADD/ADHD Proposed Disease Studies

Studies	Proposed Disease Etiology
1. Lahat, E., et. al. (1995)	brainstem dysfunction
2. Castellanos, F.X., et. al. (1994)	caudate nucleus dysfunction
3. Giedd, J.M., et. al. (1994)	corpus callosum
4. Levy, F. (1991)	dopamine
5. Greenblatt, J.M., et. al. (1994)	folic acid imbalance
6. Heilman, K.M., et. al. (1991)	frontal lobe
7. Zametkin, A.J., et. al. (1993)	brain metabolism dysfunction
8. Amen, L.E., et. al. (1993)	prefrontal cortex
9. Arnold, L.E., et. al. (1994)	serum lipid
10. Murphy, D. (1997)	serotonin

above-mentioned machines have a 78 percent accuracy rate, but Barkley (1995) and Swanson (1998) then contradict this when they state that these findings cannot be used at the clinical level. If these findings can be made in laboratory research with such a high accuracy rate, then they should be useable in the clinic, but they aren't. In other words these so-called findings are unsubstantiated and worthless, and making such claims is irresponsible and misleading to the public.

Even though no study, out of hundreds, can be pointed to as finding any real disease, it seems that the sheer volume of the number of studies is succeeding at convincing professionals that something must be there. Volume is convincing in the absence of established fact. DuPaul (1998), a disease advocate, stated in a debate with me that "We haven't found it yet, but I believe one day we will." At this time, however, the claims of disease remain unjustified. Thus far, no medical test to detect ADD/ADHD exists.

Research, using MRI, conducted by Deborah Yurgen-Todd (1998) claims that the brain anatomy of *all* teenagers is different from adults, and that teen brain functioning is different from that of adults. One can therefore conclude what we adults have long suspected, that adolescence itself is a disease. Apparently, it must be contagious, because many adults, when in proximity to a teen, seem to also get sick. Perhaps it may be wise to protect society by placing all teens in isolation until they are twenty-one. What do you think?

Also, there is no psychological test for ADD/ADHD! If you've read my other books on the subject you'd already know this, but for parents reading this for the first time, I'll bet this shocks you. Your teen was probably given a battery of psychological tests, followed by a definitive pronouncement that your son or daughter *has* ADD/ADHD. No such test exists. Somewhere, in that so-called battery of tests, was a questionnaire that *you* filled out, and the labeling was based on that report! I'll return to this issue shortly, because I want to point out more shocking inconsistencies you haven't been told.

Look again at the *DSM-IV* criteria for ADD/ADHD in box 2.1, and notice something interesting. The listed criteria, such as not paying attention to details, loosing things, being disorganized, fidgeting, leaving his seat, running about, blurting out answers, and so forth, were developed for young children, below age twelve. They really don't apply to teens. Any teen engaging in such behaviors would daily meet with the wrath of his fellow students.

Notice that the diagnoses of inattentiveness, ADD, is separate from the hyperactive, ADHD, behaviors. I admit that the ADD inattentiveness criteria can apply to teens. Lots of teenagers don't pay attention in class; my college classes are filled with them. But would that mean that all these teens are ADD? Colleen Alexander-Roberts makes an outlandish statement that "thirty-three percent of the general population in the United States may be affected" by ADD! (1995: 8). Do we have a serious disease epidemic, or is it possible that there are lots of teens today who are bored with school and hate difficult schoolwork? Is ADD a disease, or is it a modern-day attitudinal and motivational problem?

Now look very closely at the ADHD criteria. Notice the pattern of behaviors listed: pushes in line, gets out of seat, walks around the room, blurts out answers, and so forth. I've been practicing for almost thirty years, and I hardly ever see a teenager who engages in this type of behavior. Any teen who would act so absurdly would probably be beaten daily by other teens. These criteria apply to young children, and it is a real stretch to attempt applying them to teenagers, but that is exactly what many writers and researchers are doing. In my nearly thirty years of practice, I just don't see teens who fit this description.

In order to compensate for the absence of substantive diagnostic criteria, and in order to force the ADHD label onto teenagers, these same writers and researchers have devised a number of checklists and questionnaires. These new questionnaires include the Diagnostic Interview for Children and Adolescents, the ADHD Behavior Checklist, the Conners-Wells Adolescent Self-Reporting Scale, and many more. Since there are no agreed upon *DSM-IV* criteria that apply to teens, I fail to understand what standards were used to make these checklists valid. While they haven't been validated against any agreed upon criteria they are nevertheless used in making the diagnosis of ADHD in teenagers. Again, I remind you that when a teen is given a battery of tests, the diagnosis of

ADD/ADHD is based on these nonvalidated checklists, and no psychological or medical test exists.

What is the purpose of the other tests in a battery? Several are tests for the level of academic skills in reading, math, spelling, and so forth. Research has shown for years that personality tests are worthless (Mischel, 1977).

What is really going on? As stated earlier, we are now finding that we can't get children off the drugs, and therefore the drugs must continue into adolescence. Is it possible that all these checklists are a mad dash to justify continuing the use of drugs?

ODD and CD

Now, look closely at box 2.2, for ODD, and box 2.3 for CDs. Notice that ODD presents a behavioral profile, such as losing temper, arguing, being defiant, blaming others, and being spiteful and resentful, that is considerably more severe than ADD/ADHD. The hallmark of ODD teens is that they are nasty to adults, especially parents. However, few writers conceptualize ODD as a disease or biologically based disorder. How is that possible? Is it not inconsistent to consider the milder forms of misbehaviors—ADD/ADHD—as diseases, and the more severe form of ODD not as a disease? If you find this mind-boggling, so do I. If you don't get it, neither do I. I ask that my fellow professionals note these inconsistencies.

Consider also CDs. These behavioral patterns, such as bullying, threatening, carrying weapons, physical cruelty to other people and animals, setting fires, stealing, and lying, also are not considered diseases. The hallmark of CDs is law breaking, sometimes in dangerous ways, and yet as a more severe pattern of misbehaviors, they also aren't considered diseases. Notice the inconsistencies in psychiatric diagnoses. The severity pattern escalates from ADD/ADHD to ODD to CDs, and yet only ADD/ADHD are considered diseases. Is this due to the fact that there are drugs to control the milder ADD/ADHD behaviors, but no drugs to control the more severe ODD and CD behaviors? That is exactly what is going on in the psychiatric and pharmaceutical industries!

Reification is a term that means, when something is given a name or a label, it is then perceived as real, even though it isn't. Are we reifying the terms *ADD/ADHD*? Words also have denotative and connotative meanings. Denotative meaning is the exact dictionary meaning. Connotative meaning is the implied meaning. For example, the word *red* denotatively means a color, while connotatively it can mean anger. No proof exists that the terms *ADD/ADHD* mean *disease*, but connotatively it sounds like, or seems to imply, *disease*. Because of this problem, in many of my writings I've suggested that the terms be changed to Inattentive/Highly Misbehaving (IA/HM). Notice that the terms *IA/HM* no longer seem to connote diseases.

As you read the criteria for ODD, I'll bet you'll discover that is why you are reading this book. I'll bet you have a teen who is rude, inconsiderate, verbally abusive, and doesn't lift a finger to help with housework? Am I correct?

The Relationship of the Three Labels

The three labels form patterns of misbehaviors that escalate in severity, with ADD/ADHD being the mildest, ODD next, and CDs being the most severe. Thus, they are merely behavioral labels describing increasing degrees of inattention and obnoxiousness, and not increasing symptoms of diseases.

As I stated previously, ADD/ADHD are labels that represent children who are inattentive and highly misbehaving. If this pattern is not ameliorated by the time these children turn thirteen, then the pattern changes, or switches. The inattentiveness in school may continue, because most of these children still hate schoolwork. But the pattern of misbehaviors changes more toward a profile of oppositionalism, belligerence, and defiance, namely, ODD. This doesn't mean that all children diagnosed as ADD/ADHD at the age of thirteen become ODD, but a significant percentage do. Some researchers classify this change instead as comorbidity, which means coexisting diseases. Flick (2000) rates comorbidity at 67 percent. To me it isn't comorbidity as much as the fact that these teens continue not to pay attention in school, and become more obnoxious at home.

Many ODD teenagers never presented a problematic profile before age thirteen. I've had many parents describe their child as "a model child, who suddenly turned into a nightmare at thirteen." This makes sense, since the influence of the peer group becomes stronger around age thirteen, and along with it comes the defiance. Parents are no longer considered as knowing anything, because the teen's friends say otherwise, and many teens side with their friends. Part of the problem of friends gaining in importance to teens is that many of these other teens do not have parents who have been there for them. Their need for family and comradery is provided increasingly by the peer group. Then the peer group determines their values, dress, and code of behavior. The percentages of children with no previous diagnosis, who at thirteen began manifesting an ODD behavioral pattern, are not available. This may be a result of insurance companies' past refusal to pay for an ODD diagnosis (therefore few in practice made it). Only recently have they begun paying for treatment of ODD, and therefore the frequency of the diagnosis is increasing.

In this book, you'll be learning how to get both ADD/ADHD and ODD teens completely under control. Hairsplitting between the diagnoses isn't important, because what you will learn works in either case. CDs generally don't respond well to any treatment techniques. Sadly, these teens are more hardened, and often wind up in detention centers, where they are made even worse. My work focuses more on teens who are more salvageable and controllable, the ADD/ADHD and ODD teens.

Beware of the term *comorbid*. It is frequently used. Technically, this term means coexisting diagnoses, but often it is used to imply coexisting diseases. For example, many books recommend a *comprehensive battery of psychological tests to diagnose comorbid conditions. Comorbidity* is a term that is very useful in mainstream medicine, to indicate two or more coexisting diseases. However, used with ADD/ADHD, ODD, and CD it is misleading, since none have been established as diseases. This word game often confuses parents when it is used to justify a diagnosis like ADD/ADHD. The parent may hear that "Your teenager has three comorbid conditions, ADHD, ODD, and depression"; since direct evidence is not available, such as a psychological test or an MRI, it is a roundabout and confusing way to snow parents and convince them their child has ADD/ADHD. *Comorbidity* is a loose term that connotatively implies the presence of coexisting diseases and a psychobabble term used to mystify and snow not only parents but the professional community as well. Comorbidity used as a term in real medicine does mean coexisting diseases, but in psychiatry it simply means that a teen has a greater repertoire of misbehaviors. If a teen is diagnosed as ADHD, ODD, and CD, then he has a combination of misbehaviors, which include being highly misbehaving, disrespectful, and breaking the law. He does not have several separate diseases, but rather a broader range of obnoxious and troublesome behaviors.

There are often interesting connections between ADD, ADHD, and ODD. A teen who hates school, and conveys his boredom by impatiently tapping his pencil, wiggling his foot, staring at the ceiling, and frequently looking at the clock, will probably be labeled ADD/ADHD. The teenager who misbehaves at home, talking back to his parents, being sarcastic and disrespectful, cursing at his parents, locking his room door, and blasting hard rock music, will probably be labeled as ODD. If he's rude both at home and at school, then he'll probably be labeled as having the comorbid conditions of ADD/ADHD and ODD. That's all there really is to it. If he doesn't pay attention and is rude *only* at home, he's labeled as ODD. If he doesn't pay attention and is rude *only* at school, he's labeled ADD/ADHD. If he is a pain at home and at school, then he is labeled as having the comorbid conditions of ADD/ADHD and ODD.

What concerns me most is that the term *comorbidity* is being used to justify giving the teen drugs, such as stimulants for ADD/ADHD, antidepressants for depression, and strong tranquilizers for ODD. Be careful of the term *comorbidity*, therefore, because it may be used to snow you into allowing your child to be placed on several dangerous psychiatric drugs.

WHAT IS REALLY BEHIND MANY TEENS BEING LABELED AS ADD/ADHD AND ODD

Chapter 4 presents the familial and societal conditions that are causing so many teens to be labeled with such a wide variety of diagnoses. It's not a prevalence of a wide variety of diseases in their bodies but a disease of society that underlies much of their problems. I'll discuss de facto neglect, where parents are too busy to give adequate time and nurturance to their children. Is it any wonder that teens don't respect their parents? Also, junk media teaches disrespect. Listen to the words in their songs and look at the TV shows timed for them to see after school, when parents aren't home. Years of children being in day care does not help matters. Does day care instill the deep values of loving family, and loving to learn? By the time our youth become teens they are empty inside and have a host of very confused values. It also doesn't help that the extended family is gone. Grandparents were an important source for love and nurturance; now they live many states away. The extended family helped teach strong values, and this too is gone. Is it our sick and decaying social and family structures that are making our teens so nutty, or is it diseases within their bodies and brains, which no one seems to be able to find? You be the judge.

Sadly we are increasingly relying on pills to fix all these social and familial problems! It seems to me that our young are becoming scapegoats. We constrain them with powerful chemicals for problems we adults have created.

What Teens Need

By the time a youngster reaches the teen years, it is essential that she have a strongly cultivated set of values to sustain her both in school and in her personal life. Schoolwork is hard, and it takes a powerful set of goal-oriented values to sustain a youngster through a long academic day. She needs values, such as a love for learning, a love for reading, and respect for authority in order to perform well in school. Too many of our teens don't have these values, and too many are being simplistically labeled as being diseased in order to explain why they are doing poorly and behaving disrespectfully.

The Mentality of ADD/ADHD and ODD Teens

I see ADD/ADHD and ODD as cognitive problems. Cognitions are the thoughts and beliefs that underlie all behaviors. Teens labeled as ADD/ADHD and ODD have a consistent pattern of cognitions.

1. *They don't think.* You may find this difficult to understand, but many of these teenagers spend a considerable amount of time each day simply not actively thinking. When they drive, they rush through traffic without actively assessing the danger they create for themselves and others. They blast their music to shut out thought. In school they attend to the music in their head, instead of on difficult school material. At home they mindlessly watch junk TV, with no thought about helping you as you are breaking your back waiting on them. I remember a therapy session with an attractive fifteen-year-old girl. I asked her if she watched the shuttle take off last night. She replied, "What's that?"

   Somewhere between the ages of eighteen and twenty-one teenagers begin to activate their thinking processes. It is during this time that parents make a transition from protecting their young from the consequences of their behaviors, to allowing the consequences to take effect. It is when consequences become real that teens begin to think, assess, figure out, evaluate, and so forth. As they learn that there can be negative consequences for stupid, irresponsible behaviors, they begin to actively think. As you'll learn in chapter 5, by imposing serious consequences on their inconsiderate and irresponsible behaviors, we can make them start thinking a lot sooner.

2. *They hate schoolwork.* Notice that I didn't say they hate school. Being at school can be fun, because they can "hang" with their friends, which is ever so important to teens. The hardship and drudgery of schoolwork is, to them, a different matter. Too many of our teens hate schoolwork; therefore, they simply tune it out. Other books explain away their ability to outsmart video games, but fail at schoolwork, as a mysterious, selective

disease called ADD/ADHD. The reality is they turn their minds on to those things they like and shut them off to those things they hate, which is usually schoolwork. ADD/ADHD is a cognitive-motivational problem. Does this make more sense to you than the incredibly selective disease theory?

I'm an educator. I love learning. Most of my waking hours are devoted to reading, learning, and teaching. I want our young to love learning, but too many of them don't, and I don't blame them. Later we'll discuss why education is failing to turn on our young to learning. I want to make it clear that it is not the teachers I fault, Lord knows how hard they work; it is the politicians I blame, and later, I'll explain why.

3. *Too many teens are not future focused.* To focus on future goals as potentially rewarding, while forgoing numerous present reinforcers, requires a strong set of values about education, along with a deep belief that with hard work these goals are achievable. Too many teens couldn't care less what happens beyond the next nanosecond, and "hard work" is an alien phrase that has no meaning. School isn't easy, and it requires tremendous self-discipline to succeed. Such discipline requires a strong set of values that have been slowly nurtured, over many years. With parents and family not being there for the young, too many haven't been taught to develop these values.

4. *They don't like reading.* The vast majority of ADD/ADHD teens I've worked with do not like reading. I must admit that I have had a few that did enjoy reading, but they are the exception. There are numerous and complex reasons why many teens do not like reading. Television and video games provide easy diversions, and too few parents put sufficient restrictions on the time spent in front of the screen. Many parents themselves are couch potatoes, and don't demonstrate reading as an important, enjoyable, and highly entertaining substitute for the boob tube. However, the educational system is equally to blame. Summer reading lists are often filled with noble, but elitist books, books that are so difficult to read that young people cannot get immersed into the story content. They are diverted into deciphering the meaning and pronunciation of every other word. I would prefer that books be easy and fun, sufficiently easy so that a youngster can become so absorbed in the story line that he literally cannot put down the book. Reading lists and point systems are equally counterproductive. Young people go through the motions of reading just

to gather points for some prizes, and few read for relaxation and enjoyment. I wish that school personnel would reexamine their reading policies, and make fun and enjoyment a priority over elite classics. If a youngster learns to love reading, he will eventually be ready for and seek out the classics. I ask for patience in the name of helping our young people develop a love for the written word.

5. *They don't respect authority.* Too many young people no longer respect authority figures, and when told to disengage from misbehavior, they won't. They will ignore the teacher or the principal, or they will stop only momentarily, only to reengage in misconduct as soon as the authority is gone. Respect for authority is a value; failure to do so is not a disease, but the result of a weakened value system in modern society.

We don't have an epidemic of diseased teenagers; we have, instead, an epidemic of lost children. We have been failing them, but this does not have to continue. This book is about solutions, and indeed there is much we can do, which is what this book is all about.

Behavioral Treatment Issues

Current popular behavioral treatments for teen ADD/ADHD don't work. Almost all the books on treatment of *childhood* ADD/ADHD state that currently popular behavioral treatments have about a 40 percent efficacy rate (NIH, 1998), which means they don't work. Then these same authors, having admitted these treatments don't work, go on in their books to teach parents how to implement the very same techniques. Behavioral treatments for teens labeled as ADD/ADHD are even less effective, around a 20 percent efficacy rate, and still authors proceed in teaching parents how to do these very same behavioral interventions that admittedly don't work. These authors almost always conclude that if the behavioral methods don't work, then medication will be necessary. Parents are therefore cleverly corralled into only one conclusion: drugs are essential.

Drugs for children subdue and constrain their acting out behaviors with about a 70 percent efficacy rate. Admittedly, they constrain behavior, but my issue is that they aren't healthy and the child learns nothing about self-control or how to study and develop important academic skills, such as deep concentration and memorization. However, *the drug effectiveness rate* for teenagers presents a drastically different picture. The medication efficacy rate for teen ADHD is only about 50 percent and only about 30 percent for ADD (Flick, 2000).

Thus, when it comes to treating teenagers, the diagnostic labels are a muddle, the behavioral interventions don't work, and the medications aren't much help either. I therefore fail to understand the point of the books on treating teen ADD/ADHD that are currently proliferating on the bookstore shelves. Physicist and philosopher Thomas Kuhn (cited in Oliver, 1999) has an interesting point of view about paradigms in science. A *paradigm* is a prevailing or dominant belief in a science. Kuhn points out that a prevailing paradigm is a prevailing opinion accepted by a scientific community, rather than a reference to objective scientific norms. Such is psychology and psychiatry's position on ADD/ADHD. It is the paradigm that these behavioral patterns are diseases, made without substantive proof, and this in turn has led to treatments that not only do not work, but in fact make children and teenagers worse. My work is based on a completely different paradigm, namely, that these young people are not sick, they are not handicapped, they can function, and with the right consequences, they do. And that is what you will be learning, a new parenting/treatment approach that works and produces results without any need for drugs. As you implement this new treatment and see real results, your paradigm will change too.

ENTER A SCARY NEW STRATEGY TO MAKE ADD/ADHD LEGITIMATE DISEASES: ATTEMPTS TO MAKE A CONNECTION TO AUTISM

In the late 1970s and early 1980s Russell Barkley (1981) began a tireless campaign to convince the American public and professional community that ADD/ADHD were diseases. At first he had no support, no evidence for his claim of disease. In 1993, a very poor piece of research was published by research physician Alan Zametkin et al., claiming to have found the magic bullet by using PET scans to identify areas in the frontal part of the brain that appeared to emit unusual metabolic readings in adults who were formerly believed to be ADD or ADHD. This article has been completely discredited in scientific circles (Breggin, 1998). Nevertheless, it was this event that catapulted a number of researchers to begin using the cornucopia of new computerized medical machines to similarly produce volumes of widely diverse claims. Hundreds of studies have appeared suggesting an overwhelming myriad of brain malfunctions, erratic physiologies, imbalances of neurotransmitters, and pathologies of brain anatomies. Not one single study merits credibility, but sadly the sheer volume seems to be winning over misguided and misinformed believers.

In 1998 the National Institute of Health (NIH) held a consensus conference in an attempt to make sense of the overwhelming volume of material. The team of experts, reviewing all the research and all that the researchers had to say, made the following statement in their summation report:

> At this time, we do not have a diagnostic test for ADHD (Biochemical, physiological, anatomical, genetic, etc.). Therefore the validity of the disorder continues to be a problem. (p. 3)

Russell Barkley is representative of the confusion, the contradictions, and the misleading statements and claims that represent the total lack of science that has created the quagmire in which we now find ourselves. Closely examine the following statements made by Dr. Barkley:

> ADD and ADHD are diseases. (*ADHD—What Do We Know?* Video, 1992)

> Children whose problems with attention, over-activity, and lack of inhibition reach a certain level have a developmental disability known as *attention-deficit/hyperactivity disorder*, or ADHD. (Barkley, 1995, vii)

> We now understand that many children with ADHD have an inherited or genetic form of the disorder, that many do not outgrow their problems by adolescence. (Barkley, 1995, viii)

> ADHD children look normal. There is no outward sign that something is physically wrong within their central nervous system or brain.
>
> Yet I believe it is an imperfection in the brain that causes constant motion and other behavior that people find so intolerable in a child who has ADHD. (Barkley, 1995, 17)

> I believe the disorder stems from under activity in an area of the brain.
> (Barkley, 1995, 19)

> *ADHD may simply represent a human trait and not a pathological condition in most cases.* As we just saw, which of us end up with ADHD seems to be determined much more by genetics than by environmental factors. In that sense, ADHD may be viewed as height, weight, intelligence, or reading ability, to name a few traits that are largely (but not wholly) genetically determined: . . . we differ in how much of it we inherit. . . . What is considered "abnormal" for any trait is simply a reflection of where we draw a line on the continuum for a trait, we label them as having a disorder. Such labels not only are based on a somewhat arbitrary measure but also obscure the fact that those with ADHD do fall along a dimension of normal abilities. To put it another way, we all have a degree of this ADHD trait, and those with ADHD simply represent the extreme. (Barkley, 1995, 65, emphasis added).

> This means that ADHD should not be considered some grossly abnormal patholog-ical condition—in fact it is a condition not qualitatively different from normal at all. (Barkley, 1995, 65)

His next statement is crucial for understanding the meaning of all this meander-ing rhetoric:

> As such, the *developmental disorder of self-control* may be the most accurate name for ADHD. (Barkley, 1995, 61, emphasis added)

Note the next piece of rhetoric:

> Misled by research reports that lab measures have found differences between ADHD and non-ADHD children and by the fact that ADHD is a biologically based disorder, many parents ask for medical tests to confirm the diagnosis of ADHD. At present, there are no lab tests or measures that are of value in making a diagnosis of ADHD, so blood work, urinalysis, chromosome studies, EEGs, averaged evoked responses, MRIs, and computed tomography (CT scans) should not be used rou-tinely in the evaluation of ADHD children. (Barkley, 1995, 122)

In this statement, and in a similar statement by Swanson at the 1998 consen-sus conference, Barkley apparently is stating that there are abnormalities that re-searchers can readily find in the recesses of their laboratories but cannot reproduce at the clinical level. In other words the findings are fictitious and worthless.

The *DSM-IV* also states, "There are no laboratory tests that have been estab-lished as diagnostic in the clinical assessment of Attention Deficit/Hyperactivity Disorder" (p. 81).

Apparently, Barkley is shifting away from his improvable disease claims, since hundreds of studies have been unable to validate the existence of any disease. What then is Barkley's purpose in redesignating ADD/ADHD as a "develop-mental disorder?" The answer may be unfolding with the recent publication of the *DSM-IV-TR* (2000). In the *DSM-IV* the defining criteria for ADD/ADHD are introduced with the statement, "six (or more) of the following symptoms of *inattention* . . . is maladaptive and inconsistent with developmental level" (p. 83). However, the latter part of the statement in the *DSM-IV-TR* (2000) now appears in bold type: "is maladaptive and *inconsistent with developmental level.*" This heightened evidence may mean that Barkley is now beginning to maneuver to have ADD/ADHD declared as a developmental disorder, and even as one of the pervasive developmental disorders, in the *DSM-V*. These are disorders related to autism.

The term *disease* has traditionally been undefined in psychology and psychiatry until a recent paper by Stein and Baldwin (2000), but the term *developmental disorder* is completely vague and undefined, but seems to have some head-nodding consensus that it *is something real* within the mental health community. Just vaguely labeling something as a disease or developmental disorder seems to reify, or make real, its existence. Note the term *reification*, which means to regard or treat an abstraction, such as just giving something a name that sounds real, as if it indeed has concrete or real material existence. In psychology and psychiatry this seems to happen time and time again. Since Barkley has not succeeded with reifying ADD/ADHD as a disease, he may succeed by using a backdoor and calling it a *developmental disorder*. Is it only in the mental health literature that one can get away with such ill-defined psychobabble and throw about terms that have no real operational definitions, that is, scientific basis?

A Mother Enters the Autism Arena

A new, recently published book, by Diane M. Kennedy, called *The ADHD Autism Connection*, helps the Barkley campaign and scares the hell out of me. This is a mother who writes a book attempting to make connections between ADHD and *all* the pervasive developmental disorders, which include autism, Asperger's syndrome, and Rett's disorder. Pervasive developmental disorders involve *extremely severe impairment* in social contact with reality, social isolation and withdrawal, aversive response to touching or affection, repetitive behaviors, and arrest of language development, with either speech not being directed toward others or mindless repeating of what others say, called echolalia. Autism, box 2.4, symptoms appear within the first few months after birth; Rett's disorder, box 2.5, appears later, but there is a marked deceleration of the baby's head growth within a few months after birth. Asperger's symptoms, box 2.6, involve marked impairment of the withdrawal behaviors that look like autistic behaviors, but language and cognitive development do not seem to become impaired. Childhood disintegrative disorders begin after age two, box 2.7. These children are withdrawn from reality. How dare these writers suggest that children misbehaving in school and not paying attention in class equate to these very serious disorders. First of all, the pervasive developmental disorders never disappear when watching TV, or playing video games, or when the principal walks into the classroom, as my friend Mike Valentine points out in his book *How to Deal with Discipline Problems in the Schools* (1987). The pervasive development disorders involve children who have lost touch with reality. In what way are ADD/ADHD kids out of touch with reality? They hate schoolwork, and they don't respect authority; they can

---

BOX 2.4
Autistic Disorder

A. A Total of (or more 0 items from (1), (2), and (3), with at least two from (1), AND ONE EACH FROM (2) AND (3).

(1) Qualitative impairment in social interaction, as manifested by at least two of the following:

(A) Marked impairment in the use of multiple nonverbal behaviors such as eye-to-eye gaze, facial expression, body postures, and gestures to regulate social interaction

(B) Failure to develop peer relationships appropriate to developmental level

(C) A lack of spontaneous seeking to share enjoyment, interests, or achievements with other people (e.g., by a lack of showing, bringing, or pointing out objects of interest)

(D) Lack of social or emotional reciprocity

(2) Qualitative impairments in communication as manifested by at least one of the following:

(A) Delay in, or total lack of, the development of spoken language (not accompanied by an attempt to compensate through alternative modes of communication such as gesture or mime)

---

watch TV for hours, play video games for hours, and suddenly become well behaved when the principal walks in the room.

Before I even opened Ms. Kennedy's book, I knew what I'd find. In the last chapters she endorses just about every type of medication of which one can think. She doesn't stop with advocating the stimulant drugs for ADD/ADHD; she goes on to endorse tranquilizers, antidepressants, sleeping medications, and even the antipsychotic drug Risperdal. Diagnosing ADD/ADHD as a form of autism in order to sell all types of drugs appears to be the new game in town. It is a dangerous game that risks the health, well-being, and souls of our children.

THE BIPOLAR SCAM

There is still another scary movement on the horizon, aimed at diagnosing children and teenagers as having bipolar disorder, the new term for manic depres-

(B) In individuals with adequate speech, marked impairment in the ability to initiate or sustain a conversation with others

(C) Stereotyped and repetitive use of language or idiosyncratic language

(D) Lack of varied, spontaneous make-believe play or social imitative play appropriate to developmental level

(3) Restricted, repetitive, and stereotyped patterns of behavior, interests, activities, as manifested by at least one of the following:

(A) Encompassing preoccupation with one or more stereotyped and restricted patterns of interest that is abnormal in either intensity or focus

(B) Apparently inflexible adherence to specific, nonfunctional routines or rituals

(C) Stereotyped and repetitive motor mannerisms (e.g., hand or finger flapping or twisting, or complex whole-body movements)

B. Delays or abnormal functioning in at least one of the following areas, with onset prior to age 3 years: (1) social interaction, (2) language as used in social communication, or (3) symbolic or imaginative play.

C. The disturbance is not better accounted for by Rett's disorder or childhood disintegrative disorder.

sion, box 2.8. Remember the case of Angela, diagnosed bipolar, who I successfully treated after she had been taken off all drugs? Again, there are two basic reasons for this deadly game; one is to push powerful psychiatric drugs, and two is to hide the fact that too many psychiatrists and psychologists are too poorly trained to know how to effectively treat teenagers and children with more sophisticated techniques of psychotherapy. Drugs are the quickest, easiest, and most simplistic way of constraining, subduing, and confining children's and teenagers' out of control behaviors, but they are also the least healthy for the bodies and minds of our young.

The book that scares me the most is authored by Demitri F. Papolos and Janice Papolos: *The Bipolar Child: The Definitive and Reassuring Guide to Childhood's Most Misunderstood Disorder*. I only hope that by mentioning these books, I don't help escalate sales!

BOX 2.5
Rett's Disorder

A. All of the following:
  (1) Apparently normal prenatal and perinatal development
  (2) Apparently normal psychomotor development through the first 5 months after birth
  (3) Normal head circumference at birth
B. Onset of all of the following after the period of normal development:
  (1) Declaration of head growth between ages 5 and 48 months
  (2) Loss of previously acquired purposeful hand skills between ages 5 and 30 months with the subsequent development of stereotyped hand movements (eg., hand-wringing or hand washing)
  (3) Loss of social engagement early in the course (although often social interaction develops later)
  (4) Appearance of poorly coordinated gait or trunk movements
  (5) Severely impaired expressive and receptive language development with severe psychomotor retardation

---

Let me explain in as simple language as I can what must occur in order to make the accurate diagnosis of bipolar disorder. There are two forms of the disorder, bipolar I and bipolar II. It is absolutely essential that in order to diagnose either type a child must have at least one or more episodes of *severe* depression that is not precipitated by stresses, such as loss of a friend, loss of a loved one, school failure, or unaffectionate parents. The episodes must appear spontaneously and must be so severe that the teen or child *cannot* function, with depressive symptoms that include loss of appetite; loss of energy to the point of hardly being able to get out of a chair or bed; withdrawal from friends and family; crying easily and frequently; severe feelings of anxiety; having trouble falling asleep and when he does, waking up several times during the night and again having trouble falling back to sleep; weight loss; strong thoughts of suicide; and severe inability to concentrate, even while watching TV or trying to play a video game. In bipolar I the manic episode(s) is severe, where the youngster cannot sleep for days, has an abundance of boundless energy, makes up wild schemes, and then goes into the depression, and in type II the manic episode(s) are less severe, called hypo-

BOX 2.6
Asperger's Disorder

A. Qualitative impairment in social interaction, as manifested by at least two of the following:

   (1) Marked impairment in the use of multiple nonverbal behaviors such as eye-to-eye gaze, facial expression, body postures, and gestures to regulate social interaction

   (2) Failure to development peer relationships appropriate to developmental level

   (3) A lack of spontaneous seeking to share enjoyment, interests, or achievements with other people (e.g., by a lack of showing, bringing, or pointing out objects of interest to other people)

   (4) Lack of social or emotional reciprocity

B. Restricted repetitive and stereotyped patterns of behavior, interests, and activities, as manifested by at least one of the following:

   (1) Encompassing preoccupation with one or more stereotyped and restricted patterns of interest that is abnormal either in intensity or focus

   (2) Apparently inflexible adherence to specific, nonfunctional routines or rituals

   (3) Stereotyped and repetive motor mannerisms (e.g., hand or finger flapping or twisting, or complex whole-body movements)

   (4) Persistent preoccupation with parts of objects

C. The disturbance causes clinically significant impairment in social, occupational, or other important areas of functioning.

D. There is no clinically significant general delay in language (e.g., single words used by age 2 years, communicative phases used by age 3 years).

E. There is no clinically significant delay in cognitive development or in the development of age-appropriate self-help skills, adaptive behavior (other than in social interaction), and curiosity about the environment in childhood.

F. Criteria are not met for another specific pervasive developmental disorder or schizophrenia

---

BOX 2.7
Childhood Disintegrative Disorder

A. Apparently normal development for at least the first 2 years after birth as manifested by the presence of age-appropriate verbal and nonverbal communication, social relationships, play, and adaptive behavior.

B. Clinically significant loss of previously acquired skills (before age 10 years) in at least two of the following areas:
   (1) Expressive or receptive language
   (2) Social skills or adaptive behavior
   (3) Bowel or bladder control
   (4) Play
   (5) Motor skills

C. Abnormalities of functioning in at least two of the following areas:
   (1) Qualitative impairment in social interaction (e.g., impairment in nonverbal behaviors, failure to develop peer relationships, lack of social or emotional reciprocity)
   (2) Qualitative impairments in communication (e.g., delay or lack of spoken language, inability to initiate or sustain a conversation, stereotyped and repetitive use of language, lack of varied make-believe play)
   (3) Restricted, repetitive, and stereotyped patterns of behavior, interests, and activities, including motor stereotypies and mannerisms

D. The disturbance is not better accounted for by another specific pervasive development disorder or by schizophrenia.

---

mania, that is, less than full manic. But in either case the depression must appear so severe that the youngster appears to be in a prolonged and ongoing state that looks almost as if he were catatonic—in a stupor and unable to move.

Teenagers and children have mood swings. The mood swings of teenagers are related to the normal changes their bodies are undergoing, the stresses of schoolwork, the pitfalls of being popular, and their emerging independence from their parents. It is very dangerous to label these normal behaviors as bipolar, which means that they will then have to live with the label for the rest of their lives, and also be placed on a lifetime regimen of very dangerous and powerful psychiatric drugs.

A second source for the labeling of bipolar disorders has to do with the ADD/ADHD label. Psychologists and psychiatrists, as I have repeatedly stated, have a poor track record of behaviorally treating children called ADD/ADHD, and they therefore rely on stimulant drugs to constrain their unruly behavior. The doctors and parents eventually discover that they can't get their kids off the drugs when they become teens. Often a rebound effect occurs, where the symptoms are exacerbated when attempts are made to stop the drugs, because their bodies have become used to their presence. In addition, their bodies develop a tolerance until, over time, the drugs are useless and the children once again become disruptive, inattentive, and unruly. Once the stimulant drugs no longer work, the shrinks may then switch the diagnosis and tell parents that their child has become bipolar or that the ADD/ADHD had *transmuted* into a bipolar disorder and that a new family of drugs will have to be tried. Drugs, drugs, drugs seems to be all that poorly trained and helpless shrinks know how to do with these children. And, to make matters even worse, Demitri and Janice Papolos are advocating the use of electroconvulsive shock, ECT, involving 70 to 180 volts of electricity shot through the brains of these children. God help us!

I recently informally polled fifteen of my fellow psychologists, all with more than twenty-five years' experience, about how often they might encounter bipolar disorders in adults, teens, and children. They reported an average of five adult cases in their *entire careers*, less than one teen case in their entire career, with most stating that they had never seen a true bipolar teen case, and none in children. I, personally, have seen only four bipolar adults, who fit the precise criteria, in my thirty-year career, and have never seen a bipolar teen or child. I would like to know where the Papoloses have seen all these child bipolar cases? Over the years I have informally asked this same question of psychiatrists with whom I have worked, and their typical answer is that they have seen hundreds of adult, teen, and child bipolar cases. Is this because, unlike psychologists, they have not been adequately trained to treat problems of the mind, that is, psychotherapy, and therefore must declare a diagnosis that seems like a disease of the brain, in order to justify the use of powerful drugs? I've seen numerous cases of children and teens who are highly misbehaving and moody, but who do not fit the distinct criteria to be labeled as bipolar. It is bad enough that we freely label youngsters as ADD or ADHD, but the bipolar label is serious business, and should be made only when a distinct and clear pattern has been established. Instead, the Papolos couple stretches normal child and teen misbehaviors and emotions into declaring something that is quite serious. These children and teens will have to carry that

BOX 2.8
Bipolar Disorder—Single Manic Episode

A. Presence of only one manic episode and no past major depressive episodes
Note: recurrence is defined as either a change in polarity from depression or an interval of at least 2 months without manic symptoms.
B. The manic episode is not better accounted for by schizoaffective disorder and is not superimposed or schizophrenia, schizophreniform disorder, delusional disorder, or psychotic disorder not otherwise specified.

Bipolar Disorder—Most Recent Episode Hypomanic

A. Currently (or most recently) in a hypomanic episode
B. There has previously been at least one manic episode or mixed episode
C. The mood symptoms cause clinically significant distress or impairment in social, occupational, or other important areas of functioning.
D. The mood episodes in criteria a and b are not better accounted for by schizoaffective disorder and are not superimposed on schizophrenia, schizophreniform disorder, delusional disorder, or psychotic disorder not otherwise specified.

Bipolar Disorder—Most Recent Episode Manic

A. Currently (or most recently) in a manic episode.
B. There has previously been at least one major depressive episode, manic episode, or mixed episode.
C. The mood episodes in criteria a and b are not better accounted for by schizoaffective disorder and are not superimposed on schizophrenia, schizophreniform disorder, delusional disorder, or psychotic disorder not otherwise specified.

Bipolar Disorder—Most Recent Episode Mixed

A. Currently (or most recently) in a mixed episode
B. There has previously been at least one major depressive episode, manic episode, or mixed episode
C. The mood episodes in criteria a and b are not better accounted for by schizoaffective disorder and are not superimposed on schizophrenia, schizophreniform disorder, delusional disorder, or psychotic disorder not otherwise specified.

Bipolar Disorder—Most Recent Episode Depressed

A. Currently (or most recently) in a major depressive episode
B. There has previously been at least one manic episode or mixed episode.
C. The mood episoded in criteria a and b are not better accounted for by schizoaffective disorder and are not superimposed on schizophrenia, schizophreniform disorder, delusional disorder, or psychotic disorder not otherwise specified.

Bipolar Disorder—Most Recent Episode Unspecified

A. Criteria, except for duration, are currently (or most recently) met for a manic, a hypomanic, a mixed, or a major depressive episode.
B. There has previously been at least one manic episode or mixed episode.
C. The mood symptoms cause clinically significant distress or impairment in social, occupational, or other important areas of functioning.
D. The mood symptoms in criteria a and b are not better accounted for by schizoaffective disorder and are not superimposed on schizophrenia, schizophreniform disorder, delusional disorder, or psychotic disorder not otherwise specified.
E. The mood symptoms in criteria a and b are not due to the direct physiological effects of a substance (e.g., a drug of abuse, a medication, or other treatment) or a general medical condition (e.g., hyperthyroidism).

mislabel for the rest of their lives, not to mention unnecessarily staying on psychiatric drugs, also for the rest of their lives.

A few months ago, I presented before one of the Virginia State Legislature subcommittee's on the excessive use of psychiatric medications, particularly the stimulant drugs for ADD/ADHD, and on the diverting of these drugs for recreational use by preteens and teens. When I entered the committee room there was an army of pharmaceutical suits, that is, shrinks and lawyers, as well as representatives from several pro drug organizations. The following dialogue took place between a psychiatrist and me:

Psychiatrist: It is extremely important that we identify these children earlier in life in order to start treatment as soon as possible.
Me: How early?
Psychiatrist: At about two or three years of age.
Me: Are you saying that you want to start children on amphetamines at the ages of two or three?
Psychiatrist: Yes! It is very important to recognize the disease as early as possible.
Me: And when do these children come off the drugs?
Psychiatrist: Never! It is a disease that they will always have, and the medication will always be necessary.
Me: So, are you saying that you want to start children on amphetamines at ages two or three and never get them off?
Psychiatrist: Yes.
Me: Are you aware that the diagnostic criteria for ADD/ADHD apply to younger children and are completely inappropriate for teenagers?
Psychiatrist: Yes, but the diseases transmute to different forms, often necessitating the application of other medications. ADD often become ADHD in teens, and ADHD often becomes ODD, or the disorders can also transmute into things like bipolar disorder, or other forms of psychosis.
Me: I'll bet you make the pharmaceutical company executives very happy. Do you believe in legalizing street drugs?
Psychiatrist: No, of course not.
Me: Are amphetamines rampant on the streets?
Psychiatrist: Yes.
Me: Isn't that legalizing amphetamines? Have you read any of my books or my research?
Psychiatrist: No.
Me: What if I was to tell you that these children and teens can be completely treated without medication?
Psychiatrist: That would be impossible.
Me: Would you like to see the thousands of letters I have, the thousands of letters that newspaper columnist John Rosemond has, and the research that says otherwise?

Psychiatrist: No!

Me: So you're not interested in anything other than drugs! What if I told you that it is possible to train school counselors in these behavioral techniques, and that they can, in turn, then train therapists and parents to work with these children without drugs? One therapist training dozens of counselors who can then train hundreds of parents.

Psychiatrist: That would not be cost effective.

Committee State Senator: It sounds very cost effective to me doctor.

Psychiatrist: (Sitting silent and saying nothing.)

Me: Would that hurt your income, pride, or both, doctor? What if I were to train you for free?

Psychiatrist: (No response.)

If your child is labeled as having some type of pervasive developmental disorder, such as autism, and/or bipolar disorder, I ask that you seek out second and third opinions, and to help you I'll give you two ways to find qualified diagnosticians:

1. Contact the Council of the National Register in Health Service Providers, specialty in psychology, in Washington, D.C., phone 703–783–7663, and ask for a referral to a cognitive/behavioral psychologist near you. When you contact the therapist ask his or her views on all of these mysterious diseases and on the use on psychiatric drugs. If he or she successfully treats most cases without drugs then you may have found a more objective doctor to give you a second opinion.
2. Contact my website: www.theparentacademy.com

There are three new diagnostic labels appearing on the psychiatric quagmire horizon.

Auditory Processing Disorder: Auditory processing disorder is not recognized in the *DSM-IV*. It sounds fancy but actually has little or no meaning other than to snow parents and professionals and introduce another way to convince them to put kids on psychiatric drugs. It seems to mean just about the same thing as ADD, which merely means that a child does not pay attention and does not follow instructions. Whatever silliness this may or may not mean, it does not matter, because children have completely improved using my CSP, Caregivers' Skills Program, and the teen REST program presented in this book.

Sensory Integration Disorder: Sensory integration disorder also has no recognition in the *DSM-IV*, and it too seems to be unclear about what it means. I recently had a four-year-old little girl who was referred to me with this diagnosis, even though she was legally blind, deaf, and mute. I wondered what senses she couldn't integrate, touch and smell? Her blindness was corrected with powerful glasses, and she improved greatly with the CSP. The stuff I read about this label appears to be pure psychobabble. It seems to refer to children or teens who are a bit clumsy, that is, not good at sports, and who have poor handwriting, of which most labeled ADD or ADHD are, especially since they hate schoolwork and perform school-related tasks as hastily and quickly as possible. There seems to be a new substitute label for bad handwriting, known as *dysgraphia* or *agraphia*. I have never failed to improve a child's or teen's handwriting, once appropriate consequences were placed on them. I've often told parents, "Now, watch this new, mysterious disease disappear."

Adult Onset of Attention Deficit Disorder: During the last several years a new phenomenon has emerged when I give speeches. Invariably, an adult raises his hand, stands, and says something, such as, "Dr. Stein, I'm a practicing physician (or any profession), and I recently discovered, from a psychologist friend of mine, that I have adult onset ADD. I started taking Adderall, and it has made all the difference in my life. I feel so much better, and my work has improved." I reply, "My goodness, I hope you're not a brain surgeon! How did you ever make it through medical school, you poor thing?" I then proceed to tell him and the audience that I am the proverbial absent-minded professor. Every morning, I have to go back and forth to my car in order to retrieve something I forgot. My secretary has to constantly remind me where I filed things. She tells me that I couldn't survive without her, and she's right. Do I have adult onset ADD? No! Is my schedule too busy and the daily hassles of modern life too excessive? Yes! Can I keep it all in my head? No! That is why God invented PalmPilots! Would taking a drug with four amphetamines in it make me feel better? Yes! Would it make me more awake and alert? Yes! That is exactly why Freud took cocaine during his early career, to make it through his busy day. He renounced this later, when he experienced the adverse effects setting in. I point out that there is no test for ADD, for adults, teens, or children. What these question askers are experiencing is nervousness and anxiety from an out-of-control lifestyle. Drugs make us feel better. I then add, "What would you think if I drank whiskey all day? It's legal, and I don't even need a prescription. What, prey tell, is the difference? You and I would be taking a mind-altering drug just to make it through the day. Is that not addiction? Would we both not be drunks? Perhaps, sir, your diagnosis is not ADD, but instead ADD-I-C-T."

I ask parents and professionals not to get snowed by these new, fancy-sounding labels. Appropriate consequences and not drugs offer the quickest and healthiest solution, which is covered in this book.

In the next chapter I'll explain the types of psychiatric drugs and why they are so powerful and so dangerous. If they were safe, as I stated earlier, I wouldn't have bothered writing this book.

A PARODY ON LABELING

I wish to borrow a parody from the writings of educator and psychologist Mike Valentine (1987). Valentine paints a portrait in words about how out of hand labeling can get. Imagine that the following scene takes place in a traffic courtroom, where our make-believe teacher, Miss Snodgrass, is being cross-examined by the prosecuting attorney:

Prosecutor: Miss Snodgrass, would you please tell the court what the speed limit is on Interstate Highway 95.

Miss Snodgrass: Why, it is seventy miles per hour.

Prosecutor: At what speed were you traveling when Trooper Snooper clocked you?

Miss Snodgrass: Seventy-five miles per hour.

Prosecutor: Are you aware that you are a law-breaker, and therefore a criminal?

Miss Snodgrass: But, I was cruising at exactly the same speed as the rest of traffic.

Prosecutor: Blaming others eh? Blaming others is a common trait among criminals. Have you been driving in this manner for very long?

Miss Snodgrass: I usually drive at the same speed as everyone else. I try to blend in with the traffic patterns.

Prosecutor: So you admit to being a repeat offender! Does that bother you?

Miss Snodgrass: Well, not exactly. I don't feel I'm a repeat offender.

Prosecutor: It doesn't bother you? Therefore you don't have a conscience! Do you realize that makes you a psychopath, or what we now call an antisocial personality disorder?

Miss Snodgrass: (She starts to laugh.)

Prosecutor: Why are you laughing?

Miss Snodgrass: I think you're ludicrous. This is all so ridiculous that I think it's funny.

Prosecutor: So, you think serious things are funny. Do you do that often?

Miss Snodgrass: Yes, it is the way I react to the ludicrous.

Prosecutor: I believe the state-appointed psychiatrist would find your behavior as manicky and delusional. I believe that would qualify you as a bipolar disorder! (Turning toward the psychiatrist.) Do you agree doctor?

Doctor: (Nods.)

Prosecutor: Your honor, I believe that Miss Snodgrass displays all the symptoms of a criminal mind, a psychopath at that, and also of being a bipolar disorder. I think she is a danger and menace to society. I request that she be remanded to a psychiatric facility for further evaluation and treatment.

Judge: The court wishes to address the good psychiatrist, Dr. Nottso Sober. Doctor, what is your opinion?

Dr. Nottso Sober: I do agree that she is manifesting dangerous symptoms of antisocial personality disorder and bipolar disorder. I think it is important to evaluate her, and start her, as soon as possible, on mood-stabilizing medication and electroconvulsive shock treatments.

Judge: Miss Snodgrass, I order that you be remanded to the state hospital for further evaluation and treatment, and may God rest your soul.

(The deputies handcuff and then drag Miss Snodgrass from the courtroom. She starts screaming that everyone in the court is crazy. Everyone in the court looks back and forth at each other nodding sagaciously that, indeed, a proper and wise decision has just been made.)

THIS BOOK

In this book, you will learn a completely different, drug-free parenting approach, called the REST program (Real Economy System for Teens). It gives you powerful tools to control your teen's behavior, both at home and at school. Within a few weeks your teenager will be treating you with respect and courtesy, and will be helping with the many chores at home. Your teen's participation in school will improve dramatically, as will his grades. Whether your teen merits a label, as ADD/ADHD or ODD, doesn't matter, because as you'll soon learn, all misbehaviors and disrespectful conduct will stop, and schoolwork will improve. As you get your teen's behaviors under control, the door will open for a closer, more loving relationship, and deeper communications.

You're also going to learn how teens think and what they believe. You're going to learn how to reach your son or daughter, to influence their sometimes-nutty belief and values systems. You'll be learning how to help your teen develop healthy friendships, while having fun and developing a spiritual meaningful life.

In the next chapter, we'll look at psychiatric drugs, and why I have such deep concerns over their current rampant use.

3

Psychiatric Drugs: What You Need to Know, and What You Aren't Being Told

I have been teaching psychopharmacology for twenty years, and therefore I feel qualified to know a thing or two about psychotropic drugs. I wish to open this chapter by making clear my position about the proper uses and abuses of psychiatric drugs. I am not a fanatic. I rarely see things as either completely black or white. I endeavor to be a realist and see things as they are. I believe that the pharmaceutical companies have done many wondrous things. They have given us medications, such as antibiotics and cardiovascular drugs, which save lives. I believe that they are frantically searching for psychiatric drugs that are both effective and safe. However, the problem is that we aren't there yet. Almost every textbook I've ever used in psychopharmacology states that *all* psychiatric drugs have toxic properties. In some way they are poisonous, and if taken over a long period of time can pose risks for the health of the body and/or the brain. When adults choose to take psychiatric drugs for themselves, I believe that they have a right to do so, but I also believe in full disclosure of all the facts about the drugs to help in that decision. All too often that is not the case. Information for the patient consumer is unclear, or not made available, and therefore the consumer is prevented from making an educated decision about their use. I therefore believe that easy-to-understand full disclosure of all facts about the risks of the drugs should be made available to adult patients, and then the patient can decide if he or she wishes to take those risks.

If an adult is in severe anguish from depression or anxiety, I am not opposed to the brief use of drugs to lessen the pain. However, the choice should be well-informed. If the patient decides to take the drugs, then I suggest they only do so for as short a period of time as possible. Six months to a year is relatively safe. Unfortunately, too many patients never stop taking the drugs, and it is long-term use that can increase the hazards.

The decision that parents make regarding placing their children or teenagers on psychiatric drugs is especially sensitive because research shows that their bodies, brains, and nervous systems are particularly susceptible to the short- and long-term adverse effects. Some of these adverse affects can involve serious health risks, and in some instances even death. In addition, some of the drugs prescribed to young people are highly addicting and can open the door for a lifetime of addiction and abuse problems. Psychology and psychiatry have extremely poor track records for treating abuse and addiction problems, and therefore the very drugs they are recommending can trigger a problem from which there may be no return. As you read this chapter I think you'll begin to understand more about the risks of these drugs and think twice before allowing your youngster to start on them. In order to help you make healthier choices, this book, and my other writings, offer solid and far healthier alternatives.

I take serious exception to the pharmaceutical company executives, the psychiatrists, and the psychologists who have participated in the overwhelming volume of shoddy research to make misstatements and misclaims about the discoveries of the causes of psychiatric disorders in order to get them classified as diseases and to justify the use of psychiatric drugs. This has become even more unethical since two primary targets are children and teenagers, increasingly becoming enormously lucrative markets. Psychologist Lloyd Ross (personal communication, October 4, 2003) has stated, "How do these executives and doctors sleep at night knowing what they are doing to the bodies and brains of our children?"

Another area of concern is the poor behavioral treatment research. It seems that psychologists and psychiatrists participating in this money game are not finding adequate behavioral treatment alternatives and therefore are contributing to the necessity of using the drugs. I believe they could be doing far better work on psychological treatments and markedly decrease the excessive reliance on the drugs, but I think they don't want to because they are growing rich by being financed in a variety of cleverly concealed ways by the pharmaceutical companies. Both treatment and disease research are increasingly moving away from proper science and instead are becoming propaganda-marketing tools that are proving to be highly successful in selling psychiatric drugs. This is especially Machiavellian when the bodies and brains of children and teenagers are targeted and is bringing shame on both the professions of psychiatry and psychology.

I also take exception to the numerous hoards of psychiatrists, psychologists, and physicians who are too readily accepting this unethical research without critical and careful examination of the evidence itself. There are far too many sheep in my profession blindly following the few unsavory wolves. I personally know several major figures who serve on ethics boards, and who know the requirements of proper research, but are turning a blind eye on all this garbage research in order to maintain their lofty positions and not insult their "friends." I am especially offended by the fact that much of this propaganda "research" is aimed at our young, our children and our teenagers. The philosopher Pirsig once warned us, "Do not fool with science, or science will make a fool of you."

THE BRAIN VERSUS THE MIND CONTROVERSY

The brain is the physical organ located between the ears. The mind is something mystical, magical, and wonderful, of which we hardly know anything. Drugs are simple. They affect the brain. All psychiatric drugs, no matter the class or the category, whether they are stimulants, antidepressants, or tranquilizers, have one basic, common property: they allay anxiety feelings, and in turn produce a constraining or subduing effect on behavior. They calm us down. However, we learn nothing from drugs! The mind does not benefit from drugs. Drug companies are desperately trying to convince us, the public and even the professional community, into believing that mind problems or psychiatric problems are disease of the brain, for the sole purpose of selling more and more drugs.

I want to make an interesting point. Psychiatric drugs, no matter the category, *intoxicate* us. In other words, when taking a prescribed dose, we are mildly intoxicated, or *drunk*. That may shock you, but nevertheless it is accurate, and when your child or teen is placed on any psychiatric drug, you, the parent, are helping to keep him in a mild state of drunkenness. The shrinks may balk at this, but it is true. At the lower doses, it is analogous to driving a car just below the legally drunk limit. At higher doses, the impairment may be analogous to driving under the influence, DUI. Many pharmaceutical labels warn about driving while taking these drugs, and they especially warn not to mix them with alcohol, which potentates, or increases, the drugs intoxicating properties.

The *disease–pill* connection is remarkably simplistic. Pills constrain the brain and, in turn, behaviors. But it is the mind, the soul, and the spirit, especially of the young, over which we wish to reign. Winning over the mind is extraordinarily complex. Controlling the brain is a mechanical thing; influencing the mind requires great sophistication. A mechanic can fix the brain, which is what most doctors are. Helping someone's mind requires considerable knowledge, scholarship, learnedness, and wisdom. If a child is placed on pills for several years, and then taken off, the parent soon discovers that his or her youngster has learned nothing. The emotional and behavioral problems that were there at age six or sixteen will still be there at twenty or thirty, because it was only the brain that was tampered with, while the mind learned nothing. If a therapist truly wishes to be "good" at his or her craft, and to truly help children, teenagers, or adults, then that therapist must have spent years studying not only psychology, but philosophy, theology, sociology, history, literature, and numerous other scholarly disciplines. Pills are easy. Real therapy is complex, sophisticated, and difficult. I ask parents to make a choice. What is it that you wish for your teen? Do you wish to merely control his or her brain, or do you wish for him or her to *learn* how to live life? If you want your child constrained, then the pills can do that easily. Or, do you want your child to grow and learn, both emotionally and spiritually? If you answer yes to the latter question, then pills are not your answer.

Pills even interfere with the growth of your youngster's mind. When pills allay anxiety or depression, they reduce the youngster's motivation to learn how to overcome the problems that underlie the anxiety. Life is tough and sometimes produces anxiety or depression. How does a pill teach a youngster to cope with life? School-related learning, studying, and preparing for exams are anxiety-laddened activities. Anxiety is a necessary part of trying to master complex concepts. Once insight occurs and the student conquers a new concept, a delicious feeling of victory results. A natural feeling of calm and self-assuredness follows mastery. Pills rob a youngster of the willingness to fight this battle; they take the edge off motivation, and ultimately off the sense of conquest. Many books about children and teens talk about how important the pills are for helping them with schoolwork and therefore with improving their sense of self-esteem. I will point out how pills actually interfere with mastery of complex concepts, called cognitive toxicity, later in detail. How does it help a youngster when he or she cannot deal with complexities? Real self-esteem comes when mastery over difficult concepts is really achieved. When a child discovers that he can conquer difficult material, he will truly feel good about himself and about his God-given abilities. This is true self-esteem.

In addition, some pills interfere with the ability of the mind to function. Pills can make thinking foggy. They can make it more difficult to problem solve or to develop the insights necessary to deal with life and to self-control behaviors. Some pills can give a misleading and false sense that they enhance learning, particularly the stimulants. Research shows that stimulants produce "cognitive toxicity," enhancing the learning of simple tasks, such as copying letters from the blackboard or adding simple numbers, but interfering with the ability to perform higher-level learning skills, such as interpreting a poem, writing an essay, understanding a piece of literature, or mastering a complex science concept. Mental patients often refuse to take their pills because it interferes with their ability to think clearly. Pills take the edge off our most miraculous, God-given gift, our higher level of intelligence. Did you read the book or see the movie *A Beautiful Mind*?

The core of my work and research is to develop and document alternative behavioral treatments for children and teenagers in order to reduce, or completely eliminate, reliance on psychiatric drugs. Research shows that the bodies and brains of children and teenagers are more at risk for the deleterious effects of psychiatric drugs than adults. What I present in this book as solutions has been researched and documented; however, the work of science is never finished, and I therefore encourage other scientists to research and improve what I present here. I offer my help, free of charge, to any scientist who honestly and honorably endeavors to hone and improve my work. I want the children to benefit. That is my wish.

In this chapter, I hope to educate you in the available facts about the drugs being used on our young. This is information that I believe you, as parents, need to know in making your decision about placing your youngster on these drugs. I hope that the rest of the book gives you sufficient tools for dealing with teenagers so that you won't even need to consider using any of these drugs.

DRUGS DO NOT CORRECT CHEMICAL IMBALANCES

Allow me to immediately dispel one of the most popular myths about psychiatric drugs, that they correct chemical imbalances in the brain and nervous system. The so-called scientists and purveyors of this myth know better. They know that this is an utter lie. Let me explain how they camouflage the real data to snow you with this disinformation.

Until about several years ago we knew about only two dozen chemicals in the nervous system, called neurotransmitters. Therefore, all of our chemical theories involve these few chemicals. In the last few years we have discovered over 125 new chemicals, most of which we haven't a clue about what they do. In addition, the genome project predicts that we should eventually discover over two hundred of these chemicals. Most human behavior appears to involve some type of complex interaction of all of these chemicals, which we haven't even begun to decipher. Therefore our current chemical theories and drug correction theories are incredibly simplistic and inaccurate.

Now I'll show you how our modern-day pseudoscientists perform a slight of hand or illusion on you the public, and even on the professional community. They obtain radioactive samples of a particular neurochemical and inject a small amount into a research subject. They then track the injected chemicals using sophisticated computerized machines, such as an MRI, magnetic resonance imagery, to certain areas of the brain and nervous system, and most particularly to precise areas of the nerves called receptor sites. They then inject radioactive samples of a particular drug, such as an antidepressant, and sure enough the drug goes to the very same brain areas and receptor sites. Voilà, a chemical imbalance is declared corrected! Not quite! The part that these pseudoscientists don't tell you is that we cannot directly measure the amounts of any of the neurotransmitters, because their amount is so slight. However, we can measure their residue, or metabolites in the blood, after they've been used by the nerve cells. When we do this latter step we find that for any given psychiatric disorder and for any given neurotransmitter it turns out that one-third of diagnosed patients have less of any given transmitter, when compared to non-patients; one-third have an equal amount; and one-third have more. Therefore, the chemicals can't be correcting a so-called chemical imbalance because there are no differences in amounts or levels (Barlow and Durand, 2001; Valenstein, 1998).

We can look at this in another way. If a drug constrains a behavior or reduces a feeling, it cannot possibly be interpreted as correcting a chemical imbalance of a particular psychiatric disease. If you or I took a drink of whiskey, which is a tranquilizer, and it reduced our anxiety and certainly altered our behavior, can we then interpret that to mean we have some type of psychiatric anxiety disease? This is called *allopathic logic* by Baldessarini (1985) and *ex-juvantibus reasoning* by Valenstein (1998), and any scientist worth his salt knows this. The misuse of this logic is disinformation and is unethical.

WHY IT BECOMES DIFFICULT TO GET TEENAGERS OFF THE DRUGS

An escalating problem has been unfolding. We are now beginning to find that when children are placed on psychiatric drugs it becomes difficult to get them off as teenagers and young adults. There are several reasons for this.

1. *The Rebound Effect:* Whenever a psychiatric drug is used the body fights back in order to maintain equilibrium, and if you remember your high school biology, this is called homeostasis. The body does this by increasing

its own production of chemicals that have the opposite effect. If tranquilizing drugs are given then the body produces stimulant chemicals. If stimulants are given then the body produces tranquilizing chemicals. If the prescribed drug is suddenly stopped, then the body remains saturated with the opposite chemicals, which then causes an opposite reaction, both emotionally and behaviorally. If a tranquilizing drug is stopped the youngster will become agitated. If a stimulating drug is stopped the youngster will become depressed, a common reaction to trying to come off the stimulants and antidepressants. This phenomenon is called a *rebound effect*. If parents aren't taught about this effect they might buy into the shrink's pitch of, "Now do you see how much better your son did on the medication, and why he needs to stay on it?" The good news is that eventually this rebound will subside. In order to avoid this rebound it is best to have a physician *gradually* take a youngster off any of the drugs.

2. *Medication Dependency:* Medication dependency has nothing to do with drug addiction. This is a belief that the child and the parent develops that he cannot function properly unless he is on the drugs. This is balderdash! I've been successfully treating children and teens for many years without any need for drugs. Do you want your child to develop this medication dependency belief and remain on a psychiatric medication for the rest of his life?

3. *Addiction:* Parents are told that these drugs are not addicting. This, too, is inaccurate. Every textbook I've ever used in my psychopharmacology course states that the stimulants are among the most addicting drugs known. The reason for this is their psychological addicting properties, caused by their calming and energizing effects. The reason parents are told that these drugs are not addicting is because the standard for addiction is often based on physical addiction, but in the psychology of addiction, physical addiction is far less important than psychological addiction. It is the psychological addiction that gets most people hooked on any particular drug. Few alcoholics ever become physically addicted to alcohol, but they all become psychologically addicted to its sedating properties. The gauges for physical addiction are the opiate drugs, such as heroin, morphine, and codeine. Withdrawal from the opiates entails weeks of severe flu-like symptoms. Few classes of drugs produce these flu-like symptoms; that is why patients are told they aren't addicting. Nevertheless, there are powerful but more subtle withdrawal symptoms from almost all psychiatric drugs, which include sleeping problems, feelings of nervousness, vivid dreams, agitated behaviors, gastrointestinal discomfort, and so forth. In

some instances these symptoms can last for weeks or even months. In other words, the person just plain doesn't feel good without his drug and may seek relief by wanting to go back on the drug. Therefore, the drugs literally feed on themselves; they upset the body's natural balance, cause subtle but long-term discomfort, and increase the desire to go back on the drug, and then stay on it. Do you think that this makes the shrinks and pharmaceutical companies happy? Or do you think they cry all the way to the bank?

4. *Tolerance:* Drug tolerance occurs when the body's production of opposite chemicals catches up with the foreign chemical given to the patient. Whenever this occurs the drug's beneficial effects cease and the dosage has to be elevated, or a new, more potent drug tried. Increasing the dosage or placing a child on stronger drugs often increases, as we'll soon see, long-term health risks.

Let's take a look at some of the health risks of the different categories of psychiatric drugs.

THE INSIDE "DOPE" ON PSYCHIATRIC DRUGS

Health is my main concern regarding the use of psychiatric drugs. They are not healthy. No drug, of any type, is healthy, whether it is an antibiotic, aspirin, or cold medication. Taking medicine is always a trade-off of risks and benefits, and it is best to reserve the taking of any medication until it is an absolute must. A good physician is one that is extremely reluctant to prescribe medication, and does so when and if his patient really needs it. Psychiatric drugs are particularly risky. It is best that the patient work with an excellent, well-qualified therapist before starting any psychiatric drug. Earlier I gave you some means for finding truly qualified therapists to help you with your teen.

Let me introduce you to a term I believe you will find extremely important to know about and keep in mind at all times, *iatrogenic illnesses*. These are real health and disease risks that are produced by the drugs themselves. The longer a drug is taken, especially psychiatric drugs, the greater the risk becomes of iatrogenic illnesses, where different systems of the body will actually begin to develop problems or even fail. It is because of iatrogenic illnesses that parents are careful with the foods that they feed their children, or the water they give them to drink, or the preservatives they try to avoid. Parents often go to great lengths to protect the health of their children but then are talked into placing their youngsters on very unhealthy psychiatric drugs.

Drug Types

There are five basic categories for psychiatric drugs. They can be divided even further, but it is not my intention to make you go though an extensive psycho-pharmacology course. The five categories are: *stimulants*; *mood stabilizers*; *anti-psychotic drugs*, also known as the major tranquilizers; *antidepressants*; and *anti-anxiety drugs*, also known as the minor tranquilizers.

Drug Effects, Efficacy Rates, and Risks

Drug effects involve what the drugs are intended to do, while the efficacy rates involve how well they do as is claimed and the risks involve the potential iatrogenic problems that could develop. The longer one is on a drug the higher the possibility of developing iatrogenic problems, and this is especially problematic with young people, because, as I pointed out, there is a powerful campaign to get them on the drugs at younger and younger ages, and then to keep them on the drugs for longer and longer time periods. Iatrogenic risks are called side effects, which include short-term side effects that show up immediately, and long-term side effects that don't show up until years later.

Stimulants

Effects: The stimulant drugs are usually used to treat attention deficit disorders, that is, ADD, attention deficit disorder, and ADHD, attention deficit disorder with hyperactivity, and, more recently, to control ODD, oppositional defiant disorder. *Efficacy:* The stimulants at first control ADD and ADHD at about a 77 percent rate, but the rates rapidly fall. ADD falls close to about 10 percent, since there is an initial rise in academics, which completely evaporates for most children over time. The rate for ADHD falls to about 44 percent. It is important to note that the cognitive/behaviorally based treatment efficacy rates based on my work for ADD and ADHD, called the CSP or Caregiver's Skills Program, exceed 95 percent for children, and the program in this book for teens, the REST program, exceeds 80 percent, and improvements are maintained over long periods of time, with no health risks. If I have cooperative parents, who are willing to put the time and effort in for their child or teen, drugs are not needed at all! The fact that you are reading this book already indicates that you are part of the latter group. *Risks:* The risks for stimulant drugs are numerous. Short-term side effects are documented fully in table 3.1, and include stomach irritability, sleep problems, lethargy, drowsiness, tics, growth suppression, abuse and addiction, cognitive toxicity, and possibly even psychosis, known as amphetamine psychosis, which can occur at higher doses. Little is known about long-term side effects, since few researchers, especially the pharmaceutical company researchers, have any investment in doing long-term research. However, suggestive findings include suppression of the immune system; cardiovascular problems, such as thin heart walls and enlarged heart; and liver problems. Liver problems have been known for a long time, but recently some lawyers have been telling me that there may be suppressed studies, not made public, indicating severe liver problems and even deaths due to liver failure. I am particularly concerned about the growth suppression issue, since these drugs directly reduce the production of growth hormone, which causes the suppression not only of height, but body trunk size, and head and brain size. Parents are reassured that their children will catch up once taken off the drug, but the children aren't being taken off the drugs; common sense dictates to me that we are messing with God's plan for the development of the brain and body during crucial developmental years. The addiction

TABLE 3.1
Side Effects—Stimulants

Symptoms	Ritalin	Amphetamines
Depression	8.7%	Less than 1.0
Irritability	17.3	39.0%
Confusion	3.9	10.3
Mood changes	10.0	25.0
Agitation & Restlessness	6.7	10.0
Tics (dykinesias)	9.0	Less than 1.0
Lethargy & Drowsiness	18.0	11.5
Loss of appetite	26.9	23.1
Loss of weight	13.5	29.5
Nausea	11.6	5.5
Blood pressure increase	15.8	10.0
Cardiac arrhythmia	5.5	Less than 1.0
Angina	4.4	Less than 1.0
Abdominal pains	11.6	5.5
Cognitive Toxicity	40.0	40.0

(Breggin, 1998; Maxmen, E., 1991; PDR, 2001)

and abuse issues are also of deep concern for me, since this class of drugs includes the most psychologically addicting drugs known. Again, the pharmaceutical researchers assure parents that these drugs, at the prescribed doses, are safe. We have no way of knowing which children have an addictive potential, for there are no psychological or medical tests for this. What youngster with an addictive predisposition is going to stay at the prescribed dose? And once a child becomes a teenager, who, pray tell, is going to control them to prevent abuse? Please don't forget what I previously mentioned—cognitive toxicity is around 40 percent.

The Mood Stabilizers

Effects: The mood stabilizers are used to treat bipolar disorders. I pointed out that there is a new and frightening movement to diagnose these disorders in children and adolescents. These drugs have a powerful sedating effect. Often the diagnosis is changed from ADD/ADHD to bipolar disorder in order to justify changing the category of drugs when the stimulants have failed to work. The reality is that bipolar disorders are so rare in children and teens that in over thirty years of practice I have not witnessed one case diagnosed either by myself or any other doctors until only very recently when this new trend started taking place. In addition, I rarely have witnessed the diagnosis of bipolar disorder being made accurately. Most of the time it is made because the psychiatrist or psychologist is clueless about behaviorally treating ordinary teens who tend to be moody. And, it is well known that teen moodiness is part of their normal course of emotional and physical development. Placing them on extremely powerful drugs, and labeling them as bipolar, possibly for the rest of their lives, when it is not merited, enormously scares me. I recommend second and third independent diagnostic opinions before ever allowing your child or teen to be diagnosed as bipolar and placed on this category of drugs. *Efficacy:* The efficacy rates, collectively, for this group of drugs is about 30–60 percent. However, their effectiveness appears to decline over time and fails completely within five years in about 70 percent of the cases (Barlow and Durand, 2001). *Risks:* Short-term risks include foggy thinking, tremors, sleepiness and lethargy, and, for some of the drugs, toxicity that can be life endangering. The doses of the drugs have to be closely monitored because of the toxic risks, and this is especially problematic in teenagers since their bodies' change so rapidly, requiring constant readjustments. Long-term risks include liver problems and even liver failure, and possible damage for higher-level cognitive abilities. *Important Note:* Part of the pattern emerging for the treatment of teens diagnosed as bipolar is electroconvulsive therapy (ECT). Before frying your teen's brain with this form of so-called treatment, I suggest you do a great deal of reading about what it involves and what it does. This new trend is a deadly precedent.

The Antipsychotic Drugs, or Major Tranquilizers

Effects: These drugs are used to control schizophrenic symptoms, but are sometimes also used when a child or teen cannot be controlled for ADHD-type behaviors. Again, I warn parents that the diagnoses of the schizophrenias are often made when the doctors cannot get a child under control. Their aim is to constrain the child's behavior in the name of treatment, and believe me these drugs are so powerful that they will constraining even a *raging bull. Risks:* The risks of these drugs with children, teens, and even adults are so great that it isn't even worth listing. These drugs are too dangerous in the bodies of young people. The greatest risk involves irreversible brain damage, called *tardive dyskenesia,* which shows up, after years of use, in over 60 percent of adults, and much earlier and at a greater rate in teens and children. If you have a doctor that diagnoses your teen as schizophrenic, I suggest you get a second, third, fourth, fifth, and one hundredth opinion before ever considering one of these drugs. *Important Note:* There is a tendency to hospitalize teens when outpatient treatments aren't working. There is a good chance that your child will be placed on one of these drugs should such a recommendation be made. Rarely have I seen hospital-based treatments do any good, and in fact I've seen them make young people much worse. Taking a youngster's freedom away, and subjecting them to harsh treatments, because the doctors are clueless about how to effectively work with them, makes me very angry!

The Antidepressants

Effects: These drugs are used to control depression. I wish to note that this is one area of therapy where highly effective cognitive/behavioral treatments have already been developed, making the use of drugs almost completely unnecessary. The methods for working with depressed teens will be discussed later in this book. Whenever I have seen a depressed teen or child patient, I have found that there is always a real-world reason for it. Once the reason can be correctly identified then cognitive/behaviorally based therapy can be quite effective. Too many shrinks and the pharmaceutical companies would love for us to believe that depression is a disease. It is a reaction to life's pressures. Box 3.1 shows the typical shotgun approach attempting to establish another diagnosis, depression, as a disease. *Efficacy:* Reports on the efficacy of this group of drugs is very confusing.

BOX 3.1
Antidepressants

1. 1950s-MAO inhibitors—increase norepinephrine
   A. Tyramine—toxic levels
      Foods—beer, wine, cheese, chocolate, yogurt, raisins, yeast
   B. Marplan—isocarboxazid
      Parnate—tranylcypromine
2. 1960s-Tricyclic antidepressants
   A. Catecholamines—norepinephrin, dopamine, serotonin, and histamine
   B. Cognitive toxicity
   C. Elavil—amitriptyline
      Tofranil—imipramine
      Sinequan—doxepin
3. 1990s-SSRIs—selective serotonin reuptake inhibitors
   A. Increase serotonin
      Prozac—Flouxetine
      Paxil—Paroxetine
      Effexor—Venlafaxine
      Zoloft—Setraline
      Luvox—Faverin
      Celexa—Citalopram Hyydrobromide
4. Wellbutrin—Bupropion—action unknown, suspect dopamine, serotonin, and/or norepinephrine
5. Buspar—Buspirone—action unkown, suspect serotonin

Some report that these drugs produce little difference than placebos, sugar pills (Breggin and Cohen, 1999), while others indicate about a 50 percent efficacy rate (Barlow and Durand, 2001). The effectiveness of these drugs with younger teens and children may not exist at all (Barlow and Durand, 2001). *Risks:* There are three categories of antidepressants, and some report that the newest groups, related to Prozac, are safer than the older ones. However, it appears that no matter which group is used these drugs can be very risky. Short-term risks may include agitations, sexual dysfunction, sleep problems, dry mouth, blurry vision, and gastrointestinal problems (see table 3.2). The risks of suicide and homicide appear to be quite high. Approximately half of all mass school shooters had been on psychiatric drugs (O'Meara, 2004). The relationship between teen suicides and homicides and certain psychiatric drugs is unclear. In 2003, England banned the prescribing of SSRI antidepressant drugs for anyone under the age of eighteen because of the possible exacerbation of violent behaviors (D. Woodhouse, personal communication from the UK, October 13, 2003), and in America the Food and Drug Administration (FDA) has issued a strong warning. The drugs that appear to be correlated with increased risk are the SSRI antidepressants, selective serotonin reuptake inhibitors (see table 3.2), and the stimulant drugs, which include Ritalin (see box 3.2), a drug with very similar physiological effects to cocaine, and the amphetamines, used to treat ADD, attention deficit disorder, and ADHD, attention deficit hyperactive disorder (Breggin, 2001). The problem seems to occur in those individuals who are in a clinical depression and who develop side effects of akasthisia, agitation, nervousness, and anxiety (Breggin, 2001). Akasthisia involves a strong feeling of restlessness and irritability, and when this is combined with an already existing depressed emotional state and the additional side effects of heightened nervousness and anxiety, and agitation, the ability to maintain rational control over one's behavior may be considerably reduced. Akasthisia occurs about 15–25 percent of the time with the SSRIs and about 6.7–10 percent of the time with the stimulant drugs. In addition, stimulant drugs can cause or exacerbate depression between 1 and 8.7 percent of the time

BOX 3.2
Drugs Used to "Treat" ADD/ADHD

1. Ritalin (methylphenidate)-effects are pharmacologically identical to cocaine
2. Concerta—time release ritalin
3. Focalin—strong version of ritalin
4. Adderall—contains benzadrine (amphetamine) and dexedrine (d-amphetamine) plus 2 more amphetamines—a combination 4 amphetamines
5. Dexedrine and dextrostat—both dexedrine
6. Desoxyn and gradumet—both methamphetamine
7. Atomoxatine—strattera—an old antidepressant

TABLE 3.2
Side Effects SSRI's

Symptoms	Percentage
Headache	20.3
Nervousness	14.9
Insomnia	13.8
Anxiety	9.4
Tremor	7.9
Drowsiness	11.6
Fatigue	4.2
Sedation	1.9
Hypomania & Mania	1.0
Agitation	5.0
Abnormal Dreams	5.0
Akasthisia	15.0–25.0

Digestive Side Effects	Percentages
Nausea	21.1
Diarrhea	12.3
Mouth Dryness	9.5
Anorexia	8.7
Dyspepsia	6.4
Abdominal Pain	3.4
Vomiting	2.4

(Breggin, 2001, 2002; Mosby 2004). If a youngster is placed on a combination of a stimulant drug and an SSRI then there is a potentiation, or multiplier effect, that can be considerable but cannot be precisely determined (Breggin, 2001, 2002; Mosby, 2004). It is therefore important to ascertain whether or not a youngster who demonstrates most of the risk factors mentioned is also demonstrating these side effects. Barlow and Durand (2001) report that sudden deaths with these drugs have occurred, particularly related to athletic competition, and may involve cardiovascular problems. Long-term risks may include feelings of paranoia and anger with increased risks of hurting oneself or others, and possible brain damage (Breggin and Cohen, 1999). Some writers claim that it is easy to stop taking antidepressants, while others claim it is extremely difficult to get off them. I personally have witnessed that it often takes months to get off antidepressants, with patients reporting marked rebound effects, including vivid night-mares, difficulty sleeping, feelings of agitation and nervousness, and increased feelings of depression.

The Antianxiety Drugs, or Minor Tranquilizers

Effects: The antianxiety drugs are used to control nervousness. If a child or teen manifests anxiety then there is *always* a reason, and once the cause is clearly iden-tified, behavioral treatment is relatively easy. As I stated earlier, if I have two cooperative parents, there is little reason that we cannot have success without using drugs. *Efficacy*: The efficacy rate appears to be about 50 to 57 percent, but as tolerance escalates rather quickly, the efficacy rate also declines to about 37 percent. When any of these drugs are used as a sleep aid they seem to readily induce sleep, but also seem to interfere with normal sleep patterns, and in chil-dren and teens this in turn interferes highly with school performance. *Risks*: These drugs produce significant feelings of drowsiness and interfere with cogni-tive abilities, and induce fuzzy and cloudy thinking, which interferes with school-work, and are therefore rarely prescribed for teens. In addition, they exacerbate depression. However, they are prescribed for children and teens in conjunction with the stimulants and/or antidepressants to help with the sleep problems caused by the stimulants themselves. This is exactly what Elvis Presley did, took drugs to wake up and more drugs to go to sleep, and look what happened to his health. The literature seems to be contradictory; there are some claims that these drugs are not addicting, while there are other claims that they are highly addict-ing. Any drug that can help reduce anxiety as well as this group of drugs has to be highly psychologically addicting. Short-term side effects are numerous and include feelings of hostility and rage, lethargy, drowsiness, irritability, impair-ment of cognitive functioning, and possible increase in feelings of depression and suicide. Long-term risks seem to be sparse, but at higher doses there are studies that seem to indicate possible permanent brain impairment.

THE PHARMACEUTICAL COMPANY MONEY FLOW

I want to show you how pharmaceutical company money is tainting the research being passed on to you as gospel. I want you to remember a simple formula: 1:1,000, that is, the ratio of 1 to 1,000. Would you invest one dollar, knowing that within a few years it will yield you a return of one thousand dollars? If it were a fairly safe investment, I'm certain that both you and I would indeed do that. This formula applies to the pharmaceutical companies, but the figures are much larger. They easily and willingly invest millions of dollars, pocket change to them, in order to increase the likelihood of a return of billions of dollars, the 1 to 1,000 ratio, by using the money to insure psychiatric drug sales to children and adolescents. Let's see how they do it.

1. *Money for the American Psychiatric Association:* The American Psychiatric Association receives millions of dollars in direct support to maintain its very existence from the pharmaceutical companies (Breggin, 1991; Valenstein, 1998).

2. *The American Psychological Association:* The psychologist's counterpart APA is the American Psychological Association. It is now on a quest to get psychologists licensed in all fifty states to write prescription for psychiatric drugs. I did some figures just to see how prescription writing would alter the income of the average psychologist. In the area in which I teach and practice the hourly rate for therapy lies between $75.00 and $90.00, but with prescription-writing privileges, and merely doing medication checks with patients, the hourly rate will rise to about $240.00. In addition, the right to write prescriptions will open the doors for hospital admitting privileges, with significant income increases for merely doing hospital rounds and talking to patients the first thing every morning. I was shocked, when in 2001, I saw for the first time an expensive, multipaged ad for Concerta, which is slow-released Ritalin, in the psychologist's newsletter, the *APA Monitor*. The pharmaceutical companies want psychologists to get prescription-writing privileges and will help in every possible way. I hope that by having greater training in psychotherapy methods, psychologists will turn out to be far more restrained about writing prescriptions than psychiatrists, but only time and money will tell. I am afraid, however, that in the future, psychologists will be too quick to add to the problem of drugging children and teens.

3. *CHADD:* One of the most brilliant marketing tools I have ever witnessed is the creation of CHADD, Children and Adults with Attention Deficit Disorders. This is a parenting organization in the schools, second in size to the PTA. Innocent parents are the target for sophisticated propaganda in order for them to become believers that ADD/ADHD are diseases and that the best, and safest, solution, is psychiatric drugs. Parents are so well indoctrinated that they literally become militant against anyone or anything that compromises what they have been brainwashed into believing. Guest

speakers, professional research literature, and in-house literature have all been designed to win them over, and it has succeeded (Breggin, 1990; Breggin, 1998; Valenstein, 1998). I have spoken before a few members of CHADD, and in each instance they seemed to show up ready for the kill, but I succeeded in winning them over once they heard my presentation. They often left angry, discovering that they've been had by the pharmaceutical companies. However, they are now a formidable lobbying group that is pro-disease and pro-drugging of children and teens. What could be a more effective marketing tool than enraged, innocent, and duped parents?

4. *Professional Speakers for Doctors and Parents:* Professional speakers are abundantly available, and highly paid, by pharmaceutical company money in order to convince doctors and parents, at large conventions or small meetings, about the treatment efficacy and safety of psychiatric drugs. Most doctors know very little about the original research literature on drugs and depend on the pharmaceutical company sales representatives, and professional speakers. The speakers made available are the very same ones who make the remarkable discoveries of psychiatric diseases, and who find that cognitive/behavioral therapies don't work unless the drugs are added to the treatment regime. And they are very convincing (Valenstein, 1998). Several physicians have informed me that they are paid $600.00 merely to attend a lavish and expensive dinner and listen to a fifteen-minute presentation on the efficacy and safety of a particular psychiatric drug. However, the doctor must sign a confidentiality agreement, not to divulge the receipt of the check. Even more lavish avenues for propaganda have been established involving all expense-paid vacations to exotic places in exchange for merely listening to a few brief presentations (Breggin, 1998; Valenstein, 1998; and other anonymous sources).

5. *Advertising in Professional Journals:* Professional journals are extremely important within the scientific communities. They are where scientists publish their research findings in order to communicate to the scientific community and to have their research reviewed by their peers. The problem in psychiatric journals appears to involve a past history of financial troubles, only to be rescued by the pharmaceutical companies taking out expensive advertisements. These advertisements have now become a tradition, and appear to not only sell drugs but also to open the journals to readily compromising the articles they permit to be printed. Peer review safeguards have been diminished and undermined by these expensive ads. There have been instances of psychiatric journal editors serving on the boards of pharmaceutical companies (Breggin, 1991). I have witnessed

large volumes of very bad research getting published supporting the efficacy and safety of the drugs, and the existence of nonexistent diseases. De-Grandpre (1999) has called this "junk science," while I have called it "unethical science" (Stein, 2001). Volumes of lousy research are now succeeding at selling drugs, which is compromising psychiatry and psychology to such a degree that I can hardly accept or believe much of what I read in the research literature. This state of affairs both makes me sad and sickens me. How could there be so many willing researchers and writers targeting the bodies and brains of our young in order to make money?

6. *Grant Money:* Researchers need money in the form of grants in order to finance their research, and research is necessary for survival in the academic world. The easiest place to get research money is through the pharmaceutical companies, but the findings better make the executives happy or the money may disappear permanently (Valenstein, 1998). However, I am glad to say that only a couple of dozen researchers have been responsible for the garbage that is being turned out at a production-line rate. Either the lawyers will eventually get them, or God will, and it gives me comfort to be a believer.

I think by now you realize that the science of psychiatry, and rapidly psychology, is not what it appears to be. I hope that you question the disease theories and think twice before allowing a doctor, whether it is your family doctor or a psychiatrist, to place your youngster on a psychiatric drug. I'm one of the few psychologists left who hasn't stopped believing in psychology. I believe that with our collective intelligence we can develop far better cognitive/behavioral treatments and rely less on drugs. That is what this book is all about. I present parenting methods, to be used by parents and therapists, that are based on research not influenced by the pharmaceutical companies and that I believe will prove to you that our youth can be helped without the need to resort to powerful drugs. If you read on, you'll learn how it is done.

In the next chapter we'll look at the real causes of the escalating rate of teen emotional and behavioral problems.

4 | Modern Causes of Widespread Teen Problems

In this chapter we're going to explore the social and familial stresses that underlie why today's teens are so confused. The first task in therapy is to identify what is causing the problem. Once it is clearly identified we can change it, thus suggested solutions will also be covered. If you are a willing parent, then this chapter should help you begin to identify what may be going wrong in your teen's life, what you can change, and therefore what you can do to win back your teen.

STRESSES ON THE FAMILY

Cultivating and nurturing beliefs and values in teens requires a great deal of time, patience, love, closeness, and communication. It requires a stable and calm environment that fosters a meticulous and painstaking molding of a teen's character. Unfortunately, our modern world is anything but calm and stable. Consider the daily routine, or should I say hassles, of the two-parent family or, even more difficult, the single-parent family. Is this your life?

The alarm sounds at six o'clock. You rush to dress, wake up the children, and help them get dressed. Everyone rushes to eat breakfast. To get to work you probably have to leave before your teen. Little conversation has occurred, then your teen is left alone to lock the house and meet the school bus.

After three o'clock your teen returns to an empty house. Typically, she'll watch TV or visit with friends. You return at six. The house is a disaster from the morning. A frantic rush is made to prepare dinner, which is then usually eaten while everyone watches TV. Following dinner is kitchen cleanup, homework, and an attempt to straighten the house. Finally, it's bath time and then bedtime.

Weekends can be equally stressful; they include housecleaning, laundry, grocery shopping, and so forth. Does all this sound familiar?

Loss of Communication

This type of schedule is stressful to all family members. There is little or no time for you and your teen to talk. Without adequate time for communication, there is little chance to influence your teen's values and beliefs.

Tension

There are additional problems with this type of stressful schedule. Tensions run high when everyone is rushed. Tempers flare, and often, angry verbal exchanges occur. This is the breeding ground for frayed nerves and tension between parents and teen. If a teenager is nervous and feels distanced from his parents he will perhaps search for relief in all the wrong places and with all the wrong people. Thomas Moore, in *Care of the Soul* (1992), calls this harried lifestyle and neglect of children the "modernist syndrome."

Neglect of the Soul

Abraham Maslow taught that being loved is a need, which is something necessary for survival. Where, in this schedule, is there time for closeness, love, and, as Thomas Moore points out, care of the soul?

De jure neglect involves not providing food, clothing, and shelter for a child. This can be handled by the judicial or legal system. However, *de facto neglect* is the nonfulfillment of emotional needs, which involves the absence of love, tenderness, and nurturing that all children so desperately require. De facto neglect is usually unintended. It happens when our busy schedules whirlwind our lives out of control. Often parents are not even aware of how little time is available for their teenagers.

Terrible things can happen to the soul of a neglected youngster. In my research I have found that extensive de facto neglect is almost always a major part of the background of teenagers who have serious behavioral and emotional problems, such as loneliness, dejection, and ongoing depression. This emptiness in a teen's soul often results in a search to fill the void in any way he can, such as with drugs, to soothe the pain; affiliation with the wrong peer group just to be loved; having sex just to be close to someone; and venting anger by committing delinquent acts.

Quality time is not a sufficient solution. The reality is that for many families there isn't even much quality time. Teenagers need much more than mere quality time: they need lots of our time. Teens often feign independence by no longer allowing you to hug or kiss them in public. This is only bravado; they still want and need expressions of affection. My teen sons no longer permit me to walk in public with my arm around their shoulders. This is merely a superficial display of independence. In private, they still like to sit near me while reading or watching TV.

Parents often say to me that their teen doesn't want to be with them, and all she seems to want is to be with her friends. Yes, peer relationships are important to teens, and they do prefer to spend most of their free time with their friends. However, do not underestimate a teen's need to know that you love him. He still needs time with you every day. He needs to talk to you. He needs to feel important to you. He needs to know you are always there for him.

These things can be accomplished. There are a number of potential solutions.

SOLUTIONS FOR THE HECTIC LIFESTYLE

I'm going to offer you ten potential solutions to having more time for your teens. Some of these solutions are relatively easy to implement and some are quite difficult. You can choose those that are practical for you and that you think can possibly fit into your lifestyle. Don't feel pressured to adopt these solutions, but at least give each of the strategies some serious deliberation. However, if your teen is already manifesting serious behavioral and emotional problems, such as marked depression or drug dependence, you may have to seriously consider adopting some of the more drastic solutions.

THE TEN STRATEGIES FOR MORE TIME WITH YOUR TEEN

1. Get everyone up early enough in the morning to have breakfast together. Make it happen. Make it a routine that will continue until your teen leaves home. Talk about the news, the weather, about your teen's day, about something you read or learned, or simply joke and start the day on a light chord. Whatever you do, do not sit there like silent robots saying nothing. Just light conversation will do nicely. This is a pleasant way to start the day, and it is less stressful on the digestive system.

2. When talking to her, do not lecture. The worst thing you could do is use any time you have with your teen for getting on your podium to teach and preach. Nothing turns a teen off more. Listen, ask, inquire, share, laugh,

have fun, and enjoy each other, even if it is only during a twenty-minute breakfast in the morning. Just start the day by connecting. A close relationship with your teen will give you more influence with her than your lecturing.

3. Have dinner together each evening *at the table*. Shut off the TV. Most families eat dinner while watching television. Sit and talk with each other. Be interested in what your teen has to say. Teens usually love to talk. They want to share. Ask him about his day, how his friends are doing, or how his girlfriend is doing. The dinner table is a good place to facilitate this conversation.

4. Have him help with dinner preparation and cleanup. I know your reaction is, "fat chance." I promise that later in the book I will teach you how to make this occur. However, he may surprise you. If you teach him how to cook, he might enjoy your positive reactions to his preparations. Mild conversation during preparation and cleanup can be enjoyable for both of you. Look at the values being automatically transmitted during this time, such as sharing, creating something for other family members, responsibility, closeness, enjoying conversation, the importance of cleaning up and neatness, a positive work ethic, and love.

5. Two of my dear friends in Vermont, Pete and Shirley, taught me a valuable lesson with their children. All three of their children are now highly successful and wonderful adults. Every night Pete and Shirley would spend ten or more minutes talking with each of their children at bedtime. They did this even when there were houseguests. They sat by the side of their teen's bed and just talked casually about anything. If you adopt this, remember don't lecture. Listen to her—that can be the best skill you ever develop. Be interested in what she has to say, and, when appropriate, ask if she would like any suggestions. Most of the time it is best to keep these quiet bedtime talks light. The main goal is not to impart facts but to cultivate a close relationship. I have suggested this to many parents, and they have reported considerable success in improving their relationship with their teen. My boys are now sixteen and eighteen. Every night at bedtime we adjourn to my room and talk. They are always eager, at these times, to share.

6. Observe your worship day. We will delve more deeply into spiritual issues later. Presently, we are focusing on the economics of family time. Worship days can be pleasant for the whole family, and later in their lives these can become warm memories of family life for your teen.

This is the day I get out the Crock-Pot. It is easy to throw everything one needs into one of those things and come home after church to a wonderful and leisurely family midday dinner. After dinner, take a long, slow walk together. Make this day one of leisure, of a slow pace, of a wonderful meal together. Try to have all your chores and responsibilities for the week finished so that you can be entirely free on worship day. Make this a day of rest and replenishment for you and your teen. Savor this day for connecting and closeness between you and your teen. It doesn't get any better than to have a family day for worship and time together.

Spiritual issues grow in importance to your teen when they are associated with warm occasions. Do you recall those occasions when your family spent a day each week in this way? Can you make this happen? Worship, contemplation, walking, and talking and just being together can happen. With some planning, is this so hard to do?

Look at the values transmitted during this day: love of God, fellowship, love of family, relaxation, enjoying nature, listening to God's voice from within, quiet time, and meditation.

Do you also need one day of complete rest for the well-being of your soul? So did God.

7. Is it possible for one of you to either quit work entirely or perhaps work part-time? This is not as absurd as you may initially think. This is only a suggestion and not a demand. It is best if a parent is home after school for his teen. I am an egalitarian, so I don't care which parent. Family economic counselors are showing that many families are actually losing money by both partners working. They point out that if you take certain steps you may actually do better financially. When they review your budget they take every little detail into consideration. Try the following exercise:

   I. List the expenses for operating your car just to go to and from work:
      A. Gas
      B. Tolls
      C. Depreciation in the value of your car by frequent use and lots of mileage
      D. Wear and tear on your car by frequent stop and go driving in heavy traffic and thus more car repairs
      E. Parking fees
   II. How much money is spent for clothing for your job?
   III. Can you cut food expenses?
      A. Families on the run frequently eat fast food, which can be expensive.

    B. By staying home and planning meals considerable money can be saved.

    C. You will have time to clip coupons for reducing grocery expenses. Some families are experts at this.

IV. How much do you spend on day care expenses for the younger children?

This can offer a major financial cut.

V. Can you possibly provide day care for a few other children, or practice a computer, home-based job?

    A. This can provide additional income.

    B. There are numerous tax breaks available if you do this; such as

        1. deductions for deprecation of the part of your home used for day care or your work

        2. deprecation for when you use your car for day care or work-related duties

        3. deductions for toys and play or any job-related equipment

        4. food allowances, etc.

VI. Can you reduce lunch expenses?

    A. If your spouse works fairly close by, perhaps she can come home to eat with you.

VII. Can you downsize?

    A. In order to maintain a large house and fashionable cars, many families live on the financial edge.

    B. Many American families live month to month, only three weeks away from bankruptcy.

    C. Is living this way so essential that you sacrifice the well-being of your children?

    D. Can a smaller house and less expensive cars allow one of you to stay home for your teenagers?

Please think about this. Do a careful budget. Think of other savings and short cuts. Consult with a financial counselor. You may be surprised to discover that financially it is better for one of you *not* to work outside the home. I know it is scary to reduce your cash flow, but economically it may actually be the smart thing to do, and it not only gives you more family time but also reduces stress on everybody. It is certainly worth considering.

8. Find an activity that your teen would love to do with you at least one day a month. Of course, stay within your financial means. I practice and teach in a rural college town. Dads constantly go hunting and fishing with their sons;

why can't daughters go too? I don't hunt, but I do take my sons skeet and trap shooting or target shooting and I am very safety conscious. When would a daughter decline to spend an afternoon shopping and having lunch alone with her mom?

The potential list is endless: hiking, camping, fishing, canoeing, visiting museums, going to a movie together, playing pool, playing golf, just playing catch, and working on the car together. Can you think of more? Only your imagination and money can set limits. If you choose the right activities, you may be surprised to find that your teen would love to have such special days with you.

When you spend a day with your teen have fun and be fun. Joke, laugh, cut-up, be light-hearted, and relax. Put your arm around his shoulder. Be affectionate. Let him know how deeply your love him. If you do this, you will soon see miraculous changes in the way he behaves toward you, and your nerves will be far less frayed.

9. Trim your schedule of extra commitments that are detracting from the time you have for your family. It is important to be a church deacon; to be in the Rotary Club, Lions, or Junior League; to do volunteer work at a hospital; and to participate in neighborhood or community projects. But, can you handle it all and have sufficient time for your teen? I have had numerous cases where parents were overcommitted. It may be that only one favorite project is all you can handle. Your children need to come first. Please think this over.

10. Reduce your teen's organized activities. It is a curiosity that as our schedules have become increasingly stressed, we have added even more burdens by scheduling our children into organized activities, such as Little League, soccer, tennis lessons, music lessons, karate, and football. We want our children to have every advantage to fulfill their potential in every possible way, but time with us is equally as important. They need time to relax and to just have time to be a kid. Perhaps one organized activity a season is all your family schedule can handle.

All the suggestions are designed to help you build close and loving relationships with your teens. If you become close to them, you can influence them. In order to instill in them the values you want them to have, you must build a close family unit first.

As I said before, I am well aware that teens want to be with their friends. But they also want and need some time with you. The suggestions I gave you are quite practical and do not detract significantly from the time your teens have with their friends.

There is an additional bonus—all these suggestions may help reduce some of the stress in your life too. Sometimes you can, indeed, "have your cake and eat it too."

Moving

My hunch is that the initial reaction of most readers when encountering moving as an issue for teens would be something along the lines of incredulity at anyone focusing on such a trite, trivial, irrelevant, and unimportant concern. But as you read and allow me to develop my ideas, I think you will understand and appreciate the importance of this issue.

Twenty percent of America moves from city to city each year. The United States Postal Service reports that forty million families change addresses each year. National and international mega corporations often require executives to move if they are to earn promotions. Those desiring to attend graduate programs, such as in medicine, dentistry, law, or various doctoral degrees in philosophy (PhDs) may be admitted to programs necessitating long-distance moves. The military is well known for constantly moving its personnel at all ranks.

What Happens When You Move

The implications and impact of moving for teenagers can be devastating. We need to look at what a major move means to a teenager.

The only time I recommend for a family to move is when a teenager is deeply involved with a deadly peer group, where drugs and crime are their creed. Moving may be necessary to sever these bonds and to cut the stranglehold the group has on your teen. But for most teenagers moving is not a good thing.

Loss of the Extended Family

Sociologists define the extended family as the largest component of the family, consisting of grandmother, grandfather, aunts, uncles, and cousins. The enormous escalation of moving, which began in the late 1960s, has broken the backbone of the extended family in America. How can the family stay close to each other when its members live in distant places? My extended family is now spread throughout New York, New Mexico, Virginia, California, Washington, D.C., Florida, and I don't know where else.

In some instances a concerted effort may be made by a few family members to stay in touch and remain as close as possible with distant family members. Usually this only works for one generation. Eventually and inevitably the family ties erode.

Traditionally, the extended family served as an important source for support and for the transmission of important values to the young. Children and teenagers learned much of their beliefs and values from all family members. For most teenagers these traditional ties, the lessons they learned from people they loved and the sense of comfort from such an important source of support, are now gone. Today, most grow up without an extended family. Without this support structure, teenagers may grow up feeling alone and lonely. This can add to the risks involved in their searching for comfort and support in all the wrong places.

Important values were taught to the young by grandma, grandpa, and other family members. Now there is a loss of learning values from extended family members, which only adds to the confusion of modern teens. How can teens learn what is important in life and what is right or wrong if there are no close people left to teach them? It is a favorite cliché for politicians to advocate the return to family values. But, how can this happen if family members are scattered and unavailable for our young?

Loss of Friends

No one need tell you that friends are very important to teenagers. But perhaps peer relationships take on considerably more importance when viewed in the context of our harried lifestyles and the loss of the extended family. For years many of my teenage patients kept repeating, "My friends! My friends!" which would irritate me. I'd think, "Why don't they give consideration to their family like my generation used to?" Then one day I realized that, for today's teens, friends have become their family. Their needs were no longer being met either by their immediate family, who were too busy, or by their extended family, who were too far away. If one considers how important friends are to teenagers, it is not difficult to deduce how devastating a move can be.

Deloris and Suzanne

The father of Deloris, age fifteen, and Suzanne, age sixteen, initiated contact. I met with him and his wife before seeing each of the girls. They reported the common scenario of oppositional-defiant teens with disrespect, who engaged in frequent arguments, temper tantrums, sarcasm, eye rolls, and hate stares. Both girls were described by their parents as "boy crazy." Boys and friends seemed to be their only interests. Their rooms were pigsties. Their grades consisted mostly of Cs and one or two Ds. Both girls had been caught shoplifting, which confused their parents since finances were not a family problem. The girls usually got whatever they desired. After their trials they were both placed on probation. However, no substantial changes resulted. After school each day they met with their friends just as they did before probation, and they rarely got home in time for dinner.

I met with each girl separately. I found both to be extremely attractive. My rapport with each of the girls was excellent from the first sessions. I trained their parents in the REST behavioral program described in chapter 5, designed for controlling oppositional-defiant, or any difficult, behavior. After training, the program was implemented. In addition, I saw the girls separately. It took a few months of hard work, but the improvements were considerable. The arguments stopped, the girls came home on time, they kept their rooms neat, and their grades improved to mostly Cs and a few Bs.

A year after completing therapy, the father called and requested a visit. I met with him and his wife. Everything had been going well with the girls. However, they wanted my opinion about moving to a new state, which meant a promotion for Dad. They were concerned about a move's potential impact on the girls. I emphatically pointed out that such a move would uproot the girls from their friends, their boyfriends, their school, and their familiar surroundings and would probably prove to be very detrimental to the gains we had made. They moved anyway.

Another year later the mother called requesting the name of a therapist in their new area. Everything had not only degenerated but had gotten considerably worse. Both girls had again been arrested for shoplifting, they were refusing to go to school, and Suzanne had gotten pregnant and had an abortion. I searched for the names of some therapists and wished them luck. A few months later I telephoned, and I'm sad to say matters were still quite bad.

Loss of Stability

Don't be deluded by the pseudoindependence of teenagers. What this means is that they often act as if they're cool and self-sufficient, but they really aren't. It's important to remember that they are still children. The major changes in their lives that moving creates can be very traumatic. They need their family. They need their friends. And they need a feeling of security—where their surroundings are stable, reliable, and consistent.

Waking up each day to a familiar environment is reassuring and comforting. A teenager does not have the inner resources to have everything that is familiar to her ripped out from under her. Moving into new and unfamiliar surroundings can be quite terrifying for a teen.

A move away from secure surroundings can result in an emotional upheaval, manifested in anxiety and depression. Sometimes this inner turmoil is also manifested in overt acting out behavior, in a condition known as *neurotic delinquency*. This is where a teenager who has never committed a seriously wrongful act suddenly explodes and begins committing behaviors that violate the law. In these cases acting out is often viewed as a cry for help. It is not uncommon for this pattern to unfold following a major move.

Mark

I remember Mark's case from many years ago because his plight touched me deeply. He was seventeen when I first saw him. His parents described him as a wonderful young man. He had excellent grades, played high school baseball, dated, and was popular. In the middle of his senior year, his father was transferred.

When the family arrived in the community in which I was practicing, Mark went "ballistic." He refused to go to school, he constantly yelled and screamed at his parents, and he spent long hours locked up in his room. For several nights in a row, while his parents were asleep, Mark went out and committed a series of acts of vandalism. He threw rocks through the windows of the local high school; he turned over soda machines at a variety of locations; he drove the family car through someone's yard, wrecking their fence; and one evening he took a long walk with several cans of spray paint, painting one long line on every wall or fence he passed.

Mark's pain was evident from his first session. He was furious over the move. Everything that he loved and was familiar to him was suddenly gone. After several sessions, we got past his anger and reached the level of his pronounced depression. Many sessions were spent with Mark vacillating between sobbing and expressing his anger. I acknowledged his feelings. He had a right to his anger at his parents. His depression was actually a grieving process. Finally, we began talking about the issue of change in one's life. I taught him that instability and change were now the norm in this country, and I shared that I didn't like it anymore than he did. Eventually the thing that finally helped him to be more rational was being reminded of the obvious reality that a major change was going to occur in the next year anyway, when he'd be going to college. For fun, we both watched the movie *American Graffiti*, which is a comedy about a group of teens adjusting to the coming changes at the end of the senior year. Eventually his feelings subsided, and he regained rational control. He had to repeat his senior year in his new high school. He then went to college.

Mark's case demonstrates the impact of drastic change on a teenager. Mark perhaps was somewhat prepared for the move to college, but the sudden upheaval and loss of his familiar world came too quickly and was a complete surprise to him. This resulted in a drastic loss of emotional control. It would have been best if his dad could have stalled the move with his company until the end of Mark's senior year. Mark would then have been more mentally prepared. But corporate leaders are often unsympathetic to the family needs of their employees.

Solutions

I hope that what is written here about the impact of moving on the young and on the family touches the hearts of parents, and corporate, military, and academic leaders. If we are going to reestablish the extended family in this country and avoid the painful effects of moving on the young, we must take steps to curtail the mobility of this country.

Moving is not yet as pronounced a problem in European countries because most countries are only the size of our individual states. Therefore, a move within many countries is only a short distance. But as mega corporations abound in the emerging Euro-economic market, I suspect this problem will begin to plague them too. For other large countries like Russia, China, and India, mega corporations are only beginning, but they too will most likely begin seeing this problem.

What can we do? I think there are some sensible solutions we can consider.

1. *Refuse to Move.* A recent article in *USA Today* stated that for the sake of their families a growing number of corporate officers are declining promotions in order not to move. My friends, Pete and Shirley, who live in Vermont, made this decision twenty-five years ago. Pete worked for a major corporation. He and his wife declined any promotions that necessitated moving. They put their children before their ambition, and I believe it paid off. Their adult children are very successful and wonderful. I hope more families make this same decision. Might a move for the sake of the company be injurious to the needs of your family?
2. *New Corporate Policy.* Whenever possible I would hope that corporations adopt policies where promotions can be made within a limited region and

thus require only minimal distance moving. Many corporate leaders are sincere and caring individuals: they just haven't seemed to understand what long-distance moving has been doing to the American family and to our youth.

3. *New Policies for the Military.* The military needs to also look at its policies. I have many students who were army, navy, or air force "brats," and almost universally they report how devastating it was for them to move every three years. Perhaps the military brass will look at the policy more closely.

4. *Come Back Home.* We need to deeply instill in our teens a strong sense of love and commitment to their families. Let them know that, after completing their education, you would hope their dedication to the family would lead them to want to begin their careers by settling within close proximity to their family. Perhaps they will value their family so much that holding it together would be of paramount importance.

5. *Research on the Impact of Moving.* Considerably more research is needed on the impact of moving on adolescents. If, as I suspect, research shows how detrimental moving is on the young, perhaps it will be more convincing to make all of us pay closer attention.

Our teens cannot comprehend what a healthy family environment is if there are no available family role models. They will remain confused and not understand healthy family values without a family surrounding them to teach them. They will not feel secure and loved if there is no family to give them that security and love.

Media

If the theme of this book is to focus on the confusion of our teen's values, beliefs, and thoughts, then we can't bypass the impact of the media on them. Research shows that teenagers spend more time with the television than with their fathers. They watch TV between five and seven hours each day. Is what they are watching on TV consistent with the kind of values we want them to learn?

The impact of television on the minds of the young is powerful. Many years ago psychologist Al Bandura initiated research on the impact watching TV violence had on the young in learning aggression. His research supported the relationship between media violence and aggressive acts.

Why don't all young people become violent after watching TV? Those teenagers with strong family backgrounds are least likely to act out. Those with weaker family ties are more prone to being suggestible victims of inappropriate media role modeling. If there is a combined lack of appropriate role models coupled with feelings of aloneness, then the likelihood of internalizing what they see in the media becomes more pronounced.

Consider also that in addition to violence our teens watch show after show flooded with sexual content, crime, and poor language. How very confusing the portrayal of these types of values can be for the minds of immature and suggestible teenagers. Blocking out inappropriate channels and not permitting our teens to watch certain shows are obvious steps, but, if we are not there for supervision, it isn't difficult for teens to circumvent such sanctions. Again, it comes back to the issue of how important it is for us to be with them after school.

I believe it is hopeless to attempt to get some media moguls to curtail what they show. There's too much money involved. They know how attractive sex, violence, and offensive content is, not only for the young but for many adults as well. Fortunately, there are responsible executives in media and there are alternative programs available that can offer considerable valuable material, but it still requires our presence to oversee our teens.

TOXIC FAMILIES

Janet Geringer Woititz, in her book *Adult Children of Alcoholics* (1983), points out the impact a dysfunctional family has after children are grown. One of her most profound insights is that these adults do not have a mental model or image of what a normal family is. They don't know what healthy interactions and family behaviors are supposed to be. Consequently, they function on what they have learned and become familiar with; therefore, they in turn create another generation of dysfunctional and unhealthy families. Diane Ackerman, in her book *The Natural History of Love* (1994), states that growing up in an unhealthy family is a precursor to developing all kinds of emotional problems, neuroses, and personality disorders.

How can a teen learn the values of a healthy family when the family he grows up in is sick? The price for growing up in a toxic family is extensive. It means a lifetime of personal pain, an inability to establish healthy relationships, and the perpetuation of overwhelmingly confused and distorted values on to their own progeny.

Patterns of Toxic Families

Toxic families can range from the obvious and flagrant to the not so obvious and rather subtle. Whether flagrant or subtle, the impact on children or teens can be equally devastating. Let's look at several patterns of toxic families.

Abusive Parents

The abusive parent manifests an obvious pattern for destroying the soul of a child. Any form of abuse is horrible, whether it be physical, sexual, or mental. A teenager growing up under abuse often feels shame. Guilt is the feeling following committing a wrong act, such as hitting one's little brother. Shame is a global feeling of self-loathing. It involves a total sense of worthlessness and self-hate, and it is often one of the major results of being abused.

Carl

Carl was seventeen when I first saw him. His father came in for the first session complaining that his son was an "airhead" who couldn't do anything right. He pointed out that the boy was always forgetting things, for example, leaving doors open, not cleaning up after himself, and forgetting to take his homework to school. His dad said that Carl couldn't do the simplest thing right.

I had a preconceived idea of what I would encounter when I met Carl, and I was right. He looked like a whipped dog. He made poor eye contact, he spoke barely audibly, and he looked like he wanted to find a hole and be buried in it. Carl had been mentally abused by his father his entire life. His dad typically called him "stupid," "lazy," "dumb," and "an airhead." He was constantly berated for never doing anything right. Carl said he would get terribly nervous whenever he was told to do something by his dad, and, because of his anxiety, he'd then "screw up," performing his assigned task incorrectly. Of course, this led to even more mental abuse.

Carl hated his father, and, when he turned eighteen, he moved out. His father refused therapy for himself, and I could do nothing to salvage the relationship. After Carl moved out, the last information I received was that he had become heavily involved with drugs. He found a terrible way to handle his pain.

It is impossible for a youngster to grow up abused and escape unscathed. Completely reversing or undoing the extensive damage from years of abuse is for most victims impossible. All forms of abuse always include mental abuse. Inherent in any abuse, albeit physical or sexual, are the messages of a youngster's worthlessness, the violation of her integrity, and her being used as nothing more than an object or outlet for an immature parent.

Sexual abuse is terrible. Imagine what it must be like for a teenage girl to have sex with her father. This doesn't just violate her body; it violates her soul. How does a child ever overcome this type of trauma? Can a therapist ever help someone to overcome this damage to her soul?

Charlene

At fourteen, Charlene was referred for therapy by her high school counselor. At school she had become withdrawn. She appeared sullen and depressed. At the end of the day, she'd offer to help teachers so that she wouldn't have to go home. She was falling asleep in class and always looked exhausted. Her counselor was unable to get Charlene to admit what was bothering her.

My strategy in therapy was not to force any issues. I decided to let trust and rapport build slowly. It took months until Charlene told me what was going on. I told her I'd have to alert the authorities, which was required by law. Charlene was afraid that this would mean the end of her family, that her mother and two sisters would suffer economic hardship, and that it would all be her fault. I pointed out that there was a good chance her father would be offered the therapy and help he needed. If he cooperated, he would eventually be permitted to return home. She felt guilty about the years of involvement. I assured her that none of this was her fault. She was a child and therefore a victim of a very disturbed adult, and she should never have been subjected to this.

The court did assign her dad to a therapist, and he did cooperate. The court allowed me to continue seeing Charlene. Eventually, family sessions were held. Charlene's insomnia stopped. Her depression and withdrawal subsided. Outwardly all looked well. However, Charlene will always have memories of her father lying on top of her and entering her. Some emotional scarring will always be a part of her.

When any form of abuse occurs in a family the abuse itself is only part of the problem, because abuse is always accompanied by many other pathological interactions throughout the family. Any combination of other unhealthy interactions can occur, such as domination and control of all family members, isolation of the family away from any influence of friends or extended family, constant lying and covering up, threats, manipulation, and an atmosphere filled with tension.

For the abused child the concept of a normal family is totally muddled. To help Charlene develop some understanding of what makes for healthy families, I assigned her reading, such as Stephen Covey's *The Seven Habits of Successful Families* (1994), videos, and other learning aids. We discussed at length what should occur in the interactions of a good family. She sincerely tried to learn; I hope she did.

Alcoholic or Drug-Addicted Parents

An alcoholic or drug-addicted parent creates a confusing and unpredictable family environment. To a teenager living under this strain, the disappointments can be painful and the turmoil terribly confusing. The drugged parent may make promises when either drunk or sober and forget what he said when in the opposite state. When a teen has a baseball game or a piano recital, imagine what it must feel like when the parent they looked forward to being there doesn't show.

The pressure on a teen in this environment is enormous. Often she'll work hard to keep other kids from finding out what's going on in her home. She may avoid making friends or prevent other kids from coming to her house because she doesn't know what to expect when walking in. It's terrible pressure on a teen to keep such dark secrets.

Fighting and arguing are common in a home where a parent is drugging or drinking. The fights may be with the other children or with the spouse, but either way it's bad. This can wreak havoc on a teenager's nerves. In such a volatile and chaotic home, how can a teenager decipher what is morally right or wrong? How can she possibly understand what composes a normal and healthy family? Woititz, as stated earlier, indicates that she'll grow up not knowing what normal is; therefore, as an adult she cannot re-create a normal home for herself. This then perpetuates problems throughout her adult life.

The emotional strain is equally as bad. Imagine what it is like to have a parent that is loving and caring when sober and an angry and screaming monster when drunk. It's like being on an enormous emotional roller coaster: one moment feelings are glorious and wonderful, and the next, these feelings are smashed into the ground, being replaced with disappointment, fear, and pain.

Aloof and Emotionally Unavailable Parents

Research by Lewinsohn and Rosenbaum (1987) shows that adults with recurrent depressions often have grown up in a family where personal reinforcement, in the form of love and affection, was sparse. Teenagers want and need love. When parents are emotionally unavailable, as Diane Ackerman points out, their children may spend the rest of their lives desperately searching for love.

In my child psychopathology class my students do an interesting exercise. I have them read the true story of the son of Pulitzer Prize–winner John Gunther. In his book *Death Be Not Proud* (1963), John Gunther paints a picture of his son as an extraordinarily brave young man who maintains extremely high grades while dying from a large brain tumor. The youngster undergoes numerous agonizing operations. His skull had been cut away to allow for growth of the tumor. The book ends with Gunther's son being accepted to Harvard and then dying.

I ask my students to analyze the family dynamics. They usually see the son as brave and deeply committed to his education and to excellence. I don't. I see the son as a teenager who was desperate for love. He was desperate to excel academically. Even while in pain and barely able to function, he struggled with his studies just to win his dad's and mother's approval. The young man lived in a boarding school. His visits from either of his parents—his mom was also a renowned writer—were infrequent. When they did see him, their interactions predominantly focused on his academic performance. He learned to get some degree of consideration from them by continuing to excel, even while he was dying. I saw his parents as self-centered and unavailable. I think this story portrays the lengths to which a love-starved teenager would go just to be loved.

Overprotective Parents

Claude Steiner writes, in his book *Scripts People Live* (1972), that the worst thing we can do to our children is to make them dependent. He views excessive dependency as a major handicap that can cripple a person for life.

The teen years are the time for the transition from compliant childhood to independent adulthood. If we overshelter, overcontrol, and overprotect a teenager, then this transition will either be permanently halted or may never be made.

In *DSM-IV* diagnostic terms there is a label called a dependent personality disorder. This is the adult who is desperate for someone to take care of her. Often she will do anything just to be with someone. This type of person is a prime candidate for very unhealthy relationships, the most common of which is an abusive one. Even if she meets someone who caters to her dependency, what will result to her emotionally if something happens to that other person? Dealing with loss is difficult for anyone, but when a person's well-being desperately depends on being taken care of, the loss is far more extensive and devastating.

Leslie

Leslie was thirty-three years old when she called for an appointment. She stated she was getting married to an airline pilot from Sweden. After the marriage she'd have to live in his native country; she was frightened. Initially, I thought the prospect of this could create an understandable adjustment difficulty for anyone. After the marriage and the move there would be sizeable cultural changes that would be quite difficult. This turned out not to be such a simple case.

Additional information painted a very different picture. Leslie had her own house. In the third session she revealed that the house was owned and paid for by her parents. Leslie wore beautiful clothes, all bought by her mother. Her parents lived only one block away. Each week her mother purchased all of Leslie's groceries and then did all the unpacking and sorting. Leslie went to her parent's house almost every evening to sit and watch television. She did not work; her parents provided her with an allowance.

As a teenager her parents dominated and controlled Leslie's every breath. They did this in a gentle, loving manner, deluding Leslie into feeling falsely comfortable and secure. Her parents gave her everything. They provided for her every need. If Leslie had an argument with another teenager, her parents went to their house to "straighten things out."

At age thirty-three Leslie was totally unprepared for adult life. I thought that going to Sweden or even getting married would be a disaster for her. Leslie's level of terror at the prospect of the marriage and the move was severe. She couldn't sleep, eat, think, or concentrate. She constantly broke out in hives. Sometimes the anxiety was so great she'd vomit for hours.

Leslie got married and moved to Sweden. She was back home with her mommy and daddy within six months and divorced within another six months. I began counseling Leslie's parents. They already realized what their excessive doting had done to their daughter. They learned to gradually let go, allowed Leslie to get her own apartment and a job, and permitted her to function on her own.

The best thing you can do for teenagers is to gradually let go. Be there as a loving resource but permit them to make their own mistakes. Even though we may often think they have poor judgment, they will learn from the consequences of their bad decisions. Here's a helpful proverb: Good judgment comes from experience, but most experience comes from bad judgment.

Excessively Punitive Parents

In the punitive family, parents frequently use various forms of punishment such as yelling, lecturing, grounding, and sometimes slapping. Oddly, there is no overt verbal or physical abuse. In the punitive family, the parents believe they are using sanctioned and proper means for disciplining their teenager. Often they mean well and believe this is the right way to raise a youngster. It isn't! It's damaging and cruel.

Again, research by Lewinsohn points out that adults who have recurring depressions often were raised in excessively punitive families. Excessive punishment can also cause severe anxiety.

Joseph

Joseph was a thirty-year-old school teacher and an alcoholic. He was raised in a strict Irish Catholic family. He described his parents as well intentioned, wanting him to become a responsible and hardworking adult. They screamed at him almost every night throughout his childhood and teen years. They never hit him or called him ugly names. They saw screaming as the way to motivate him to perform well in school.

Over the years, Joseph described a heightening feeling of anxiety. As a teenager he stuttered. He developed sleep problems. He said that this emotional state kept getting worse and worse. After working two years as a teacher he began to discover that a few drinks after work temporarily alleviated his pain. The drinking escalated. Before work, he began drinking vodka to hide any odor. His drinking kept getting worse and worse.

Joseph voluntarily entered therapy. I had him enter a twenty-eight-day hospital-based alcoholic treatment program. He resumed therapy with me after his release. He also joined AA (Alcoholic Anonymous). It took two years of therapy for him to learn how to reduce his anxiety and to be able to function without drinking. Joseph would probably have to remain in AA for the rest of his life.

It is a basic and well-established principle in psychology that the key to raising a healthy youngster is social reinforcement, or, stated in laypeople's terms, *love* and not punishment. Punishment or discipline should be used with reserve and should always be administered with love.

The Peer Group

You may be the most perfect parent in the world and yet your teen may still behave badly. Besides all the influences we've covered, one more remains. Even though you may be doing a good job, the parents of your teenager's friends may not. Those friends bring with them their parents' sets of values and beliefs, which can strongly influence your child.

In chapter 8 we'll explore how to control with whom your teenagers become friends. I'll offer ways for your teenager to have good friends with good values from families whose parents you know well. In addition, I'll tell you how to do this in such a way that it will provide a rich and fun social life for your teen.

In the next chapter we'll begin exploring the most common teen problems and problem teens, and how to change them. We'll look at the patterns of teens who are oppositional and defiant, who may be failing in school, and who are currently labeled as ADD/ADHD or ODD, and learn how to control them.

5

Controlling the Very Difficult Adolescent: The REST Program for ADD/ADHD and ODD

As you learned in the previous chapters, the diagnostic labels aren't accurate, and they're really not important. The important issue is that you have an out of control teenager. She's either failing in school, rude to you, possibly rude to her teachers as well, or any combination of the three. You wouldn't be reading this book if your child were an angel. These behaviors are not the product of disease, and we don't need to drug your child to control her. In this chapter you will learn how intelligence can be used to deal with out of control teens. By the end of this chapter you will be back in control. You will reestablish yourself in your rightful place, as the boss.

Most books on the market about attention deficit disorder/attention deficit hyperactive disorder (ADD/ADHD) and oppositional defiant disorder (ODD) teens recommend negotiating with these teens to establish rules and regulations for their conduct. They claim that parents can reason with kids like this. I don't intend to reason with an immature tyrant in my own home, and I don't recommend that you do either. If these kids responded to reason, you wouldn't be seeking the help of a therapist in the first place. For the most part, these are teenagers who will not respond to reason. They will not listen to their parents, nor will they listen to a therapist. Their behavior is at the level of being abusive to all members of their family. Their behavior and conduct are beyond the level of normal adolescent rebellion. It is you, the parent, who will set the rules for conduct in your own home. You will do this with love, and with the best interests of your child in your heart. John Rosemond (2001) calls this being a "benevolent dictator," and I agree. It is time that we parents took back control, which the shrinks long ago made us give to our children. Children, with childlike mentalities, should not be in charge, dictating the rules of the home; we should.

I want you to talk with your teen. I do with mine. But, I don't recommend even trying when she is the one in control. Get their outlandish behaviors under control first, whatever the label or diagnosis, and later in the book we'll talk about how to establish healthy communications.

If you have a teen like this, you most likely are filled with conflicting emotions. On the one hand, you love your child, but, on the other, you resent him. Probably there are times when you wish you had the finances to send him to a boarding school and just get him out of your hair. In turn, you probably feel lots of guilt. After all, you may feel that no parent should feel such intense negative emotions toward their own child. It may soothe you to know that this mixture of emotions is quite common.

What can be done with a child like this? As we saw in chapter 3, drugs barely help, and they are filled with health risks. Trying to get them to sit and talk with a therapist will probably not help either. The only time you can reason with a teen like this is after *you get him or her under control.* How you can do that is what this chapter is all about.

Let me share with you what a first therapy session can be like with many of these teens. I say many, because there are some who will engage in dialogue with a therapist, but most won't. Let's proceed.

Doc: Well Johnny, can you tell me why your parents want you to come see me?
Johnny: (Stares around the room, looks at his fingernails, then roles his eyes toward the ceiling, and finally answers, shrugging his shoulders.) I don't know!
Doc: Have you and your parents been arguing a lot lately?
Johnny: (Still staring at everything, except the therapist.) I don't know!
Doc: I'd like to help Johnny, but to do that I need to hear your point of view.
Johnny: Everything is fine! (Impatient sigh, as if he'd just like to get out of here.)
Doc: Well, perhaps you can tell me something about your school?
Johnny: Yeah, it sucks!
Doc: You don't like school? Can you help me understand why?
Johnny: The teachers suck, the classes suck, the building even sucks!
Doc: But why? What's wrong?
Johnny: It sucks! (His eyes role back in his head, as if the doctor were totally stupid.)

I can go on and on, but session after session will most likely be similar. He hates school and hard work. He'd rather spend his days at parties drinking, smoking, and hanging out. Remember the song "All I Want to Do Is Have Some Fun"? Engaging a teenager such as this in a meaningful therapeutic dialogue is most likely not going to happen. The statistical evidence doesn't support those therapists who claim they can reach these teens, because their success rate is abysmal. Maybe some therapists can get them talking, but every time the sessions move toward substantive change, the teen will resort to his belligerent tactics. He'll control the content of the sessions, not the therapist.

GETTING TOUGH WON'T WORK

You probably have already discovered that the use of force or the threat of force does not work with oppositional teenagers. If you yell at them, they yell back. If you hit them, they pick up the phone and call the Department of Human Services and have you arrested, and, believe me, these kids know this routine quite well.

I've had numerous cases where parents were, by profession, police officers or in the military. They thought that roughing up their teen would drive some sense into him; one good, thorough knocking around would put a stop to his nonsense. In every case it made matters considerably worse. First of all, this is flagrant abuse. Second, the only purpose this really served was to further alienate the teen from his parents. In some instances, it did irreparable damage to the parent–child relationship.

I, too, felt frustrated with these types of cases. Over twenty-five years ago I decided to find out what treatments or therapies were available that could help with these teenagers. I went to the university library, and to my surprise I found nothing, not one research article or book that could be of any help. I was astonished. I thought there had to be a way.

I reviewed all my cases searching for some way to control these rough teens. Finally the answers began to emerge. I began developing a program based on sound behavioral principles designed specifically to control ADD/ADHD and ODD adolescents. I researched, practiced, and polished all the elements until it culminated in the program you are about to learn.

THE REST PROGRAM FOR CONTROLLING THE DIFFICULT TEEN

I introduced the concepts for dealing with difficult teens in an earlier book I wrote called *Controlling the Difficult Adolescent: The REST Program* (1990). REST stands for Real Economy System for Teens. Since writing that book, I have continued my research in this area and have made some changes that increase the effectiveness of the program for both the milder ADD/ADHD teen and the more rambunctious ODD teen. The program is both sensible and easy to follow. It provides you with a powerful tool to deal with an extremely difficult teen without a need to resort to force or confrontation. My philosophy is that we can use our intelligence instead of our brawn to get results.

In beginning our journey it is essential to separate that which we can control from that which we cannot control. We cannot control teens' minds. We can only try to influence their minds. In order to influence their minds, we must have their respect, love, and attention. We cannot have this if we are constantly engaged in battle with them. The only way to influence their minds, what they think, believe, and value, is through effective communication. These are called *life issues*. To effectively communicate, we must control their behavior at home without constant battle. These are called *home issues*. Once their behavior at home is controlled we can work toward the goal of renewing our loving relationship with them, improving conditions for better communication, and, in turn, influencing their *life* beliefs and values.

With the unreasonable teen, we must turn to the following methods as a tool for bringing them sufficiently in line to foster and enhance an atmosphere where positive communication can occur.

The Rules for the REST Program

In this program we have five basic at home rules. The rules are aimed at controlling the five behaviors parents report as being the most offensive and the most disruptive to a positive family environment. These are called the *home conduct rules*. Let me list the rules first, and then we will cover more precisely what specific expectations we can require for each rule. Then I will instruct you on how to enforce the rules. Finally, we will talk about two additional behaviors, school problems and aggression, that are of major importance but which will require additional and more stringent methods for control. In later chapters we will discuss how to handle the very serious problems of delinquency, drug and alcohol use and abuse, and teen depression and suicide. Other issues such as driving or owning a car and college will also be discussed later in the book.

Suspend any fixation you have on diagnosis, because it's not important. Once all these behaviors are under control, the reasons for any diagnosis will also disappear. Magically, there will be no more *diseases*.

THE FIVE HOME CONDUCT RULES

1. Personal Hygiene
2. Room Care

3. Major and Minor Chore Responsibilities
4. Verbal Abusiveness
5. Safety and Curfew

Additional behaviors of concern are:

1. Aggressive Behavior or Physical Abusiveness (will be dealt with in this chapter)
2. School Performance Problems (will be dealt with in the next chapter).

In chapter 7 I will address parent's concerns over the most severe behavior problems:

1. Delinquency
2. Drug and Alcohol Use
3. Depression and Teen Suicide

Home Conduct Rules

These rules are designed to control offensive and abusive behaviors that occur within the home. *Do not post these rules.* To help get your teen's mind to function, it will be his job to remember the rules; if he wishes to post them for himself, that's fine.

Rule 1: Personal Hygiene

Fortunately personal hygiene turns out to be a relatively minor concern for most parents. As we discussed earlier in the book, most teens are perhaps excessively concerned about appearance and grooming. If anything, parents usually complain that their teens spend too much time in front of a mirror or in the bathroom primping. In wanting to be attractive to the opposite sex, teens usually carefully attend to personal hygiene and are frequently blamed by the other family members for using up all the hot water when they shower.

I advise parents to use reasonable judgment in understanding teenage dress codes. There are always fashion fads. Teens are always obsessed about remaining current with their choice of clothing. As long as their fad is within reasonable standards, be tolerant. Be sensible and fair in establishing these standards. Remember that their clothing is their uniform for acceptance within their peer group. There is considerable peer pressure to meet the group's standards.

This first rule is primarily aimed at controlling dress and appearance when it reaches the level of the ridiculous. It is when half the head is shaved bald and the other half is colored orange that we move in. It is when they dress in leather and spikes, when they cover the face with excessive makeup and outlandish designs, when they pierce body parts, when they look like a hooker or a gangster, and when they cover themselves with tattoos that we must exert strong control over them.

Do not forget that these forms of dress reflect the uniform of their peer group. It will often be a glaring advertisement about what kind of practices their peer group is into, such as drugs, sex, truancy, and even crime. When you see these patterns of dress, it is essential that you know with whom they are hanging around. Actually, it is essential that all parents know their teen's friends and their parents. If the peer group is really bad, take the steps I will later advise.

In rule 1 you *do* have the right to demand reasonable dress that you judge falls within a fair-minded assessment of what today's teens are wearing. By demand, I do not mean for you to yell, scream, hit, or curse. I mean let the enforcement part of the REST program do the work for you. Losing your control only identifies you as the enemy to your teen. She will then fail to see her responsibility in any problem and you will get absolutely no where with her.

Rule 2: Room Care

The condition of a teen's room is often a major source of aggravation to parents and is a frequent reason for endless arguments. It is common for parents to be confused about whether or not they have the right to require their teen's room to be kept neat and clean. I emphatically say that if a clean room is important to you, then you have the right to require it to be that way. You paid for the house. It is your property, in its entirety. You have the right to keep every part of it as you wish.

Parental confusion over this issue usually centers on the right of a teen to have privacy. I recall many years ago a counselor on one of the morning shows advising that a teen's room is his private domain and that he has the right to keep it any way he wants. She advised parents to recognize a teen's privacy and simply shut the door. What utter nonsense! Teens do have a right to privacy. Privacy is a sacred trust. Parents do not have the right to read their mail, go through their drawers, read their diary, or search their room. Parents do not have the right to do these things any more than their teens have the right to go through their parent's belongings. Requiring a clean room has nothing to do with privacy, because that room is the property of the parents in the first place. The way a parent's property is treated is the parent's right.

How neat should the room be kept? Again, it is impossible to define precisely what is reasonable. Be fair and sensible. There is no reason that the bed cannot be neatly made, the floor cleared of objects, or books put on their shelves. You do not have to require perfection. A reasonable standard is sufficient. Rule 3 will add some additional requirements that will make it easier for your teen to maintain his room's appearance.

It is important to have a specific time each morning when room care must be completed. I suggest fifteen minutes before the school bus arrives, but it's your choice. If you do not have a set time, you will hear, "I'll do it later." Do not get into this unnecessary debate. Set a specific time; do not permit a second past that time. Be specific. Be firm. Be consistent.

Rule 3: Major and Minor Chore Responsibilities

A teen's body is probably at the peak of health more than at any other time of her life, and yet she often does little to help with the housework. Do you find that it is a battle to get your teen to take out the garbage? There is no reason your teen cannot help with the care of the house in much more significant ways than merely taking out the garbage.

Most parents work, and then, when they come home, they have to do all the housework. Why? Why can't a teen pitch in? I will bet your answer is that it is more of a hassle to get them to do anything, than it is to just do it yourself. We are going to learn how to make it an enforceable requirement without having to struggle to get your teen to assume a fair share of the housework.

In this rule, teens are required to perform and complete, with a high standard of quality, one major chore each day, except worship day, which is a day off. This chore is to be completed by a specific time and without a reminder. Examples of major chores can be:

- vacuuming the house
- cleaning one or two bathrooms
- preparing a complete dinner for the family
- dusting and polishing all the furniture
- doing some of the laundry, including proper folding
- cleaning the kitchen and washing the dishes after the family dinner, by themselves

You may think of others.

The major chore for Saturdays should always be to clean their own room to a near perfect level; this means cleaning under the bed, changing the bedding, cleaning the closet, vacuuming, and dusting. Doing this chore each Saturday helps make it easier to honor rule 2 during the week. Sunday may be a day of rest where a major chore is not required. Reverse this for families of the Jewish faith.

Minor chores are also required. Usually, I simply require that teens clean up after themselves throughout the day, such as putting their laundry in the hamper, cleaning up after a snack, and placing their dishes in the sink or dishwasher after a snack. It would be nice if they contributed to helping in other ways, such as helping with the dishes after dinner or cleaning up someone else's mess, but this usually turns into arguments and probably is not worth the effort to enforce.

Rule 4: Verbal Abusiveness

This is probably the problem that is of most concern to parents when bringing their teen to my office. Some teens can be unbelievably cruel to their parents or siblings. This rule must be strictly enforced. The teen must discontinue the practices of

- sarcastic tone of voice
- cursing
- yelling and screaming
- foot stomping, kicking furniture, or slamming doors
- eye rolls that convey the message that what a parent just said to them is remarkably stupid
- glaring hate stares
- damning statements such as, "I hope you rot in hell!"
- threats
- use of global "you" statements, such as, "You never let me do anything!"

Absolutely none of this is to be permitted.

It is essential that you teach your teen assertive methods of communication, which will be covered in more detail in chapter 9 when we'll discuss effective communication skills. Assertions should be made in the following way:

- speaking in a calm, normal, and respectful tone of voice
- being polite
- phrasing a request as a question
- Using "I" messages, such as "I'd like to go to a movie," "I don't agree with you," or "I feel angry when you don't listen to my side."

There are numerous books on assertiveness: I suggest you read some of them as an aid to help teach these skills to your teen.

If you want to teach your teen to talk to you assertively, you must learn to be a good listener. If you are closed-minded and refuse to listen to her side, you will extinguish her desire ever to try to speak with you in a proper fashion. Good listening will also be covered in chapter 9, when we'll look more carefully at communication skills.

If you have listened to your teen's side and you still do not agree with them, say "No" calmly, give your reasons, and that is the end of any further discussion. Further debate will only escalate into an argument.

It is important that when a parent says "No" a good reason or explanation be given. "Because I said so!" is not sufficient. If you do not have a sensible reason for a refusal, then reconsider your position. Perhaps you should make a reasonable concession.

Rule 5: Safety and Curfews

You have the right to know that your teen is safe and exactly where she is at all times. Parents should not have to stay up until all hours of the night worrying about their teen. This rule requires that your teen return home at the required curfew time and that you are told exactly where she will be at all times. If there is a change of plans, your teen is to call you for permission to go elsewhere.

On weekends, please try to be realistic in setting a curfew hour. Find out what the other parents are permitting. Try not to put your teen in an embarrassing situation by phoning him to come home too early. If your teen relies on friends for transportation, find out what their curfew time is. Try to match your teen's curfew with theirs so that your teen doesn't have to beg for an early ride home. If necessary, coordinate these times with the other teens' parents.

Curfew during the Week   Many teens are permitted to go out on weeknights. Parents who permit this typically report that their teen gets low grades. I am astonished that they do not see the connection. Carefully completed homework should consume between two to five hours per night. Completing a major chore takes about an hour. Outdoor free play or a school sport takes about two hours. One hour should be required for relaxed reading. There is little reason why a teen should be permitted to have several hours each weeknight for idle social time. In other words, there is little reason for teens to be out during the week. Do you carefully check their homework? If not, you should. There are two great lies that teens tell: "The teacher never gives us homework," and, "Teacher, I lost it on the bus." Are you keeping track of your teen's schoolwork? It amazes me how many parents pay no attention to their child's school responsibilities; checking their report card every six weeks is insufficient. It takes many hours for homework to be done correctly: check it every day. If your teen seems to be getting too little homework, contact his or her teachers and find out exactly what the requirements are.

Curfew time during the week should not be a contentious issue since your teen should be at home in the first place. Please make allowances for special school activities and organized church activities. An occasional night out during the week can be a treat for the teen who is performing well in school and behaving well at home, but teens should not regularly be cruising about unsupervised during the week.

There are two reasons for having the safety rule. First, I believe on weekends that as parents we should know the whereabouts of our teen. It is not merely a right to know this but a responsibility. Teens often point out to us that parents have no right to keep tabs on them and that they are old enough to take care of themselves. My observations are that teenagers do not do a very good job of taking care of themselves. Many of them drive too fast, tailgate, smoke pot, drink, go to dangerous places, and so forth. A second reason that we have the right to know where they are is for parents to know that they are safe. None of us enjoys staying awake, afraid that something may have happened to their son or daughter. We are entitled to the minimal comfort of knowing whom they are with, what their destinations are, and what time we can expect them home. It is little to ask.

Enforcing the REST Program

Now we can focus on how to get our teens to comply with these rules. Notice the acronym of the program REST—Real Economy System for Teens. In this program we control their financial resources. Many parents who use the REST program also call it the allowance program. We control the resources for obtaining all their needs, wants, comforts, and entertainment. In order to earn everything of value, they must behave properly, treat us with respect, and honor the five house rules. From this moment on you will no longer give your financial power away to an abusive teen.

Notice the common pattern of a parent with an abusive teen. The teen curses at his parent and talks in a snide and disrespectful manner, and then gets money to go to the movie. He slams doors and screams at his parents while wearing designer shirts and jeans. He doesn't lift a finger to help with the housework, and the parents in turn cook his meals, do his laundry, take care of his room, and then give him money to go to the school football game.

If you have an abusive and defiant teen, I want you to do a quick exercise. Walk into their room and observe. Do you notice a color TV, a stereo, an abundance of quality clothing, sports equipment, makeup, torn tickets from concerts, a bicycle, a skateboard, roller blades, CDs, video games, perhaps a computer, and perhaps cigarettes. Shall I continue, or do you get the point? His abusiveness makes your life a living hell. Sometimes you feel like you want to throw him out the front door. You stay angry and upset. You yell. You threaten. You ground him. Perhaps you have even smacked him. Nothing works. He does not change. Sometimes he may feel a twinge of guilt, and he comes to you saying he's sorry and will not do it any more, and, within a few days, he is back to being just as offensive as ever. Notice that all those material goods in his room show that you have given away your real power.

Some of you may have taken your teen to a therapist. The therapist and your teen spend a secretive hour each week talking, but nothing changes. Perhaps the therapist calls for family therapy sessions. Everyone collects in the therapist's office each week learning how to communicate with each other and how to understand each other's needs, but nothing changes. I am a psychologist, and I am telling you that you have no need to understand them or to communicate with them *until their abuse stops*. I do not care what deep, dynamic, psychological secrets underlie their abusiveness. It stops!

The secret to controlling teens is to make their earnings and resources contingent on their behavior. Call this an allowance program or call it the REST program, the idea is that your teen must earn the money she needs for buying everything, except food, medical care, school supplies, and shelter, by honoring the five basic rules. It is essential that you learn all the details about enforcing this because it must be done correctly or it will not work. I have been refining and improving this program for about twenty-five years. Teens can find loopholes and, when they do, the program collapses. I've learned what most of these loopholes are and so will you. Take the time now to learn precisely all the details to make the program work.

The program is designed to be stringent. The reason for this is that it is designated for controlling the abusive, oppositional, and defiant adolescent. If your teen is generally "a good kid" and only mildly rebellious, you can modify the program to be less comprehensive and less stringent. However, if you have a hard-to-live with and abusive teen, then do not deviate from exactly what I am teaching you. Be certain you clearly and fully understand each step and then enforce the program without any changes. And don't hesitate because a psychologist told you your child has a disease called ADD/ADHD, along with a comorbid disease called ODD. Rubbish! Get tough, but intelligently.

What They Must Earn

In the REST program, you provide only four of your teen's necessities—food, a home, school supplies, and medical care. Everything else must be earned. They will henceforth earn what you have been freely giving them. If they wish to be offensive, they will have nothing. If they wish to behave decently, they can easily have all their needs and wants met.

In this program, we do not reward them with extra special luxuries for good behavior. We do not bribe them to behave. I do not advocate buying them a new bike, or even a car, for behaving well, because they should be behaving well in the first place. Instead, from now on they will earn their everyday needs, which they have previously been freely getting, by engaging in decent everyday conduct. The five home conduct rules are very reasonable. From now on, they must earn the money needed for buying shoes, socks, underwear, clothing, toys, games, CDs, makeup, concert tickets, lunch, movie tickets, candy, sports equipment, sporting event tickets, car insurance, and car payments (if you wish them to have a car), gas, and anything else.

How Much

In the REST program, you should not spend more on your teen than you are at present. In fact, you probably will be spending less. Take a few hours to browse through your checkbook in order to get a rough idea of how much you are currently spending on your teen. For older teens be certain to include all car-related expenses, such as the increase in your automobile insurance. Each family needs to do their own calculations, but I will give you an estimated figure to help teach you how the program works. Most families spend about $35.00 to $45.00 per week on a thirteen-year-old. This does not include food, school supplies, medical, and home expenses. For a sixteen-year-old who drives the family car the figure may be double, at about $70.00 to $90.00 per week. If your teen has his own car, the figures can be enormous.

How the Money Is Earned

Money is given to your teen each day, seven days per week, *only if she obeys all five rules*. Years ago I tried payments for honoring three or four of the rules, but

teens calculated how much they would need for the day and deliberately dis-
obeyed one or two rules (if they thought they needed less). Therefore, the rule is
all or none, which means that if they miss one rule, they get no money for the
day.

The daily allowance must be slightly less than the amount they actually require, because the remainder is made up as a bonus each Saturday only for having a perfect week. As an example, if their financial requirement level is $35.00
per week, they are paid $4.00 per day. For seven perfect days they will have
earned only $28.00, which is below their requirement level. The remaining $7.00
is given on Saturday for a perfect week. Tough, huh?

When and How to Pay the Allowance

Their allowance is given to them in cash, in an envelope *after* bedtime. To avoid
a personal confrontation, leave the envelope on their night table. At first you
may think that this involves a lot of money. No, it doesn't. You are already giving
them this money, and perhaps more, anyway.

If they failed for the day, the envelope contains a note on an index card,
clearly explaining which rule(s) was broken. The reason for the note is to avoid
any personal confrontation that will then merely end with your teen seeing you
as "being on their case." Avoid this common misinterpretation by using the note.

If you give them the note earlier in the day, or if you yell at them any time
during the day, "all right, that's it, you've lost your allowance," your teen has
nothing to lose and will probably break every rule for the remainder of the day.
Say nothing and give them the note after they have gone to bed.

Use an index card in the following way:

Rule Broken	Reason
Rule #3	Talked nasty to me in the kitchen after school when I said you could not see your friend. I explained to you that you had a great deal of homework.
Rule #2	Minor chore not done. Towel and underwear left on bathroom floor in a.m.

How Their Money Is Handled

Help your teen open a checking account in his or her name. If your bank will
not cooperate, open a joint account. The AAA, Automobile Association of

America, now provides for teen checking accounts. One day each week is designated as banking day, and your teen deposits the accumulated cash into the account. I would recommend Mondays. Take the time to teach your teen how to record checks and balance the account. Take him or her shopping as usual, but, from now on, your teen writes the checks from his or her account to purchase whatever he or she needs.

Notice the illusion. In reality all you are doing is moving your money to a different checking account.

When I first started this program, I had three surprises. First, teens love writing their own checks at stores because it is an adult thing to do. Second, I was amazed at how many teens become careful consumers. When you spend the money, they buy only the most expensive items. When they spend their money, you will be surprised at how quickly they become careful shoppers. I have had countless parents tell me how shocked they were when they would catch their teen looking through the newspaper for sales or when their teen would ask to go to factory outlet stores. My third surprise was when teens began telling me they really liked this program. They felt freer to make their own choices. They liked writing checks. They had fun learning to be careful consumers. They now understood what their parents meant when accusing them of not knowing the meaning of money. And finally, they also liked the fact that the fights with their parents stopped.

Again, I wish to reemphasize that in reality all you are doing is transferring your money from one checking account to another. Your teen just happens to be in the middle. You are not giving money away and you are not spending more. The only shocking part is that you become very aware of how expensive it is having a teenager.

Dealing with Loopholes

There are a few things that can neutralize the program, so we need to foresee what these can be and discuss how to handle them.

Loophole 1—Windfall Money   What if Grandma wants to give your teen $50.00 for his birthday, or if there is some other source of money? When opening the checking account, also open a savings account into which all windfall money is deposited and not to be withdrawn until age eighteen. The money can then be used for college or a first apartment. Grandma can still give the $50.00, but it is deposited in savings instead of checking.

Loophole 2—Gifts   Christmas gifts, birthday gifts, or any gifts should not consist of any items you are aware that your teen either needs or wants. Those are the things they must earn. Gifts should be something creative that would make an occasion special but that they would not necessarily work for. For example, if your daughter desperately wants a bracelet, she must earn it, but perhaps a sweater can be substituted. If periodically for special occasions your teen is inundated with what they need or want, then there will be nothing to strive for, and therefore the program will have been compromised.

Loophole 3—Jobs   Most parents are thrilled if their teen wants to work. However, if they are miserable to live with, then their behavior at home must remain as a priority. They may go to their jobs only if they have had six perfect days during the previous week. If they have not, then they cannot go to their job at all the following week. If that causes them to be fired, then so be it. If they lose their job, then so be it. Not tolerating a tyrant in your home is more important than a job.

Money from their jobs is mainly deposited into savings and only a small amount may be used to supplement their checking account. The reason is simple: if they lose their job, you do not want them to have a large reserve in checking. If they do, you will have several weeks of misery until their funds become exhausted.

Loophole 4—Not Enough $ in the Program   If the amount of money they can earn is below their need level, the incentive to work will be minimized. They will not be motivated to cooperate with the program. Examine the amount they can earn, and, if it is insufficient, adjust it to a higher amount.

Loophole 5—Earning Something Special   What if your teen wants an expensive special item, such as a computer or a new bike? Ask yourself if the item is something you would have ordinarily bought for her. If it is, then make her earn it. Merely divide the cost of the item into somewhere between sixty to ninety days. Add that amount to their daily allowance, as an additional incentive, until they have accumulated enough to afford the purchase.

Let's look at an example. If your teen wants a $270.00 bike, then divide by ninety (days). This equals $3.00 per day added to the program. If they behave perfectly then they will reach their goal in ninety days; if not, it will take longer. It is their responsibility to set the money aside. Once the goal is reached, $270.00, the extra money stops. If they failed to properly save, that failure is their problem. A second chance to re-earn the money should not be provided.

Is the Program Restricting a Teen's Emerging Independence?

Before presenting a case example, I wish to mention a criticism leveled at me from a fellow psychologist. He said that the teen years are a time for emerging independence and exploration and that the program is too restrictive. I responded, "Have you ever lived with an abusive teenager?" Silence. There is nothing in the REST program that prohibits a teen's emotional and mental development. In fact, it enhances it because the program teaches them to be more responsible, polite, and appropriately assertive.

Dealing with Aggression

It is unacceptable for a parent to strike a teen, and it is unacceptable for a teen to strike a parent. Just as it is unconscionable for adults to strike a relative, friend, or a stranger, it is just as unconscionable for a teen to strike a sibling, friend, or anyone.

Many of you reading this book cannot imagine a family where physical violence happens. But as a therapist, I see it too often. One researcher reported that aggression occurred in 40 percent of the adolescent cases with which he worked. His research, however, focused on inner-city youth. In my research and clinical practice, I deal with generally middle-class youth where the aggression rate is about 19 percent. Usually the focus of the aggression involves slapping, shoving, and hair pulling. In rare cases, the aggression reaches severe levels where closed fist punching or striking with heavy objects may occur, sometimes resulting in broken bones or dangerous life-threatening physical injury. Don't assume that if your child is aggressive he will grow out of it. In fact, just the opposite happens: the violence grows progressively worse and has a very high probability of being perpetuated later in life in an abusive marriage. It must stop!

Aggression is highly resistant to treatment. Therapists rarely succeed in getting teen or adult patients to curtail their violence. Oddly many aggressors want to stop, but once their anger is triggered they lose all semblance of control. Once they explode they cannot seem to stop. As you can tell from this book, when talk and reason fail, whether with parents or therapists, imposing strong consequences may be required. That applies here doubly for aggression.

By using our intelligence, we can come up with clever ways to control an uncontrollable teenager. I found, however, that the REST program by itself did not effectively control aggression. I developed the two additional methods presented here that often produce very dramatic improvements.

Reinforcement Removal

This procedure, called *reinforcement removal*, is simple and easy to implement. Once again, we employ the control of resources, which are right under our noses. Identify six to ten objects or activities that you know are extremely important to your teenager. Write them as a list, in rank order from the most important to those of lesser but still real importance. An example might be:

1. using the family car
2. playing the guitar
3. listening to stereo
4. riding a dirt bike
5. having a telephone in his room
6. going to concerts
7. playing video games
8. using the computer

Tell your teen that from now on each aggressive act toward anyone will mean the loss of one item for exactly one year, beginning with item number eight. It is essential to begin with the least important items because each aggressive act will mean the imposition of stronger consequences. Inform your teen that if he is caught using the item during the year, it will mean the permanent loss of the item.

A few teenagers will stop the aggression when merely told about these consequences. The vast majority of teens will stop after losing three items. Only in very rare cases will it be necessary for the parents to go as high as items 2 and 1, and usually this occurs when the parents had histories of being extremely inconsistent. Teens interpret inconsistency as an invitation to test and bluff, and, when they realize their parents mean business, the aggression finally halts.

Grounding

Grounding is not an official psychological-based technique. It's merely something parents impose when angered by their teen, usually for a poor report card. Parents often take something important away from the teen for several weeks, such as the family car. Typically, when enforced in this way nothing changes. Grounding in the REST program, specifically for aggression, means a total loss of everything for at least one or more months.

If your teen has lost everything from reinforcement removal, then one month of total grounding can be added for the first aggression and two months for the second and so forth.

Total grounding in the REST program means loss of everything, including use of the car, watching TV, use of the telephone, contact with friends, everything. No mercy should be shown: aggression is too dangerous. Don't argue with your teen. Tell him in advance and silently impose the penalty.

Call the Police

It is also important to tell your teen that if he becomes aggressive to any family member, you will call the police to arrest him for assault and battery. If he becomes aggressive, do it. You are not helping your teen if you make threats and do nothing. Aggression must stop before something terrible happens.

LESLIE—AN ODD CASE

Leslie, age fifteen, came from a middle-class background. Her parents at the first session seemed warm, personable, and deeply concerned. They conveyed a typical dichotomous emotional profile consisting of love and resentment toward Leslie. People outside the immediate family viewed Leslie as a sweet and charming young lady. Her teachers had nothing but praise for her. She was an A student, active as a school leader, and an excellent tennis player who could easily qualify for a sports scholarship in college.

However, Leslie was a completely different person at home. It seemed to her parents as if Leslie could barely stand them; in fact, it was as if she hated them. She constantly talked to them with a sarcastic tone. They said that when she would glare at them with hatred in her eyes, they were actually afraid of her. Leslie's temper was infamous. She would explode in a fit of screaming, yelling, and cursing at least four times a week, and sometimes they said it could occur as much as four times in a day. When Leslie was not actively screeching or cursing at them, she stayed isolated in her room. She treated her two sisters with equal contempt. Several times a year she would become physically violent to either parent. She would punch and throw things at one of them. On one occasion, she struck her mother on the back of the head with a broom, causing her to fall down the steps and break her arm. Another time while in a rage, she threw a heavy brass candleholder at her mother, hitting her in the chest, causing her to have considerable difficulty catching her breath and leaving a severe bruise. Leslie, by the way, was referred to me by the police.

Her parents described Leslie as an impeccable dresser. However, at home she was a slob. Her clothes were thrown everywhere. She never picked up after herself. If she got food from the refrigerator, she would rarely close the refrigerator door. Her room was described as a "war zone," with deep piles of clothing.

Leslie was very popular at school. She loved going out with her friends on Friday and Saturday evenings to movies, parties, dances, skating, and bowling. She always came home on time. She and her boyfriend preferred double dating with their friends on weekends. Her parents believed they were not sexually active and indicated that Leslie was very antiabortion. They did not think she ever took drugs and that, if she did drink, there was no indication that it was more than recreational.

In the initial phases of therapy, Leslie was intent on passive-aggressing me. She slouched in her chair and answered questions with only one or two words while continuously examining her fingernails.

I informed her parents that our work would have to begin with establishing strong consequences to get Leslie under control. I assigned them to read my earlier book on the REST program. They then had a session where I taught them the full program. Weekly sessions after beginning the program were mostly with the parents to answer questions and refine the application. I spent only brief amounts of time with Leslie. Once Leslie was fully under control at home and was more communicative and cooperative, I spent more time talking to her. It was at this point that Leslie's parents and I could begin working on her values and belief systems.

The REST program was presented to Leslie by her parents, who explained the specific behaviors within each rule that would no longer be tolerated. The following is Leslie's program:

> *Rule 1: Personal Hygiene.* Leslie was to be neatly dressed and ready for school Monday through Friday by exactly 8:00 a.m.
>
> *Rule 2: Room Care.* Her room was to be cleaned by 7:45 a.m.: no objects on the floor, books placed in bookcases, her bed made, and no loose articles of clothing strewn about.
>
> *Rule 3: Major and Minor Chore Responsibilities.* The following is Leslie's major chore list:
>
> *Monday*—vacuum the entire house
>
> *Tuesday*—clean the two upstairs bathrooms thoroughly
>
> *Wednesday*—dust and polish all furniture in the entire house
>
> *Thursday*—cook family dinner and clean up kitchen

Friday—do all of her own laundry, including folding and putting articles neatly in proper places

Saturday—clean own room to perfection

Sunday—no chores

In addition, Leslie must always clean up after herself:

after eating snacks

after discarding clothing and using towels in the bathroom

after eating breakfast

after using magazines, games, or anything else in any part of the house, including in her own room

Rule 4: Verbal Abusiveness. The following are not permitted:

screaming and yelling

sarcastic tone

cursing

calling parents names

eye rolls

glaring hate stares

refusal to speak when spoken to

talking back

staying in room, isolated from the family other than when doing homework or studying (all of the above applied to her treatment of her sisters)

Rule 5: Safety and Curfews. Curfew Friday and Saturday is 12:30 a.m. She is to always let parents know where she is and call if plans are changed. No going out during the week.

Allowance: Leslie is to earn $6.00 per day plus an additional $10.00 on Saturday if she has a perfect week for a total of $52.00 per week. Leslie's telephone in her room will be in her name, and, from now on, she will be responsible for the monthly bill. She is responsible for all of her expenses except room, food, school supplies, and medical care. Leslie's parents and I decided to allow the REST program to be in effect for one month before focusing on aggression. Then the following list was added to control the aggression:

being allowed to stay on the tennis team

being allowed to take driver's education this year, and after that to keep her license

being allowed to see her friends on Sunday afternoon

having her room telephone

having her room stereo

having her room TV
having her doll collection

It took three months until Leslie was complying with the REST program seven days per week. The initial weeks were dreadful. Her tirades became considerably worse. I had warned her parents that this getting worse is a universal occurrence, often lasting for several weeks, before results begin to be evident. In psychology, this is called a behavioral burst. It was crucial that the parents remain calm and let the noose of Leslie's financial needs pull tighter and tighter, which is deliberately built into the REST program. After five weeks, her home behavior was considerably improved. She earned her allowance six or seven days each week. Then the aggression program was added. She lost five items. Then the aggression stopped. Leslie never again displayed any aggression.

After the third month, my sessions with Leslie took on a different tone. She took a deep interest in discussing my views about defining a person as the sum total of their true values and beliefs, and about how we must decide these if we are to choose what kind of person we wish to be. We discussed the issue of self-discipline in directing our behaviors. We talked about irrational beliefs, how to change them, and how to deal with irrational thinking. Since she was bright, it was refreshing for me to work with a teen who could grasp such sophisticated concepts with ease and enthusiasm.

Leslie began to understand that she already had a vested interest in some moral issues, like sex and abortion, but that her values extended to her friends but not her own family. She became increasingly appreciative of her family. As her brutish behaviors subsided, she began to talk more with her parents. They resumed being a close family.

One Sunday, before Christmas, I was in my office when the phone rang, which of course surprised me. It was Leslie's dad. He wanted to thank me for the Christmas present of giving him his daughter back. I knew in the silence that followed that tears were rolling down his face; they were on mine as well. We quietly said goodbye.

6

What to Do When Your Teen Is Failing School: The So-Called ADD/ADHD Teen

Later in the book we will talk about how to cultivate a love for learning and reading in your young. There are things both parents and educators can do to make education relevant and meaningful. I ask you to reflect on these issues: the teenager who strongly values education, loves reading, and respects authority will never be diagnosed as attention deficit disorder (ADD) or attention deficit hyperactive disorder (ADHD), while the teen who does not value education, hates reading, and disrespects authority will most likely wind up diagnosed as ADD or ADHD. These aren't diseases; they are labels that reflect poorly developed values!

But all is not lost. In this chapter we will discuss real solutions to dramatically improve school performance, and diagnosis doesn't matter. Furthermore, drugs won't be necessary. Once we get a teenager performing well in school, then reinforcements will automatically come with success, such as smiles from teachers and high grades on tests, homework, and papers. Positive feelings about herself will be meaningful because of real successes. Real success is the best way to develop real self-esteem. All these things will elevate motivation and sustain continual improvement. Once grades and behavior improve in school, the diagnostic label of ADD/ADHD will be meaningless. Your teen doesn't have a disease and can succeed in school without drugs.

At first your teen may have to work extra hard to improve deep concentration and memorization skills. These improve, and become easier with practice. Your teen has no choice; he will have to master these skills through hard work and dedicated effort. Pills only give a false sense of well-being and should not be a substitute for developing real learning and mastery of skills.

Before beginning this rather stringent program have your teen evaluated by a psychologist and your physician. We do not want to impose strong consequences on school performance until we learn if there are certain specific underlying problems that can interfere with learning. I suggest you refuse to fill out any questionnaires about your teen that could lead to his being labeled ADD or ADHD. There are three things we need to know: level of intelligence as measured by an individually administered intelligence test; an evaluation for any specific learning disabilities, such as problems in reading or math; and finally, a careful physical evaluation for vision and/or hearing impairments. I suggest that you request the psychologist not perform any personality tests because they are invalid, unreliable, and very misleading. If your teen has an average or above average intelligence score, he or she should be able to make Bs and Cs relatively comfortably. If there are no learning problems or physical problems, then we can proceed with the program.

Before focusing on schoolwork, make certain that the REST program has stabilized all behaviors at home. It is extremely important that all home behaviors be stabilized first, or school will never improve. Actually, in the majority of cases, once a teen's behavior at home is firmly brought under control, school performance automatically improves, and intervention for school work is not even necessary. If school performance does not satisfactorily improve, then begin the program.

THE WEEKLY REPORT CARD

Getting a report card every six weeks is too long a period of time to shape school performance. Parents going ballistic and grounding their teen for six weeks usually gets some temporary improvement, but this almost always falls apart once sanctions are lifted. Instead our weekly report card will remain in effect until the teen finishes high school or until he demonstrates an overall improvement in his attitude about his education. Thus, each week your teen must make a choice, goof off and face negative consequences, or give it his best effort and return home to positive consequences.

Look at the weekly report card, table 6.1. It is designed to match the report cards of most school systems. I give you copyright permission to copy it as it is or to modify it to match the grading system of your teen's school. Please note: I use a daily report card for younger children, but a weekly report is sufficient for teens.

The criterion level is that level we establish for passing or failing. In this program I recommend establishing that level at absolutely no grade below an S (satisfactory) level; this includes each category of class performance (what the

TABLE 6.1
The Weekly Report Card

DATE _____

SUBJECTS	CLASS PERFORMANCE	CLASS CONDUCT	TEST GRADES	HOMEWORK GRADES	TEACHER'S SIGNATURE

TEACHER'S COMMENTS: _____

_____

_____

E = EXCELLENT

S = SATISFACTORY

N = NEEDS IMPROVEMENT

U = UNSATISFACTORY

teacher observes in the classroom) and conduct. An N (needs improvement) or a U (unsatisfactory) in either category is considered a failure.

Test grades and returned homework grades must not fall below a grade of C. This can be set at B for teens with higher IQs. Be certain to know the school's grading system. In some districts, an 86 is a B, while in others it's a C. Conduct reflects behavior in class, while class performance is the grade for academic performance, such as staying on task, listening, and class participation. Notice that the term *class performance* has been used for many years; however, the currently popular trend is to call poor class performance ADD. Notice the dramatic shift in interpretation and perceptions. Both mean the same thing: the child is not paying attention, isn't answering questions, is daydreaming, and so forth. The term *poor class performance* places responsibility on the teen. The term *ADD* seems like a disease, handicap, or mental impairment where the poor child can't help himself. The term absolves him of personal responsibility.

The term *class conduct* has also been used for many years. This term means bad or inappropriate behavior in class, such as getting out of one's seat, talking to other students, throwing spitballs, and so forth. But now the trend is to label this as ADHD, again connoting a disease and absolving the teen from responsibility for ill-mannered behavior while in school. Are you beginning to understand the psychobabble that has been thrust upon you? Do you see how terminology can lead to misguided consequences. Poor class conduct entails discipline, while ADHD entails drugs. I've worked with hundreds of teens. Responsibility and real consequences produce far better and more substantive improvement than do drugs, and they are far healthier.

It is also useful to "require" your teen to keep a poster where all test grades are displayed. This can be posted in the privacy of their room since it is not intended for humiliation. Teens often report that they are doing well in a subject, but base their assessment on the last one or two grades received. They honestly forget earlier grades; the posting of grades helps them keep better track.

Consequences

It is essential that consequences be imposed based on each week's report card. This facilitates the teen's associating the week's work with immediate consequences. If the report is given only every six weeks, then the consequences do not match the behaviors. Six weeks is too long a time period to shape better performance. In this program, each week is new in order to shape the appropriate behaviors.

If there are two failures on the weekly report card during the week, then all weekend activities are lost. During the weekend, grounding is total, where only reading and walking around inside the house is permitted. Allow nothing! No TV, phone, games, drawing, music, friends, or even walking outside is permitted. Avoid conversations with your teen except to give directions or instructions. Don't argue. Let the REST program control any verbal abuse; let the weekly report card control school failure. Usually the mere warning of loss of weekend privileges is sufficient to raise both the grades and the conduct of even the most recalcitrant teen. Sometimes it takes several weeks before it begins to work. Remember that the REST program and the school program remain in effect simultaneously.

At first your teen may resent this program, but, once his grades improve, a dramatic attitude change will occur. Reinforce an improved outlook by showing a strong interest in his schoolwork and by giving frequent praise. Continue to practice those suggestions made earlier in this book about enhancing the values for loving education and reading.

In the next chapter we're going to look at how to deal effectively with more serious problems, such as depression, suicide, or involvement with drugs and alcohol.

7 | Serious Problems

Why do some teenagers engage in serious problem behaviors such as delinquency, suicide, running away, and heavy involvement in drugs and alcohol? In this chapter we'll look at some of the causes. We'll look at what you can do when these problems emerge. However, the best solution always lies in preventing these problems in the first place.

Developing steps for prevention requires us to understand what causes these behaviors. Understanding causality gives us the power to change or correct the causes before it's too late. My hope is that you deal with these issues early enough in your teen's life to avoid the emergence of problems.

THE THREE MAIN CAUSES OF SERIOUS PROBLEMS

Through the complex myriad of possible causes for serious trouble, there are three sets of circumstances that stand out as most common. The first and most prevalent is parental neglect. Some people who read this may think I am attacking parents and blaming them for being at fault. Yes, I am, and yes, they are. Our worst crime is that too many parents are not aware of what they are doing. Many readers will be outraged and respond by saying how hard they work at providing quality time and care for their children. Indeed they do. But it is not enough. Working every day, paying bills, staying on top of all the household responsibilities, and giving children quality time is insufficient. It takes more than that. Children require a great deal of time, attention, and nurturing. It takes lots of time and lots of attention to mold the souls of healthy children and teenagers. So-called quality time, as too many writers suggest, is just not enough. Our youth need hugs and kisses, snuggling, relaxed conversations, going for walks together, and doing special things like hiking, fishing, and family activities that are fun.

Many or most seriously disturbed kids generally have received way too little personal and social reinforcement. Remember my earlier discussion about de facto neglect? The more pervasive the neglect, the more likely serious problems will develop. Days, weeks, months, and years pass, and our young do not receive a consistent diet of warm and tender personal interactions. Without this personal element, their spirit eventually breaks, which often occurs in the teen years. If this happens, they will search for ways to stop their pain and express their anger.

In American society, we are too busy and too stressed. We have too little time for our kids. In discussions with my college students, I advise them to avoid having children after marriage until they determine whether or not they will have the necessary time to give them. I suggest that if they are busy with work and career and there is little or no room in their schedule to devote lots of energy to children, they consider not having children. This is a difficult decision that requires some honest soul-searching. Actress Bette Davis once said, "There are three parts to one's life, career, children, and marriage. I can handle two of them but not three." She said this many years before the stresses in our lives escalated to their present level.

The second major factor that underlies severe acting out is abuse. As I discussed earlier in the book, there are three types of abuse; mental, physical, and sexual. Recall that mental abuse is always present in all three. Mental abuse can range from the relatively moderate, such as calling a teen "lazy, good for nothing," "Why did I ever have you?" or "You'll never amount to anything!" can progress to even more severe levels where parents use curse words such as, "You dumb bitch!" and others I do not care to mention. Continuously yelling at a teen, or constantly berating a teen, conveys a low opinion of her. If this pattern continues, a child eventually sees herself as being a lowly and worthless creature. This breaks her spirit, and, once that happens, severe patterns of acting out will often emerge.

Sometimes mental abuse can be subtle. It can be expressed simply through body language, facial expression, looks of disgust, hate stares, or closing one's eyes as if saying, "You fool!" Teenagers periodically exasperate any parent, and it is natural for us to react in this way. But, in my practice, I have worked with parents who do this daily. A good rule to remember is that subtle can be more powerful than blatant. It hurts a child to feel that their parents convey through body and facial language that she is incompetent. Honestly examine if you practice these reactions too frequently. If you do, you will destroy your teen's spirit. You need to stop now before it is too late.

The third factor contributing to severe acting out is the teen's peer group. I have mentioned this several times because I cannot emphasize enough the power of the peers. With the wrong crowd, your teen can turn into a monster. You may be the best parent in the world, but the parents of your teen's peers may not. It is friends who will exert a powerful influence over your teen's behaviors.

In exactly what manner a teen will seriously act out can't be precisely predicted. Who she stays with often determines the possibilities. How completely her spirit is broken by abuse or neglect determines other possibilities. The combination can lead to a broken spirit where the existential attitude or deepest belief is "I'm Not OK and You're Not OK." This means that a teen loathes herself and distrusts others. She will feel pain almost all the time, and she will search for ways to stop her pain. Now let's look at some of the ways in which this search may result.

DELINQUENCY

In psychology we have a diagnosis for teens called *conduct disorder*. There are two types. Less severe forms involve teens who violate less damaging laws through vandalism or truancy. *Delinquency* is often a synonym for the more severe *conduct disorder*, where major laws are broken, ranging from burglary to murder. In addition, either pattern can occur as one of two types: the *solitary type*, where the teen acts out alone and stays alone most of the time, and the *group type*, where the teen acts out with other teens, usually in a gang.

The solitary type of delinquent or conduct disorder generally involves the most broken child. This teen's spirit has been so severely maltreated that there is hardly anything left inside him. I described this teen as the one who walks close to walls, keeps his hands in his pockets, and looks totally lost and alone. He is usually friendless. He doesn't care about himself or anyone else. He believes he has nothing to lose by either harming himself or someone else. It no longer matters to him. This type of teenager is potentially very dangerous. Can he be helped by therapy? Probably not. His spirit may be too broken. The only chance, I believe, that he may have to regain his soul is to live in a very accepting and loving environment for a very long time. This is usually not provided for him by either the legal system or the psychiatric community.

There are other teenagers whose delinquency or conduct disorders result from group affiliations. For this type of teen the severe behaviors result from the value structure of the group. The group has different names and may be referred to as a "gang," a "cult," or a "brotherhood." Some groups may not be formally organized. A teen can come from a good family and still get involved with a bad group. This is a major difference from the solitary type who always has been chronically mistreated.

In the inner cities, gang membership may be necessary for survival. In most cases, however, a teen's gravitation to a bad group can result from searching for supportive relationships. The group can serve as a teen's family. Teens that are desperate for affiliation will do *anything* to gain acceptance from the group. Sometimes initiation rituals involve assassinating a member of a rival gang, or sometimes they may involve murdering anyone at random. In addition, today's gangs engage in the most severe practices, such as selling and using drugs, committing acts of violence, carrying weapons, and committing a wide variety of crimes.

Once a poisonous peer group gains control over the loyalty and values of a teen, there is little that even a professional psychologist can do to influence him. I often recommend that families move, even though this is a drastic step. On other occasions, I have recommended that a teen be sent to live with relatives. Either recommendation is aimed at breaking the stranglehold of the group. Sometimes this works, and sometimes it does not, but if things are badly out of control, it may be the only chance.

Recently the parent of one of my teen patients told me that the school's assistant principal called to let him know that his daughter was hanging out with a very bad group of kids. The father did not know that. I am surprised at how often parents do not know with whom their teen associates. Be certain that you know your teen's peer group. Invite her friends to your home. Observe them. Listen to them. Learn their code of conduct. Be alert, and be aware.

If your teen is in a gang, do you have other possible solutions open to you? Yes. If your teen is willing, in order to meet his affiliation needs, get him into an active church or community teen program. If that doesn't work, then you may seriously have to consider moving, perhaps even to a distant location, and perhaps you can get him into a healthy teen program. If your teen is involved with a deadly gang, this may be your only hope. As drastic as it may seem, it may keep your teen out of jail or may even keep him alive.

I hope that parents will understand how crucial it is to provide a home environment where there is an abundance of family love, an emphasis on spiritual values, an awareness of who their teen's peers are, and a firm set of rules that are in effect long before the teen years. It's the combination of all of these that can prevent conduct disorders and delinquency.

SUBSTANCE ABUSE

Teenagers generally get introduced to drugs and alcohol through their peer group. Most teenage peer groups only tolerate recreational use. However, there are the "druggy" groups that are into very heavy substance abuse. Remember, as I stated earlier, the group usually wears clothing that conveys their orientation. Their clothing is a uniform, and it conveys a message. Leather apparel, pierced body parts, heavy makeup, shaved heads, or long, dyed hair are often the uniform of the "druggy groups."

If your teen is heavily abusing drugs, you'll have to take the same drastic steps I mentioned earlier to extricate your teen from the group, that is, moving and arranging entrance into a new, healthy peer group. Remember, his life is in jeopardy by taking these toxic chemicals and by being in automobiles where either he or someone else is driving while impaired.

There is an additional problem surrounding substance abuse. We have no way to identify which teenager has an addiction potential. There is no medical test or any psychological test that can measure this. Even the best teenager from the best family can become an addict once addiction gets triggered. Once the addiction process is triggered, psychology and psychiatry have a dismal rate of treatment success. There may be no way to bring them back. For the teen who has addictive proclivities, moving and a new peer group won't be enough. The most common form of introduction to strong chemicals is through the peer group. However, there is another source—your family doctor. As we discussed in chapters 2 and 3, we now have an avalanche of kids being diagnosed as attention deficit disorder/ attention deficit hyperactive disorder (ADD/ADHD), oppositional defiant disorder (ODD), bipolar or other psychiatric disorders. The drugs used to treat these disorders are more potent than marijuana. They can trigger an addiction. Think twice before allowing your younger children or teens to be placed on any psychotropic medications. Parents must learn to say "No" to drugs, even if it is the family doctor doing the prescribing.

Other Signs of Drug Abuse

Have you noticed drastic personality changes? Personality changes are almost universal with heavy usage. Impaired thinking, poor judgment, and mood swings are products of heavy use of chemicals. Chemicals literally change personalities. Heavy usage causes great wear and tear on the body and the nervous system and has a cumulative effect that can cause drastic personality changes. Parents often describe their teenager as some kind of monster when she is using. I often hear, "I don't know her anymore!" If she can stop using, her personality will then retransform to that of the nice kid you used to know. But, once she starts using again, the monster will return. Use this personality change as a gauge or warning sign that she is using heavily. Such a change is not there by accident. Stay alert.

If your teen is into heavy use of drugs because of a peer group, then moving and a new peer group are viable solutions. However, if your teen has become a full-blown, out of control addict, then solutions become even more difficult. Most addicts don't want to stop using. They crave the reinforcing effects of the drugs, namely, the escape from stress and tension and the quest to recapture a feeling of euphoria. There are steps that can be taken.

First is hospitalization. Consult a psychologist or a psychiatrist about getting your teen into a drug/alcohol rehabilitation program. Be certain your medical insurance can help with the expenses, which can be considerable. Insurance companies no longer cover drug treatment for adults, but teen coverage is still available. Be prepared. Your teen may be in the program from a month to as long as three months. Usually programs begin with detoxification, where the drugs are slowly reduced to prevent your teen from going into shock. This takes between one and two weeks. The rest of the program is devoted to intense individual and group therapy, drug and alcohol education, and entrance into an AA (Alcoholics Anonymous) or NA (Narcotics Anonymous) program. You as the parent will probably be required to enter into family counseling as well as Al-Anon, which is the AA affiliate for family members of addicts. You'll quickly be surprised at how much you have to learn. Hospitalization is only a beginning. After release, your teen will have to attend regular AA meetings and therapy for a very long time. He may have to stay in AA for life.

What if your teen won't cooperate, which is very common? How can you save him? Reasoning, pleading, threats, grounding, or even a therapist may not be sufficient to reach him. The only solution may be a Tough Love program. There are two books with this name that you may wish to read: one is written by Pauline Neff and the other by Phyllis and David York, a couple that started Tough Love programs in the 1970s when their teen became an addict. Most cities in the United States have active Tough Love programs that are listed in the phone directories.

The idea behind Tough Love involves making it extremely difficult for a teenager to use drugs and behave in rude and sometimes violent ways toward his family. Both parents and teen join Tough Love support groups. Since the teen won't go at first, the parents go to their group. With the group's support the parents stop all means of financial support until the teen stops using, attends his group, and obeys the family rules. If that doesn't work, the teen is required to leave the home. He may go to another Tough Love family's home, but the same rules will apply. He may go to a few homes until he has exhausted his welcome. At that point, the street is the only alternative. Parents find this last step difficult because of the dangers. However, Tough Love's philosophy is that the teen is dying from drug use anyway, and this may be the only way to get him started into recovery. I must confess that I don't take this last step in my practice because I consider the streets far too dangerous. There are people out there called "chicken hawks" who are experts at seduction into prostitution and other crimes to pay for a teen's addiction.

I developed the REST program as an intermediate step before Tough Love. I simply add a rule for no drug use. Sadly for drug addictions, I've only gotten moderate results. AA or NA is essential for any recovery approach. It took peers to get a teen into using; it will take a peer group on the same journey toward recovery to get him out. Since AA and NA are spiritually based programs, I believe this helps a teen to gain strength in battling the powerful compulsion toward drugs.

The major drawback is that none of these programs, hospitalization, AA, or NA has long-term success records. Recidivism is high for teenagers who are addicts. I am so sorry that this is a bleak picture, but it is our current state of treatment, or lack of. It is reality.

TEEN SUICIDE

About five hundred thousand teenagers between the ages of fourteen and twenty-one attempt suicide each year, and about twelve thousand succeed. If you suspect that your teen is suicidal, seek professional help without delay. If a mental health professional believes it is necessary to hospitalize your teen, don't fight her. Putting a teen in the hospital can safeguard him until whatever crisis that precipitated an attempt to die has been ascertained and controlled.

In making an assessment for potential suicide, a professional would determine the level of risk. At the lowest level is a teen thinking about dying. Actually, they probably have such thoughts periodically and that is no cause for alarm. The next higher level would be having a plan, which means they have thought about how they would actually do it. At this level, there is cause for concern. The more detailed the plan, the greater the risk. Preparation means the highest level of risk. This means they have done things specifically to get ready for committing the act, such as hoarding pills, hiding a gun, or buying single-edged razorblades. If there is any indication of preparation, hospitalization is necessary. I allow for hospitalization at this level, as I do for addiction, because there is a clear risk to life.

Misconceptions about Teen Suicide

I'd like to dispel some confusions and misconceptions about teen suicide.

No Test for Suicide Risk

First, there are no psychological or medical tests that can accurately predict which teen is a potential suicide risk. There are available suicide risk questionnaires, but if a teen wishes to hide his intent, these may not discover that.

Depression versus Hopelessness

Second, depression is not necessarily a good indicator that a teenager may commit suicide. Most studies of teenagers that concluded that teens were depressed at the time of their attempts were usually conducted in clinical or hospital settings where the patients included highly disturbed individuals, such as schizophrenic patients, bipolar or manic-depressive patients, or the mentally handicapped. In studies done on more normal teenagers, such as at schools, where these more serious impairments were less frequent, the majority of teenagers who attempted suicide were *not* clinically depressed at the time. As psychiatrist Aaron Beck (1975) points out, a much better indicator is a deep sense of *hopelessness*. In hopelessness there is sadness, but the clinical signs of depression—which include frequent crying, lack of energy, inability to sleep, loss of appetite and weight, extreme anxiety, poor concentration, and isolating oneself—are not fully present. The hopeless youngster feels a combination of sadness and apathy but is not necessarily clinically depressed. He doesn't care what happens to him. Nothing has any meaning for him. To him life has been lousy and will continue to be lousy, so "What's the use?" Hopelessness means resignation, and a suicide means "Why not check out, it can't be worse than this!" However, clinical depression is still present in a significant number of cases, about 40 percent, and therefore cannot be dismissed as not being a serious sign.

The very ingredients that cause hopelessness are similar to those that lead to delinquency, gangs, and drug abuse. These include severe de facto neglect, feelings of being unloved, and possibly being abused. Suicide is only one way, from a variety of ways, that the wounded teenager searches in order to stop his pain.

Academic Failure

Another misconception is that most teenagers who attempt suicide usually are failing academically. Actually most of the youngsters who make an attempt are excelling academically; the second greatest number are those who are failing. Thus, suicide risks represent both ends of the academic spectrum. As a parent you may ask if you should not pressure your teen to excel. Is it dangerous to want them to do their best? It's not the pressure that leads to the suicide—it's the combination of pressure and the absence of unconditional love. If a child feels loved only because she excels, that could be a danger sign. But, if she knows she is deeply loved at all times and under any circumstances, even if she should fail in school, then there is probably little risk. So yes, you can encourage her to excel, but be certain to give her lots of unconditional nurturance.

Repeated Suicide Attempts

Does a history of several failed attempts mean your teen is only seeking attention and that she doesn't really mean it? Do you then not have to worry? NO! Most teens who do kill themselves have a history of previous attempts. Get these teens to a professional.

The Final Attempt

Often there is a specific event that may trigger a final and real suicide attempt, such as a breakup with a girlfriend, or the sudden separation of teens' parents. This actual, final attempt will most likely occur if the teenager has reached the end of the line, the point of hopelessness. The precipitating event may be minor, but it is the last straw. Most of the time, the buildup to the final step is gradual. If she reaches the point of hopelessness or if she becomes clinically depressed, then any negative event, even trivial, can tip the scale, such as the bombardment of negative media news, a friend getting into trouble, failing several tests, or conflict within her family. The weight of prior loneliness builds until anything can make her snap.

Should Parents Discuss Suicide with Their Teen?

If you feel that your teen has all the ingredients, such as a history of neglect, a feeling of hopelessness, a look of being lost and dejected or being depressed, then talk to her. Many parents feel they should avoid talking about suicide with their teen because that may plant the idea in their teen's head. You have to talk about it to find out what is going on. If she is healthy in the first place, talking about it will not plant the idea in her head. If she is not healthy, you need to know if she is nearing the end of her strength. When you discuss potential suicide with your teen, acknowledge her pain and assure her that help with a professional therapist will make the pain go away: that's all she really wants. It gives her hope.

Be Alert for the Added Risk of Drugs and Alcohol

Drugs and alcohol must also be a consideration in suicide. Use of chemicals can trigger depression; loss of enough rational thinking; and loss of control can push a teen "over the edge." Stay alert to any warning signs that drugs and/or alcohol are exacerbating the danger.

WHAT HAVE YOU LEARNED

I hope that you have learned about the danger signs for serious problems. You've been given directions to help with each problem, but they are not foolproof.

In the next chapter we're going to learn how to prevent serious problems. Prevention is far preferable to repair. We'll learn how to be proactive, so that we won't have to deal with becoming reactive.

8

The "1-2-3" Formula for Keeping Your Teen Away from Trouble

One: Fellowship
Two: Fun
Three: Spirituality

Does the prospect of your teenager getting into serious trouble frighten you? Of course it does. No well-intentioned parent wants their teen to fail in school, engage in lawless, delinquent acts, abuse drugs, or engage in violent acts toward others or himself. Are there any clear and pragmatic preventive measures that parents can take? I think that a major part of the answer lies in a three-part formula where we provide for our teens the ingredients of *Fellowship, Fun,* and *Spirituality.*

Some readers cringe when they see the word *spirituality.* For them it may be "Uh-Oh here comes the sugarcoating!" Many in the mental health profession scoff at the mention of spiritual issues. Psychiatrist Scott Peck in his book *The Road Less Traveled* writes that "Many psychologists and psychiatrists separate church from practice and don't connect the two." I recently read an article in one of our professional journals by a psychologist dismissing spiritual issues as unworthy for the profession of psychology to become involved with.

The practice of cognitive therapy, focusing on thoughts and beliefs, is growing as a dominant force in psychology. But psychologists fail to acknowledge the fact that spiritual beliefs form the major cognitions for the majority of the world's people. Eighty percent of the earth's population belong to some form of religion. That means that four out of five billion people are influenced by religious and spiritual issues. Put another way, this means that for 80 percent of the world, spiritual beliefs are an essential component of the way they live and behave. Even atheists often have what can be considered to be spiritual beliefs, which raises the percentage even more.

What will happen to our world if we fail to teach our youth the importance of spirituality? One only needs look at recent history. When the secular and Darwinian-like philosophies of Schopenhauer, Machiavelli, and Nietzsche dominated the minds of the Germans, ruthless, godless, and decadent conduct took over. Spinoza wrote that without a spiritually guided standard of conduct to control morality, there are no limits to destroying ourselves. Immanuel Kant wrote in the nineteenth century that in order to be happy and have order we must have God.

WHAT IS SPIRITUALITY?

There is no single or simple answer to the question, "What is spirituality?" It has many meanings, such as:

A feeling of being with God.
Belief in a deity or deities.
Transcending ordinary life to a feeling of ecstasy.
A philosophy or system of beliefs that gives us peace and serenity.
A belief system that gives us a moral and ethical code of conduct.
A moral system that controls our conduct with the fervent belief that failure to do so will engender dire consequences. Pope John Paul II writes in his book *Crossing the Threshold of Love* that "Hell is the ultimate guardian of morality."

Actually, spirituality means all of these things and perhaps a great deal more.

Foundation

Is belief in a religion necessary for spirituality? Yes and no. Scott Peck (1983) writes that a religious person may not be spiritual and a spiritual person may not be religious but yet still have a strong moral code where she values integrity, learning, growing, commitment, and nature. I have a friend who is an atheist, yet he is an extremely spiritual person because he has a strong sense of love, a dominant moral and ethical code, and a love for nature. However, I recently challenged him by asking him to look at and study the miraculous beauty of his newborn child while she is asleep in her crib and after that tell me that he still doesn't believe in God. He did, and he reported that the exercise planted some questions in him that he agreed to wrestle with.

Sometimes excessive religious fervor can reduce and even destroy our spirituality. Pope John Paul II writes that some fundamentalists violate the human rights of others; nothing can be farther away from spirituality. Rabbi Harold Kushner writes that we can destroy God's true message of love with sophisticated rhetoric.

The responsibility of raising children is perhaps our most important task in life. We devote the first twenty-one years of life to teaching and grooming them. But, have you clearly thought about what you want them to become? What type of person do you want them to be? What are you going to teach them? Are you going to leave their spiritual, moral, and religious development to chance? Or are you consciously and deliberately going to decide the kind of guidelines you want for them?

Is there a central theme or a basic idea that can guide you? Yes! Love is central to the emotional development of your child. The central principle in the spiritual foundation you teach your teenager should simply be *love*. John Paul II says that "The young need guides. They want to be corrected, to be told yes and no, and they want love." I believe that any religion or spiritual philosophy truly based on genuine *love* can't go wrong. The pope states that his church does not reject that which is true and holy in other religions, which he states is that "God Is Love."

I've treated many adults who in their youth rejected their faith because it rested on hell and damnation. To them, their early exposure to their family's religion was negative. If you want your teen to adopt your beliefs, then base them on the message of love. Attract them to your faith. Don't force it upon them. If you introduce them to faith through intimidation, in the long run you are likely to lose them. They may bolt. Rabbi Harold Kushner rejects a God that is not a God of Love. So will your teenager.

The New Testament, Matthew 22: 34–40, states:

> Hearing that Jesus had silenced the Sadducees, the Pharisees got together. One of them, an expert in law, tested with this question: "Teacher, which is the greatest commandment?" Jesus replied: "Love the Lord your God with all your heart and with all your soul and with all your mind. This is the first and greatest commandment. And the second is like it. Love your neighbor as yourself. All the Law and Prophets hang on these two commandments."

A child not taught love cannot in turn give love. If you want to raise a healthy teenager who behaves in a loving way toward you and others, then surround him in a spiritual life based on love and teach him a loving moral code. Remember the following:

$$Love = Spirituality$$
$$Spirituality = Love$$

If your teenager is filled with a strong sense of a loving spirituality, and if she conducts herself with this theme, then you probably won't ever need the services of a psychologist. There is also a more practical side to this spirituality issue that I will soon address.

PART ONE OF THE FORMULA—FELLOWSHIP

The first part of the preventive formula is fellowship. Earlier I pointed out how important friends are to teenagers; is it odd to you that I choose the word *fellowship* instead of the word *friendship*? *Fellowship* is a term more traditionally used in houses of worship. My intent is to focus on the relationship between spiritual matters and the friends your teenager hangs out with. I deeply believe that our houses of worship, that is, our spiritual homes, should be instrumental in helping teens to have friends and to have lots of good times.

For teenagers, the peer group is enormously powerful in determining their behaviors, their dress, their beliefs, and their attitudes. Please note that in this context I use the term *attitude* to mean demeanor, deportment, or the manner in which they relate to adults. You sometimes will hear a teen say, "Man you got a bad attitude," which means that your demeanor comes across negatively.

Do we, as parents, deliberately influence with whom our teens form friendships, or do we leave it purely to chance? Shocking as it may seem, we often leave it up to chance. I'm often surprised at the number of parents who know nothing about their teen's friends. Our teenagers typically form friendships with kids they meet either at school or in the neighborhood. What do you know about these kids? What are their values? What are their parents like? What are their life goals? Are they into drugs, and, if so, how deeply? Are they practicing any other illegal activities? Can you answer these questions with certainty and accuracy? If you can't, it is crucial for you to understand that *your teen's peer group can be a more powerful influence on her than you!*

In the last chapter we learned that if your teen hooks up with a bad peer group, you may lose her. Even if you are the greatest parent in the world, your teen will assume the mentality and behavior of her peer group. So, do you design who that peer group will be, or do you leave it to chance?

If you are having difficulty controlling your teenager, there is a high probability that a negative peer group has taken over. She has adopted the values, beliefs, and behaviors of that group. If the group is into drugs, your teen is too. If the group has little regard for adults, neither does your teen. If they do not value school, neither will your teen. If the group cares nothing for morality or the law, neither will your teen. Once the tentacles of the peer group engulf your teen, it will be extremely difficult for you or a therapist to reverse the damage.

Let's pretend to make an unlikely assumption. Let's assume you are a perfect parent. As I've pointed out, sadly, many teenagers from other families aren't so fortunate. Many are neglected, undisciplined, possibly abused, and probably untutored in moral values. If these teenagers become your teen's friends, you can expect to lose the battle over your teen's soul.

Do you ever go shopping at a mall on weekends? What do you see? As you are entering the mall, do you see teenagers hanging out, sitting on the ground, smoking cigarettes, wearing bizarre costumes, and looking aimless, purposeless, and lost? I've seen this scene many times. These lost souls can be the nucleus for your teen's value system. Is this what you want?

Solutions

Is there a solution to your teen's affiliating with the wrong crowd? Yes! It is our responsibility to design teens' social lives and to ensure they are hanging out with the kind of kids we want them to be with. It is here that houses of worship and community associations can make an enormous difference.

PART TWO OF THE FORMULA—FUN

Does your house of worship have a strong teen program? Does it have a program where fellowship and fun are deliberately designed and arranged and where teenagers are supervised?

Notice the word *fun*. Fun is essential for your teen. A well-conducted program can offer a rich variety of fun activities on weekends, such as lock-in parties, skating, bowling, field trips, going to movies, and on and on. What better way to win your teen than to give him a full and exciting life of fellowship and fun?

This is a magic formula. By guiding her to a peer group in a house of worship and by assuring that she has lots of healthy fun, you know who her friends are, you know what activities she is engaging in, you are controlling what beliefs and behaviors she is likely to adopt, and you are introducing her to spirituality in a positive way. Who says you can't have your cake and eat it too?

This formula ensures that our youth can make a learned association between good times and good friends within a spiritually enriched environment. Your teen can associate with other teens who you feel reasonably sure have the kinds of values and goals you want your teen to adopt. In an atmosphere of fun and friendship, your teen will be much more receptive to learning these values and morals. Wouldn't it be reassuring to know whom they are with, what they are doing, and that they are under responsible supervision?

If your house of worship or community association doesn't have a program, then try to enlist other adults to form such a program. Point out to other parents the numerous advantages. It is crucial that every Friday and Saturday evening is filled with fun activities or your house of worship or community association won't be attractive to your teen. While it will require some work on the part of all parents, you all can take turns, which means you have some weekends off while still having the peace of mind of knowing your teen is safe.

Leslie

Leslie, age thirteen, was described by her parents as a model child. They stated that they worked hard at being excellent parents. In fact, Leslie herself, at her first appointment, acknowledged that her parents were nice and that they were "always there for her." Her parents reported that ever since Leslie entered the eighth grade in middle school, a dramatic transformation was occurring. They were extremely distraught when they described that she had started smoking, become belligerent and unmanageable, and dressed, as they described, "like a little whore." She had gotten involved with a group of older kids, who they said were "about as low as you can get." Leslie was also coming home with the smell of alcohol and beer on her breath, and they were suspicious that she may have started smoking pot. All she talked about were her friends. They said it was as if she were possessed.

The peer group had taken over and was too powerful an influence. I recommended two things: first, that they move to a new school district, and, second, that since they were Jewish, they made certain that there was a strong teen program at a nearby Jewish community center. Moving was a rather startling suggestion, but I felt it was a necessary one in order to break her bonds with this particular peer group.

I continued to see Leslie. Her parents complied with my two suggestions.

They moved and joined a large Jewish community center with a very dynamic teen program. They had observed the program's activities carefully before deciding that it looked good.

In the fall, all the changes were made. At first Leslie was mad, but within two months she began a dramatic retransformation. She was constantly having fun with the group. The kids frequently called her to see if she was going to be at the planned activities. Her father said, with tears in his eyes, that he knew we won the battle when he was driving several of the teens to a scheduled activity and their conversation turned to what books they were currently reading. He looked in the rearview mirror and saw Leslie paying careful attention. Soon after that she began reading as a daily activity.

The lesson I am suggesting is to not let your teen's peer group be a consequence of chance. Design it. Make responsible decisions about where to find the kind of peers you want your teen to associate with. I keep a list of worship centers in my area that have excellent teen programs. I give parents all the information they need to make contact, observe what is going on, and make a decision about getting their teen involved. I encourage parents not to choose where to worship based just on their needs, but to also make certain the needs of their teen are well met too. While not very sophisticated theoretical therapy, it is pragmatic, and it works.

Let's look at the formula another way:

Fellowship: a carefully selected peer group

plus

Fun: providing exciting activities that a teenager would love to do, which is under supervision and in facilities provided at our houses of worship

equals

Spirituality: a joyful way to learn good values among good friends and healthy fun.

Now that you've got your teen's behavior under control and are working to fulfill many of their normal needs, it is time to learn how to grow closer with your teen. The next chapter focuses on how to communicate effectively with teenagers.

9 Communicating with Your Teen

When I first started practicing over thirty years ago, I did not know how to talk to teenagers. And did I turn a lot of them off! However, I recognized that a big part of the problem was me. I set out to learn those skills that would help me break through to as many of my teenage patients as I possibly could. I had a responsibility, and I was determined to fulfill it with gusto. Now I actually relish sessions with most of my teens. I've learned how to communicate with teenagers so that I listen to them and they listen to me. In this chapter we'll review some effective communication skills.

WHAT IT TAKES

Teenagers are walking radar machines. They can pick up on your attitude in a heartbeat. They can read you well. If they don't like you, you won't reach them. If they detect insincerity or hypocrisy, they won't communicate with you. I've learned that when I project genuine concern, a caring attitude, and love, perfect psychological technique isn't all that important. If they know you care, they'll probably be willing to engage in open, honest, and intimate communication with you.

It is from this prospective that I recommend all parents begin. Communicate from your loving and caring heart. Softness, gentleness, and genuine love are necessary to begin the process of dialogue. Robert Burns and Tom Whitman (1992) make the following and very relevant statement: "Intimate communication can be reached by those with humble attitudes."

Now that the constant *home* arguments have stopped, and your teen is doing well in school, you can work on improved communication. Remember it's their

135

life issues, beliefs, and values we want to reach, and to do that meaningful communication is essential.

COMMUNICATION BEGINS BY TRYING NOT TO COMMUNICATE

Effective communication doesn't begin at the time you are trying to communicate to resolve a crisis. It begins long before an incident or an issue surfaces. It begins by slowly and over many years cultivating your relationship with your teen.

Real communication begins with the daily practice of chitchat. This is where you spend what I call "soft time" with your teen. In other words, try to have idle conversation each day, instead of "preaching and teaching" about critical issues. Soft conversations should take place at least three times each day: at the breakfast table, at the dinner table, and when you're sitting by the side of his bed every night having delightful banter about "stuff." This is the time that you mostly devote to listening to your teen. It is at these times that you demonstrate a deep, loving interest in the events of *his* day, *his* reactions to what's going on in school, how *he* feels about what's happening in the news or sports, or how *he* feels about things other teenagers have been involved in. You are the empathetic listener who truly wants to know about *his* world.

It is OK to respond, to share, or to express your point of view. But try to keep this to a minimum. Mostly, ask and listen. You'll be amazed where these conversations go. In addition, you are teaching your teen critical thinking skills because with your gentle questions you can get them to think and rethink about whatever position they've taken. Most important, they are learning that they can talk to you and that they can trust you. In this way you are laying the foundation for the more intimate and critical communications that will inevitably come along. A deep, loving relationship lays the groundwork for those times when your teenager will really need you.

What Not to Do

Do not attempt to discuss a difficult issue when you are angry. If you do, you will not reach her. She will raise her defenses, and you will have no impact. Get your emotions under enough control to speak in a soft, assertive fashion. Let your intelligence and not your emotions govern your words.

If you have a concern do not jump on her as soon as she comes home. Let her enter the house to a loving you. Deal with the issue after she is settled and comfortable. I always find it best to let her know ahead of time that you wish to talk with her later, perhaps when her homework has been finished. An intimate conversation should be kept private. Don't try to communicate with her while anyone else, who is not relevant to the issue, is present.

If you yell at or bark at your teenager you are not communicating. As Pat Jakubowski says in his book *The Assertive Option*, she will only hear your first two sentences and nothing else. What occurs is that your teenager immediately begins rehearsing in her head her caustic rebuttal. She's stopped listening. If you wish to speak with her, then do so in a calm, normal, and respectful tone of voice.

Don't curse. It's wrong, and it sets a bad example. We usually curse in order to make a strong and emphatic impact. That's not the way to make your point. It also escalates emotions in both of you, which results in neither of you listening. Don't use global "you" statements, such as "You never do anything I tell you!" or "You're always on the phone." Especially don't use damning statements, such as "You're an idiot," "You are so clumsy," or even "You're just like your father." These types of statements are put-downs and also elevate defensiveness. Don't lecture. Nothing turns a teenager off more. It will get you nowhere.

Rather than lecturing, a much better rule for communicating is to say your point in a gentle, soft, very concise way and then to be very patient. I call this planting a seed. Your teen is listening. Just plant the seed; eventually, it will grow. She may not suddenly incorporate into her life the beliefs or values you're trying to teach her. But, as she gets older, she will remember, and what you have taught will eventually govern how she conducts herself. It sometimes takes a long time before you'll see it happening. Be patient and one day all the seeds you planted will begin to grow.

How to Initiate Problem-Focused Communication

If you have an issue you wish to discuss, do it by invitation. "Son, there's something I want to talk with you about. Can we sit down together, maybe in your room after your homework is finished?" Be polite. Be loving.

Use the formula that works best for assertions: the "I feel" plus "behavior" message. For example, "Julie, when you come in late on Saturday nights I feel really nervous. I'm scared something may have happened to you. All I ask is that you call if something has delayed you. I'd feel a whole lot better knowing where you are and that you are OK," or "Son, when you leave your room a mess, I feel angry at you. But, more than that, I worry that I'm not doing a good job as a parent in helping you to be organized and appreciate something that I think is important—neatness. Would you please try harder?"

Listening Skills

Listening to your teenager is a critical skill that you can develop. Being a good listener increases your teenager's motivation to talk to you when he feels burdened over something. He will not learn to be assertive if he knows *you* don't listen. Instead he'll resort to yelling and marked anger as attempts to overwhelm you with his power in order to get his way.

Good listening requires good empathy skills: try to put yourself in his shoes and actively interpret what his problems really mean to him. I recommend using imagery. I do this with my patients. This means that as you're listening try to form a mental picture about what is actually occurring or what the social circumstances may actually be like for your teen. This is called "active listening" or "active interpretation." For example,

Daughter: Dad, you don't understand how embarrassing it is for me to ask for a ride home at eleven o'clock.

Dad (actively trying to understand): Honey, what actually happens? I mean, why is it embarrassing?

Daughter: Because all the other kids don't have to be home until one o'clock.

Dad (probing more deeply): Well, how do they react if you ask for a ride? It's only about ten minutes of their time.

Daughter: Dad, they get pissed. They don't want to leave. If they see me approach them, they look as if the leper was coming. It's humiliating.

Dad: What if I drove over to pick you up?

Daughter: Yeah, right dad! I'd win baby of the year award. That would make things worse.

Dad: I'm trying to understand. I can see that if I were in your shoes it would be terribly embarrassing. Is there anyway a compromise can work?"

Daughter: I'd like to stay 'til one o'clock like the other kids.

Dad: What about midnight?

Daughter: Well some kids may leave earlier, but it would still be hard for me.

Dad: OK. I'll compromise. How about twelve thirty? At least I'll feel I'm doing my duty. You are younger than the other kids, but I'm trying to work with you. Will this work?

Daughter: I can live with that. Anyway, until next year.

Dad: OK, sweetheart. This will work 'til next year' and then we can talk about it again.

Dad really tried actively to understand her position. He placed his relationship with his daughter as a priority over absolutely winning what he wanted.

I know I said earlier don't negotiate. That was with the oppositional and abusive teen. If you used the REST program, arguments have stopped and now your teen should be more reasonable. If your teen is being reasonable and trying to communicate assertively, then negotiating is quite appropriate.

Be affirming. This means let your teenager know you love him and that what you want him to do is because you love him. Your position is not the product of wrath and of your being the absolute ruler. The covert or deep message you should always convey is, "I love you and I truly want what is best for you." This means that your relationship and your love for your teenager are your most important considerations. Often the issues are important because of your love. You want your teen to be happy and safe. Do you realize that your anger at him is because you think his behavior will lead to him not being happy or safe sometime in the future? When you get angry and insistent, however, you succeed in making him miserable and rebellious *now*. In other words, he gets upset and winds up doing the exact opposite of what you want—he'll deliberately do some dangerous or destructive act. Don't let your fears and your anger rule how you talk to him; let your love guide you. That is the best way to succeed in reaching him.

Your body language, tone of voice, and facial expressions convey a message. When talking to your teenager, look directly at him; don't cross your arms, which conveys an obstinate meaning; don't be sharp or caustic; don't be sarcastic. It helps sometimes to lean forward as if you're giving what he has to say your full attention and indicate that you are listening by saying, "Uh huh," "OK, go on," or "I'm listening." Validate his feelings by restating what you think he may be feeling, such as, "You're frustrated about coming home early Saturdays? Do you also feel mad at me?" Don't put him down, such as, "That's ridiculous!" or "That is dumb!" Try to listen and understand his point of view.

By doing all of these things you are also training your teenager in listening skills. If he knows from past history that you are fair-minded and that you honestly try to understand his point of view, you increase the likelihood that he will actively listen to your side.

Generating Solutions to the Problem

During the course of an exchange or debate, a time comes for solving the problem. To settle the issue, ask your teen what she sees as options. You can also express what you see as options. But, agree that some type of fair solution must be made; otherwise, the issue will remain as a sore spot for ongoing disagreements.

Honor the Agreement

Once you've come to an agreement, it is essential that you don't sabotage it. If you agreed to a 12:30 a.m. curfew, then don't pretend to forget and start requiring 11:00 p.m. again. If you do, your teen will lose faith in you, and consequently she'll close the door for future communications. Simply stated, she can't trust you. Honor is the last and perhaps most important part of effective communicating. If you are unhappy with the solution, then agree to discuss the issue again at some future time. If it looks like the solution isn't really working, then ask to discuss it again. But don't change the rules capriciously.

Other Hints

Try never to say, "No, because I said so." If you do say no to something, then say "no" with a good reason. If you don't have a good reason, then don't say "no," instead give in. Be flexible.

One of the greatest pitfalls to effective communication is *topic hopping*. This means that you get off the topic and bring up other issues. This is one of the most common mistakes for getting nowhere. For example, if you're discussing weekend curfew hours, don't switch to the topic of drinking at parties. Solve one issue at a time. You can deal with another issue at another time. Stick to only one problem at a time. If you try more, you have an argument rather than a communication.

Throughout your discourse, always stay calm and loving. Remember it is the relationship that is paramount. It is quite common for a discussion to get out of hand and turn into an argument. To prevent this, it is necessary for both you and your teenager to recognize it and stop. Take a breather. The underlying thoughts that lead to an escalation or yelling match involve focusing on one's own feelings of vulnerability, powerlessness, insecurity, and loss. When this occurs, each of you tries to escalate to a more powerful posture. If one can appear more menacing and threatening, then he falsely believes that he can overpower his opponent. Of course, when one party does this, usually the other does the same thing, and the situation rapidly escalates out of control (Jakubowski and Lange, 1978). Attorney Gerry Spence points out that this is not the way to win an argument. "Winning" according to him means winning the other person over to your side. This can occur only with calm and loving reserve. Getting angry and yelling never helps either party to win. In fact, when that happens, both lose.

This chapter isn't intended as a full course on everything you need to know about effective communications. But, I think there's enough here to provide you with some working guidelines. Some suggested readings that might help you and your teen include: *The Assertive Option* by Pat Jakubowski and Art Lange; *Your Perfect Right* by Robert Alberti and Michael Emmons; *Love Is Never Enough* by Aaron Beck.

In the next chapter, we'll look at how to communicate and relate to help your teen develop healthy attitudes for her deepest beliefs.

10 Understanding and Influencing Teen Thoughts and Beliefs

Our ultimate goal is to help your teen develop a healthy cognitive pattern, to help him develop healthy thoughts, healthy beliefs, healthy values, and healthy attitudes. Toward this goal we've gotten your teen's behavior under control to stop the arguing and to pave the way for improved communication. In the last chapter you learned effective methods of communication to better reach your teen. You've also learned that if you are to impact his cognitive development you've also got to connect your teen to a healthy peer group that will influence his behaviors and his cognitive development. In this chapter we begin to explore some of the most important thoughts and beliefs that must become part of your teen if he is to function in emotionally appropriate and healthy ways. In chapters 11 and 12 we'll focus on healthy values, and in chapter 15 we'll focus on developing healthy attitudes, the deepest beliefs.

Our job in this chapter is to uncover some of your teen's thoughts and help him to change his irrational, defeating ones to more rational, enabling cognitive patterns.

There is an interconnected relationship between beliefs, thoughts, and behaviors that is crucial to understand if we are further to uncover the mystery of how teens function. Beliefs determine the way one thinks, and one's thoughts determine how one behaves. For example, if a teenager believes that having a girlfriend is essential for being important to his peers then he'll probably be thinking that he must therefore have a girlfriend. In turn, his behavior will be directed toward getting a girlfriend. Once you understand a teen's beliefs and thought patterns, then their behaviors become less of a mystery.

Freud used the term *preconscious thinking*, which he viewed as those thoughts or beliefs that are just below the surface. According to Freud, and others, most of our beliefs are learned early in our lives. By the way, Freud never used the term *subconscious*. I prefer the term unaware to *preconscious*, which is a term with too much mystical connotation. Many of our beliefs can be readily retrieved and articulated; however, there are many beliefs human beings are often unaware that they have, and yet they are important because they dictate much of our behaviors.

Irrational beliefs often underlie some of the rather bizarre teen behavior patterns that puzzle us. In the next section we'll look at some irrational beliefs and focus on helping them develop more healthy and rational ones.

YOUR TEEN ISN'T AN ALIEN

Did you ever look at your teen and wonder, "Is she mine? Maybe she's from another planet. She couldn't be mine. It's some kind of mistake." I will bet that sometimes you have seen your teen interacting with other teens and felt an overwhelming sensation of nausea.

Teens do indeed have patterns of thinking and ways of behaving that we can designate as not quite rational. Some of these we may have to tolerate until they reach age twenty-one, when perhaps they become normal again. But some of their beliefs need our attention and our help. We can help by working with them on realigning their thoughts and behaviors into more reasonable and rational patterns. We must understand what irrational thoughts they harbor before endeavoring to help them change to more rational thinking patterns.

Therapeutic methods for changing cognitions, that is, thoughts and beliefs, are called "cognitive restructuring." Our goal is to help your teen think and behave more rationally by restructuring her cognitions. This requires using the communication skills you learned in the last chapter. Let's begin our journey into some of the more irrational beliefs, thoughts, and behaviors of our teens.

Irrational Thought 1

It is not my fault that I get into trouble or fail. It's my parents, teachers, and other adults that are the cause.

Rarely do teens blame their friends for their problems. This occasionally does occur, but it is not as favored by many teens as blaming the adults around them.

It is extremely important that you do some soul-searching to be certain that there is not some validity to your teen's point of view. While blaming parents is a common irrational thought, sometimes, as we saw earlier when discussing toxic families, the parents may indeed be the problem. One such case I dealt with, when it was the parent's fault, was quite recent.

Melinda

The father of thirteen-year-old Melinda came in to see me after I had been doing several months of frustrating therapy with the family, stating that he was very "put out" with her because he caught her drinking beer; he added that "she was slugging it down like a pro." Melinda was also continuing to fail in school and that too was upsetting him.

Sometimes when I think it may be helpful, I use strong confrontation, which is what I did in this instance. After so many sessions with little change, I finally said to her parents, "Why shouldn't Melinda drink like a pro? She sees both of you slug down several six packs almost every night of the week! What else is there for her to learn? As for failing in school, why shouldn't she? Both of you continue to work late most evenings. You aren't required to put in these late hours, and you don't really need the money. Have you shown any interest in her school-work? I told you that it was important to occasionally take her on educational day trips. In the last several months you haven't done this once. When you are home, have you shut off the TV for reading time?" They both shook their heads no. "Have you shown any interest in her reading? Have you taken her to the library or bookstore?" Again they shook their heads. "Why haven't you gotten her into a church teen program? It's been weeks. What do you expect me to do as a therapist? How can I counteract what she is surrounded by? If you don't show responsibility, why should she?" Her father responded by saying, "I guess you're right. I needed to hear that. I'd better get on the stick." He did, and finally, Melinda improved. Before dealing with the issues of your teen taking responsibility for his problems, make certain you are a proper role model.

Many years ago, William Glasser wrote a pioneering book about teens called *Reality Therapy*. One of Glasser's main issues was that teens often do not take responsibility for their problems.

Disputation as a Communication Technique for Accepting Responsibility

A good way to handle a teen's denial of responsibility is by *gently* disputing your teen's position. Disputation is a common cognitive restructuring technique. "Johnny, I love you and I know you are hurting because you are doing poorly in school. But have you listened to yourself? It's your teachers' fault. You say that they are lousy teachers. Johnny, each and every one of them? Son, I also can't buy that it's your girlfriend's fault because she wants so much of your time. When was the last time you told her you couldn't see her because you needed to study? Next, you have the excuse that you can't study or concentrate because Mom and I won't let you see your friends during the week, and that upsets you. Then you claim you're failing because you've been grounded one weekend, or because I got mad at you over something. Johnny, do you not have a role in what happens in your own life? I love you son, and I hope you will realize that it is your responsibility to do well in school. The rest of the world is not going to change for you. If you want to do well then it is your responsibility and yours alone. I'll love you no matter what, but all I ask is that you give this issue some serious thought. I worry so much about you. I want you to do well, but I'm not the one that can make it happen: everyone else is not your real problem."

In this hypothetical exchange, Dad focuses on the irrational thinking and the behavior. He does not globally put Johnny down. He does not say, "You're lazy! You'll never get anywhere in life," and so forth. He disputes Johnny's attitude with reflective questions and avoids the typical "When I was your age. . .!" comments.

When I see teens in my office, I use this same technique. I'm usually quite frank, open, and honest with them. When issues are stated calmly, soberly, and positively teens do listen. I often add, "If your goal is to get the rest of the world to change, well, good luck! That is a rather 'humongous' task, and if you can do that, let me know the secret. None of us can change the behavior of other people. The only real power any of us have is to change ourselves." If a teen is experiencing painful feelings, I instruct him to honestly face his role in generating these feelings. How can feelings change? I'll ask, "How are you dealing with circumstances? It takes courage to face your personal responsibility in your problems. It takes self-discipline on your part and personal change if your life is ever going to get any better. If you want to continue to hurt, then continue doing nothing and blame the rest of the world. It is not me that's hurting. It's you and only you, who can do something about it. I don't want you to be hurting. But, you're the only one with the power to change yourself. I can guide you, but you have to do the work."

Getting Your Point Across

It may surprise you how receptive teens can be to this point of view, but only if stated calmly and in a nonthreatening manner. Communicating is a skill and an art. It is a learnable skill, but it requires artistic finesse in its application. Being calm, frank, open, and honest is the magic key to talking to teens. Talk to them, not at them. Use disputation, not confrontation.

If you try talking to them when you are in a rage, or in the middle of a bad situation, you will get nowhere. Wait for a quiet time to sit and talk. Show your love and concern. Tell them you love them. They need to hear it. Do not assume they know it. Tell them how worried you are. Loving communications performed in this way will succeed much more than most parents realize.

If you lecture or yell, you will feed directly into their blaming mentality. When you yell, they focus only on your "being on their case." They will not be listening to you. They will not entertain the idea that they had any responsibility in whatever the problem might be. Lecturing and yelling are self-defeating. They will not be receptive. When your teen does something that you think is blatantly wrong and your immediate reactions is to explode, he will not listen: he will focus his blame on you. Reflect for a moment: I'll bet you've yelled repeatedly over the years and nothing changed. Why continue behaviors that have constantly met with failure? Try this new, more effective approach.

When you do talk calmly with your teen, validate or affirm his feelings. This means you are trying to understand how he may be feeling. For example, try, "Son, you've seemed down lately, are you? Do you think it's because of your grades? If we talk about it, maybe we can focus on a solution that will help you feel better. I love you, and I hurt when you do. I hope you know that." When you get your teen's attention, and validate his feelings, next try to get him to focus on solutions. "What is preventing you from doing well in school?" "I hate the teachers!" your son replies. "I don't think we can fix the teachers. I've had a few bad ones too. The only power you have is what *you can* do to make things better. Is there anything that you can do?" If your teen blames you or others for his problems try this calm, direct, and assertive route.

Irrational Thought 2

If there is something I'm supposed to do that I hate doing, then I'll avoid it.

Most of the time when teens think of avoiding something they hate, it usually involves schoolwork. Sadly this places them at risk for being labeled attention deficit disorder/attention deficit hyperactive disorder (ADD/ADHD). After schoolwork, household chores are probably next. The most frequent strategies teens employ for avoiding school responsibilities are excessive partying, drinking, cruising, or merely talking on the telephone for hours with friends. Many of my students do all of these.

I hold class discussions about these behavior patterns and the underlying belief. I ask my students to be honest and share whether they indeed do any of these things. I ask them if they wait until the very last moment to do their work. Most of them confess that they do. I ask them to get in touch honestly with the feelings they have while ducking their work and making poor grades. I inquire if they tend to blame their professors. When I discuss this calmly with both my students and my teen patients, they do admit to these tendencies. They also confess to feeling guilt and anxiety when they avoid hard work. Upon reflection most of them admit that their avoidance strategies only relieve tension very briefly and actually result in more prolonged bad feelings.

I emphasize to both my students and patients that tasks such as studying and homework do indeed produce anxiety. School-related tasks are typically difficult and uncomfortable things to do. However, if teens can become deeply immersed in their work, these bad feelings will quickly subside. The hardest part is getting started on the work. If grades improve as a result of developing new and more responsible habits, then they get the added benefit of moving closer to their chosen career.

As we'll learn in the following chapter on value education, only self-discipline can lead to feelings of peace and calm. Self-discipline requires courage. Self-discipline means forcing oneself to face the most difficult tasks. It is only by conquering, mastering, overcoming, solving, and completing hard tasks that bad feelings will go away. I point out to teenagers that if they continue to avoid dealing with responsibilities, then a little voice programmed inside them constantly tells them that they are doing something wrong, which then results in a constant and ongoing state of feeling bad. Avoidance behaviors consisting of partying, drinking, or meaningless activities offer only a temporary reprieve from pain. Bad feelings will encompass and pervade their lives if they continue to avoid responsibilities.

I often tell my students and patients that A students are not necessarily brighter. The basic difference is that A students have better work habits. They steadily and consistently deal with difficult work until it is mastered. Once their work is mastered, then good feelings prevail.

Tammy

Tammy was a freshman in my Introduction to Psychology course. She came to my office at the end of the semester to thank me for teaching her study skills during the first two class meetings of the semester. She said in high school she was a procrastinator but made As because the work was so much easier than in college. She told me that when she realized the amount of work and the complexity of content in all her courses, she knew she had better practice what I had taught her. By remaining current in her readings, clearing up complex concepts as the semester progressed, and beginning to study for exams several days before the test, she had completed her first semester with As and only one B. She said that she felt good all through the semester and that getting good grades helped her feel even better. She told me that, as I had promised her, she was pleasantly surprised to find that she actually enjoyed her courses. On weekends she found that she could enjoy herself more, because mentally she gave herself permission to truly relax and have fun.

I only wish more of my students would adopt this new and better belief.

Irrational Thought 3

Not Thinking.

Do you ever wonder why teens drive as they do? Why they blast their music? Why they may not know where Florida is on a map? Why they cruise, or hang out for hours in front of a mall? Some teens have literally turned off their brain. Yes, it's true: no thought.

Their minds are only preoccupied with rehearsing the top ten rock songs. Their interests lie in playing video games, talking with friends about the opposite sex, admiring the fanciest cars, or talking about which movie they'd like to see. They only focus on what trivia they value and give little or no thought to anything else. If we have failed to teach them to make important their education, their career, world events, other people, God, books, their personal accomplishment, then there is little motivation for them to think about important issues.

I recall the day many years ago while a teenage patient was sitting opposite me, I had been frustrated in trying to work with her. All of a sudden, I realized that she hardly entertained any intelligent thought whatsoever. This insight occurred when I asked her if she saw the space shuttle go up last night, and she said, "What's that?" I almost fell out of my chair.

Researchers, including myself, have been finding that the major cognitive pattern of children diagnosed as attention deficit disorders is "not thinking." This cognitive proclivity also applies to too many teens. Too many teens simply do not think. No effort is expended to learn, understand, or pay attention to anything that to them is not fun. Thinking about their future, focusing on the speedometer while in the car, and trying to understand complex concepts is not import to them nor is it fun, and therefore they exert little or no mental effort. Buddhists call this pattern of nonthinking having a "monkey mind." I think that's apt.

There are typically two main causes of this not thinking phenomenon. The first cause, as I stated, is our failure to inculcate into them important values, and values underlie motivation. How can they learn and hold dear values we haven't taught them in the first place? If we haven't surrounded our teens with the proper learning environment, how can they learn important values? If their extended family is absent, if their immediate family is too busy, if they don't have proper role models, if they are flooded with the meaningless values portrayed in the media, why should they exert any mental energy on those things that are truly important? No one expends energy or thought onto those things they don't consider important. In too many cases we have failed to motivate teens to analyze, reflect, project, or problem solve in what are truly the meaningful areas of life. Understanding anything requires energy and mental exertion, which requires motivation, and in turn motivation requires a strong set of proper values. For all too many of our teenagers, motivation is absent because they are valueless.

The second cause of this "not thinking" phenomenon is affluence. We fulfill teenagers' material needs too easily. Teens are often surrounded by material wealth, all of which has been placed there without any exertion on their part. To earn a TV in their room, a stereo, designer clothes, a telephone, and so forth all that is required of them each day is to merely roll out of bed. Why think or problem solve if there is no reason to? Are we giving them too much, too easily?

Irrational Thought 4

They Don't Value Money. "Why don't teenagers understand the value of money?" *says almost every parent.*

This is one of the frequently asked questions that I hear from parents. I answer, "Why should they?" How can they understand how difficult earning money is when all they do is put their feet on the carpeted floor in the morning and magically everything they want or need is there? No effort or planning on their part was necessary.

Here is a helpful step you can take. When I see teen patients who are performing poorly in school, I ask them what it would take to live on their own. I do a hypothetical budget with them. Together we calculate how much money it would take to be single, live in a small apartment, and own an economy car. We then compare this budget to their potential earning ability without having any marketable skills. Teens are often shocked to realize they will be unable even to manage living in a small apartment unless they start paying attention and begin to plan more carefully.

John's Budget

Below is a budget I worked on with John, a sixteen-year-old, who was thinking of quitting school. This budget helped him to change his mind.

HYPOTHETICAL AVERAGE MONTHLY BUDGET:

Apartment Rent	$500.00
Utilities	$100.00
Car Payment	$200.00
Telephone	$30.00
Car Insurance	$125.00
Medical Insurance	$150.00
Food	$225.00
Gas	$80.00
Entertainment	$160.00
Cleaners	$10.00
Clothing Allowance	$50.00
Car Repair Allowance	$60.00
(including oil changes, tires, regular maintenance, etc.)	
Household Necessities Allowance	$75.00
(pots, pans, dishes, furniture, etc.)	
Miscellaneous	$75.00
Total Monthly Expenses	$1,880.00
Annual amount needed	$22,560.00
Estimated taxes	$3,000.00
Gross annual income needed	$25,560.00

HYPOTHETICAL INCOME

Monthly (4 weeks) income ($6.00/hour)	$960.00
Gross annual income	$12,480.00
Estimated taxes (15%)	$1,872.00
Net annual income	$10,608.00

Quite an eye-opener, isn't it?

Another exercise is to have your teen help with the family's monthly bill paying. This helps them discover exactly what your actual financial situation is. Why keep it a secret? Seeing how much is coming in and how much is going out helps them understand why you get upset when they make excessive financial demands. A budget concretely explains why you are always so worried about finances. This monthly exercise frequently facilitates a better understanding between teens and parents over money matters. By fostering more understanding, arguments are often reduced.

Stop providing for all their needs; instead, put them on a modified, less stringent version of the REST or allowance program where they must earn much of the money that they require. This program will not only require them to earn money for many of the things you are now giving them but also require active thinking and planning on their part to obtain the things they need.

Irrational Thought 5

Catastrophizing.

Catastrophizing involves interpreting a mild event as major and then reacting accordingly. Teens often overreact to minor setbacks. Probably the most prominent setback for a teen is breaking up with a boyfriend or girlfriend. From a parent's perspective we see this as no big deal. "After all, it is not like being married with children and facing a divorce." But to a teenager this can be a catastrophe. There are other frequent situations that can trigger an overreaction. Perhaps, for example, you've said to your teen, "No you can't go to that party: they'll be drinking!" only to end up enduring his giant temper tantrum. Missing a party is perceived by a teen as a catastrophe.

From our perspective, much of what they catastrophize seems minor, perhaps even humorous. We may even be tempted to get angry at how silly we think they are acting. Dismissing their perceptions as trivial only serves to distance both of you. To them it's an important issue. Patiently try to understand their point of view. By calmly discussing a more rational interpretation of the situation, you may be able to defuse the situation. Let's look at a case where the ramifications of a teenager's catastrophizing almost turned into a tragedy.

Cathy

A psychologist friend of mine had a fifteen-year-old girl, Cathy, as a patient in a hospital unit. Cathy's boyfriend had ended their relationship. She had been admitted because, while clutching her boyfriend's picture to her chest, she was crying and wailing throughout the day and night. My friend, an excellent psychologist, thought that for this particular girl there was a serious risk for suicide. He ordered an around-the-clock suicide watch. One day, surrounded by two nurses while on the way to breakfast, she suddenly leaped over the stair banister and fell several floors. She did not die, but she did shatter her legs.

The moral of this case scenario is that what may seem minor to us may be of major importance to a teenager. Put yourself in "their moccasins" and try to imagine what the circumstance really means for them. For example, you may require your teen to be home early from a party. To you it's no big deal. But to your teen it may appear to be a catastrophe. From his perspective, you may be putting him in an awkward position because none of his friends with cars are required to leave until a later curfew time. Then your teen has to beg someone to take him home. This can be humiliating. In Cathy's case, my colleague correctly assessed that her parents markedly neglected her and that for her, having a boyfriend was excessively important. The loss of her boyfriend meant the loss of the only source of love she had. By fully understanding why her boyfriend was so important, my colleague correctly assessed the magnitude of her grief and what she was capable of doing.

Understanding their point of view doesn't mean avoiding teaching them more realistic thinking. If teens are to learn how to see things more realistically, they must learn rational thought. Developing the ability for clearer thinking necessitates that you try to understand their point of view and that you patiently and calmly communicate more rational ways to look at each circumstance. Over time and with patience on your part, they can learn more realistic ways to interpret setbacks.

When a teen is in my office, I patiently listen to her point of view about her problem. I validate her feelings and acknowledge that I can see how, indeed, it is a problem. I affirm her point of view. However, I point out that complications, problems, and stresses in life will never cease. These things come in many forms, and, if we habitually view each problem as a catastrophe, we will spend the rest of our lives either severely anxious or painfully depressed. A helpful imagination exercise I do with teenagers is:

> Imagine you [the teen] are standing at the bottom of Hoover Dam and you are looking up at a wall that is hundreds of feet high. Suddenly, the wall cracks open, and a giant wall of water is bursting out and is about to kill you. That is a catastrophe! Now how would you rate your problem when compared to this wall of water? Is your problem indeed a catastrophe?

After a chuckle, teens often begin to see their problem more realistically.

Adults also frequently catastrophize. This is not an exclusively teenage pattern. Ask yourself if you needlessly and excessively get upset over "the small stuff"? If you do, remember that you are a role model, and, if you overreact, why won't your teen?

Irrational Thought 6

I wear these clothes because all the other kids do.

In my research I have found that for teenagers, lack of neatness is an infrequent problem. In fact, most teens spend hours in front of a mirror primping and trying to look appealing. Yes, some teens can dress in markedly outlandish ways. If that's a problem with your teen, then remember that here too the REST program will help. However, I encourage parents to be reasonable when trying to define what outlandish means because I can't give you a standard as a basis for your judgment.

A teen's clothing or manner of dress is a uniform. It reflects the style of dress of the peer group to which the teen belongs. If they associate with relatively normal and healthy teens, I doubt you have much to worry about over their manner of dress. Teens simply have styles that may not necessarily agree with our tastes. However, as you are aware, there are some teen groups with some rather drastic modes of dress. Their clothing, or uniform, can reflect a group that practices some undesirable behaviors. For example, some groups are rather wild and may be involved in drugs, acid rock, cults, hate groups, and so forth. They wear clothing that reflects membership in their group. If your teen is dressing as if she belongs to one of these groups the odds are that either she does or that she aspires toward membership. Fortunately, most teens are not into these more drastic behaviors and their dress merely reflects what is in vogue. Use good judgment. Be careful before drawing conclusions.

If your teen is dressing in a very bizarre way, then you may, indeed, have something to be concerned about. Is your teen involved in a group that is into some serious problematic behaviors, such as drugs, violence, vandalism, crime, and truancy? If he is, then it is imperative that you get him out of that group. It is doubtful that any therapist or any behavioral program will overcome the influence and power that the group can exert over your teen. If you discover that your concerns are accurate, then recall our earlier discussion involving getting them into a new peer group in a church or community center. As I also stated, in extreme instances, it may even be necessary for you to move to a new neighborhood and a new school district. Your teen's membership in a truly bad group may necessitate such a drastic change. Fortunately, these more severe cases are not very frequent. Stay alert to what your teen's clothing is communicating.

Irrational Thought 7

I can't help it, that's just the way I am and I'll always be that way.

Teenagers often think they can't change. Some of them don't want to change.

I am in a position, as a therapist, to more readily challenge this irrational thought than are most parents. When talking with teenagers, I can cite numerous case examples of teens who have successfully made remarkable changes. Thus, I'm in a position to reinforce the message that change is realistic.

I often hear, "It is not possible for me to change." I then reply, "Not only is it possible for you to change, but you are going to whether you want to or not." I'll ask them to project to ten years, twenty years, or thirty years from now: do they see themselves then as being exactly as they are now? Most say that is silly because they will be middle aged, and, of course, they will be different. I then ask them if they want merely to let these changes happen or would they rather design the specific kinds of changes they would like to see happen. At this point, most teens just sit quietly, then, after a while, often say, "I never looked at it that way."

Then I will usually say, "So far we've been talking about long-term changes, and you're beginning to see that you will change whether by deliberate choice or by letting the events of life dictate that change." I ask them to think about short-term or more immediate changes. I want them to reflect on doing some changing now. I often ask, "Is the way your life is going now truly making you happy?" Those teens that are not happy and are experiencing emotional pain, such as anxiety, depression, or guilt, will probably welcome change. They want to know anything that they can do to feel better and make the pain stop. But, this only applies to a few of my teen patients. Most of the teens I see as patients are not in pain and do not want to change at all. This does not represent the majority of teenagers, just the majority a therapist sees as patients. These teens did not volunteer to come to therapy. They wound up in my office by being dragged in by their parents because of their obnoxious behaviors. These are the oppositional defiant disorder (ODD), oppositional, or ADD/ADHD teens. Typically they'll say, "I'm fine and perfectly happy. All I want to do is be with my friends and have fun. I just want you and my parents to leave me alone!"

Oppositional-defiant, ODD, and ADD/ADHD teens are neither in pain nor do they desire to change. It's the parents who are in pain and want them to change. Some think that opposition, inattention, and anger masks hidden pain: it does not. The opposition and anger are part of a power struggle to get their way, and do as they wish. Typically there is little incentive for them to change. All their needs are being met. They remain quite comfortable without having to do well in school and with being very difficult to live with at home. Change means nothing to them. They have no meaningful consequences for their lack of thinking or for their inconsiderate behavior. In the absence of distress, there is no incentive to change. For oppositional teens, the irrational message usually is, "I'm not going to change and you can't make me!" For the ADD/ADHD teen, the message is "I hate school. It means nothing to me. All I want is to have fun. Leave me alone." I'll bet that for most of you, these are the reasons you picked up this book in the first place. If a teen is hell to live with and failing in school, then make her change with the REST program. Teens in pain with depression and anxiety are more amenable and receptive to help. They want to learn how to function better and make the pain go away. Who wouldn't want pain to stop?

A teenager in pain must understand that change takes courage and hard work. Personal change is the most difficult work anyone, teen or adult, will ever have to do. In the old days of psychiatry, we thought that all a patient had to do to get better was to lie down on a couch and talk. But we've discovered this form of therapy doesn't work. We now know that it takes self-discipline, hard work, and lots of effort for adults or teens to change self-destructive patterns of thinking and behaving. Therapy is like a teacher–student relationship. The therapist helps the patient discover irrational cognitive patterns and offers alternative and more rational ways to interpret events. *We can force behaviors to change; we can only influence cognitions to change.* Cognitive change will usually happen only with considerable dedication and effort on the patient's part. If a teen wants his pain to stop, this is what it takes. No magic cures exist.

Irrational Thought 8

I absolutely must have a boyfriend (or girlfriend) or I am worthless.

Having a boyfriend or girlfriend, for teenagers, is often a badge of status among their peers. It sends a message to their peers as well as to themselves that they are attractive and desirable. In addition, when a teenager's hormones surge, an enormous and almost uncontrollable drive is unleashed. Having a boyfriend or girlfriend can also compensate for some of the loneliness modern teens feel. In our culture, when we aren't providing the affection that teens desperately need, they often seek out members of the opposite sex for comfort.

There are two components necessary to address in discussing a teenager's desperation for someone. First, it is important to provide a loving, nurturing, and secure family environment. Only a loving family provides the necessary security that makes it less crucial for a teen to desperately seek someone to love.

The second component, as I said a moment ago, involves having a boyfriend or girlfriend as a badge of prestige or self-worth. But this doesn't necessarily have to be the case. Having a boyfriend or girlfriend is nice but not essential. A true and more meaningful sense of self-worth comes from accomplishment. A deep immersion in industrious occupations, such as schoolwork, sports, and hobbies, provides a more consistent and substantial foundation for self-worth. The most important message for a teen is that if they are happy within themselves, they will not desperately need someone else to "make them happy." They won't need a prestige badge. Having a relationship can add to an already fulfilling life; it is not a substitute. A relationship should not be the sole measure of one's self-worth.

An important lesson for teens is that being happy within themselves by being productive and industrious increases the chances that they will choose better partners for a relationship. When one is content from within, one will not be desperate for a relationship. When one is desperate, one will grab whatever comes along instead of being selective.

Happiness from within must be earned. In order to earn it, one must have goals and the willingness to immerse oneself in achieving those goals. When self-fulfillment is a priority, then the desperate need to be in love will not be overwhelming.

Irrational Thought 9

Life should be fair and easy and I should get what I want when I want.

Are you frustrated with your teen wanting all of life's goodies right now? Do you realize you're probably feeding into this? Many of us too readily provide all of our teen's material desires. Do you believe that your teen should not struggle as you did? Numerous philosophers, theologians, and writers tell us that God uses struggle to mold us. Struggle requires us to make use of our own brains, our wits, and our bodies to overcome the hurdles built into life. It is this battle that brings out the best in us and gives us a sense of accomplishment, self-worth, and dignity. Immanuel Kant wrote, "struggle forces us to exert and reach levels of newer powers." When life is too free and easy, humans can automatically gravitate to lower and lower levels of functioning. Our mind and soul are like muscles that atrophy if they never get used. The result of an absence of struggle is feeling lost, aimless, and purposeless in life. These lead to an ongoing emotional state of listlessness, apathy, and mild depression.

A few of my teen patients initiate seeing me because they have this vague feeling of unhappiness and confusion. They describe themselves as having a combined sense of restlessness and boredom. I often ask if this also feels a little bit like feeling down or sad. They look surprised and ask, "How did you know?" I then suggest that they compare the number of hours that they feel good to the number of hours that they feel not so good. The scale usually leans dramatically toward not feeling well most of the time.

I emphasize to teens that it is the hurdles and obstacles in life, the things that demand our utmost attention and energy, that bring us into focus! These hurdles are what mobilize us and make us function at our best. Putting our heart and soul into overcoming hurdles actually makes us feel so much better. I ask them to try it for two weeks and report how they feel. Some teens, of course, refuse to do this, but some comply. Those that try it and pay careful attention to their mood usually report feeling better. Often they're quite surprised. In discussing this phenomenon, I point out how difficult it is to initiate work on a project, but once underway a magical transformation takes over our feelings. We begin to feel constructive, focused, and even excited. In physics there is the concept called *inertia,* which means that an object that is not in motion tends to stay not in motion, and an object that is in motion tends to stay in motion. To start an object into motion takes extra special force. It also takes an extra special conscious effort on our part to get us into motion and start work on a project, but, once we get going, it becomes easier to stay in motion and the result is much better feelings. We actually feel alive. Excessive idleness is a great enemy of emotional well-being. When looked at in this way, hurdles are a great blessing.

I sometimes share with teens that for years I was in full-time private practice in a very affluent neighborhood. My adult patients generally fit into two categories, those who overworked and stayed exhausted and stressed, and those who had nothing to do all day but stay neurotic. Psychologists sometimes refer to the latter group as the "worried well." Contentment necessitates a delicate balance between industrious occupation and having healthy and relaxing fun. Too much of either is destructive.

I have many teenagers who have little motivation. All they desire is to "hang out." Most of the time these kids harbor ongoing feelings of sadness and listlessness. I tell teens that the world is complex and conquering it can be tough, but, as Harold Kushner states, "God gave us a lot of excellent equipment" designed just for that purpose. God wants us to use our equipment. When we do, we feel better. We feel a sense of accomplishment and a well-earned positive self-image. When we don't use our equipment, we feel useless and walk around with an ongoing negative self-image.

I have some students that openly resent and rebel against the hard work of college. They get mad at professors who demand a lot. They want to get through the system quickly and effortlessly. These students spend more time avoiding work than it would take to tackle it, master it, and get through it. By resenting and dodging these obstacles, they are missing out on an important lesson of life. It is the very process of conquering obstacles that gives a sense of meaningfulness and personal growth. The studying, reading, and hard work can lead to the joy of accomplishment. It gives humans a sense of personal growth, which cannot happen in any other way.

At the beginning of each semester, I have a discussion with my freshmen students. In this discussion, I emphasize the message about the rewards of hard work. I emphasize that easy routes to success are very rare. Only a tiny fraction of people win the lottery or inherit wealth. If they want the so-called good life, there is no easy way to get it. I don't like the emphasis on material success, but unfortunately many of them only relate to this type of approach.

Many college students refuse to go to graduate school because it means additional years of hard work. I tell my students that whether or not they go to graduate school, they will not escape hard work. If they enter the business world right after college, the corporate store will make them "work their buns off." They will face working nights and weekends if they wish to survive in the business world. Graduate schools in law, medicine, psychology, or any other field are equally tough roads. Owning one's own business also consumes all of one's efforts. There is no easy way! I whisper to them, "But there is a special secret." Choose what you love doing, pursue it with a passion, and enjoy the journey. The learning and the mastery that it takes to conquer a chosen goal will require all their intelligence and all their effort. If they have chosen well, then conquering each hurdle will result in wonderful feelings of accomplishment, growth, and joy. The message I am trying to get my freshmen to learn is "roll up your sleeves now, dig in," commit yourself to the hard work of college, and one day you may be surprised to discover that you are actually enjoying the journey of learning itself. If they choose to detest and resent the work, then they will probably suffer. If they choose to be passionate and work hard, they will probably feel good. Some of my students report to me years later how valuable this lesson has been in their lives.

Irrational Thought 10

Life should be free from pain.

For some teens, the demand that life should be pain free may be irrational, but, for others, it is realistic. Too many of our youth are truly in pain today, and they are not equipped to handle it. In my practice I see the raw side of life. I see young people in deep grief over the separation and divorce of their parents. I see teenagers angry, confused, and depressed when their father, who may be living with another woman, does not call them or have anything to do with them. I see teenagers who feel empty inside because neither of their parents gives them any time or attention. If they get attention, it comes in the form of yelling and hurtful accusations. I see teens who are beaten. I see teens who discover they have a sexually transmitted disease. I see teens who watched their parent waste away and die from a terrible disease. I see teens who have seen their parent shot to death in front of them. How can we explain such a world to teens who are legitimately filled with so much pain? How do we help them cope? My answers depend on the circumstances precipitating the pain.

If the pain is the result of natural causes such as the death of a friend or parent, or illness, I try to deal with it through the teen's spiritual resources. Nature has no conscience. Bad events in nature happen by mere chance. They strike one person but not another. It is not God that causes these terrible events. They just happen. God does not control the world he set in motion so long ago. However, God gave us two very important pieces of equipment; a soul and intelligence. Within our soul lies the power to make decisions. Unfortunately, the human race often makes bad decisions. If people had decided long ago to invest their energies in curing diseases, we might have prevented some of the losses of loved ones. Instead, humans choose to use their collective brainpower to make sophisticated machines with which to fight each other. The collectively bad decisions of the human race have precipitated much of our own suffering.

However, if the source of a teen's pain is caused not by nature but by the significant adults in his life, then I do not tell him to understand his parent's stupid behaviors. As Laura Schlessinger tells us, when we do stupid things, we do not deserve to be let off the hook. When adults have affairs, drink excessively, and are not present to meet the needs of their children, then a child's wrath is justified.

I counsel teens to learn from their parent's mistakes. If a parent beats them, abuses them, drinks, or uses drugs, then I don't protect that parent. I don't justify their parent's behavior. I literally pray with teens in the course of these horrible events that the teen will find the inner resources and strength to overcome the shortcomings of their environment and do something meaningful with their lives. They can either drown in self-pity or overcome their suffering by doing meaningful things for their own benefit. They can choose between hatred and building a new life for themselves. The choice is up to them. I offer to help them with these decisions.

David

Both parents of sixteen-year-old David were severe alcoholics. When they drank, which was daily, they mentally abused him. They called him "stupid, piece of sh———t, no good, a pain in the ass," and told him they wish they never had him.

And so on. This teen's pain and anger were justified. I told him that when I listened to him, I felt some of the pain, too.

His parents would not cooperate with me in any way. It was useless. All I could do was comfort him. I told him the best way out of this and his only solution was for him to take control of his life and make good things happen. I could not prevent the pain he was experiencing now. It was real and it was valid. He did have many God-given assets. He had lots of intelligence, and he was a good student. He was a voracious reader. He was a good athlete. With this equipment, he could develop a plan that would eventually get him out of his painful circumstances and produce some joy in his life.

David remained a patient until he left for college. Our sessions focused on his education and the spiritual issue of finding comfort in God. I told him psychology had little to offer in the way of relief from his pain but that God did. One Sunday he met me at my church, and I introduced him to the teen group. He attended regularly. Part of our strategy was for David to stay away from home as much as possible. He studied in the local library. He participated in the teens' group activities. Like most of the people in the congregation, he loved the positive and motivating sermons of our minister.

All this helped reduce the pain in his life. He followed this same formula in college and then in law school. He is now an attorney. I believe he has an excellent marriage and is a wonderful father to his two sons. He turned his pain and adversity into victory. I view this young man as extremely courageous; I hope that his story serves as an inspiration for other teens.

We, as parents, must try to combat any of our shortcomings that may cause pain for our teenagers. I wholeheartedly believe that we need to seriously look at the issues we talked about earlier such as reestablishing the family in America; making wiser decisions about marriage and trying to reduce the divorce rate; making certain that our kids get the time, love, and attention they so desperately need; and carefully helping them to have proper amounts of fellowship and fun in healthy environments. All these steps may reduce some of the pain we perpetuate for our teens.

Then there is the flip side, the side where a teenager's avoidance of pain, which usually means avoiding the discomfort of hard work, in life is irrational. By avoiding pain, a teen actually creates his own pain. By hating school, avoiding hard work, indulging in alcohol, and not thinking about goals for his life, he creates his own pain. Failing in school hurts. Being idle produces feelings of aimlessness, apathy, emptiness, and sadness. Alcohol and drugs are used to avoid pain. But alcohol and drugs actually cause pain in numerous ways, such as by not taking care of his responsibilities and setting the stage for definite failure; by ravaging his body so that he cannot play sports; by not feeling well most of the time because of the toxic effects of chemicals on both the body and the emotions; by risking the possibility that he may become addicted; and by engaging in bad behaviors that he may not do when sober.

When teenagers avoid the discomfort of hard work, time passes, they accomplish nothing, and they then wind up as an "I could have been. . . ." They spend the rest of their lives hurting because they feel like dismal failures.

Teens have to take responsibility for some of the pain they experience. Teach them that it is in their power to prevent much of this. Blaming others or blaming an unfair world does not change anything. Facing problems and overcoming them takes courage. If a teen does these things, life will not necessarily be exempt from pain, but a significant percentage of it may be reduced.

REVIEW

I'm going to use the case of Dan to serve as a review of most of the irrational thinking we just covered. It will also demonstrate how I dealt with a teen in great pain.

Dan

I saw Dan when he was sixteen. His parents contacted me for help after Dan drove their car into a tree at a high speed in a suicide attempt. Amazingly, he did not suffer any injuries, but the attempt was serious. He intended to die. Dan's parents were highly religious and regularly attended church with him. He reported that his suicide felt "like a religious insight," where he felt a compulsion to be with God.

His parents reported that in school Dan was the class clown, and teachers constantly complained that his antics disrupted their classes. The school psychologist had labeled him ADHD. (Note: Ask yourself if a pill would sufficiently resolve Dan's complex problems.) While the other kids would laugh at some of the things he did, it was apparent that they did not like him, which resulted in his having no close friends. Both of Dan's parents worked and donated much of their free time to their church. Thus, Dan spent most of his time, when not in school, alone and lonely.

Dan's first session consisted of an angry tirade directed at just about everyone in his life. He said his grades were poor because the teachers couldn't teach and they were "always on his case," a phrase I frequently hear from teenagers. The kids at school picked on him, and periodically he would "give them what they deserved by kicking the sh——t out of them!" The other kids were idiots. He claimed, "they had their little groups and wouldn't let anyone in." All his parents ever did was yell at him; of course, he hated them. He saw no reason for living.

Dan saw himself as worthless. He had little self-esteem. If ever I saw a teen in pain, it was Dan. The following is from Dan's third session:

> Dr. S.: Dan, did you really want to die?
> Dan: I don't know. I think so. It felt like God was telling me to drive the car into the tree.
> Dr. S.: If you had died, what would have happen?
> Dan: I'd be with God and out of this f——king place.
> Dr. S.: So you see death as easing your pain?
> Dan: (With tears running down his face) Yes!
> Dr. S.: You want to die, but you don't want to die?
> Dan: I don't know. Sometimes, yes, sometimes, no. I don't know.
> Dr. S.: (With tears running down my face) Dan, I don't want you to die. I'm not in your shoes, so I can't fully understand the pain you're in. I sense it's quite a lot (*validation*). I've had pain in my life, so I'm no stranger to what you might be feeling (*sharing*). Dan, listen to me. Are you paying attention? (*I wait until I sense he has moved his focus from his own thoughts and feelings to what I have to say. The artistic part of therapy is good timing and good communication.*) Dying is the ultimate solution to your pain. I know that. But there are solutions you haven't thought of. They are not easy solutions. Much of it will require you to be open and honest about what is causing much of your pain. In other words, it means facing some of the things that "you" are doing to contribute to your pain. Once you know what these things are, you have the power to change them. If you change them, you will have less pain. There are also some things I'll need to do with your parents to help make things better. I have to be careful here because you're blaming them and everyone else around you, and your pain is only some of their fault, but not all of it. Will you agree to not do anything to kill yourself, at least for now, and give me a chance? (*Contract between patient and therapist—not to die.*) (Dan nods.) Not good enough, Dan, I clearly want your word.
> Dan: (In a soft voice) OK.

In separate sessions I began working with Dan's parents to get them to shift some of their time from church to Dan. I reminded them that Dan is God's gift to them, and they have the responsibility to meet his needs. While they agreed to this change, it still was not enough. There was the more difficult task of getting them to change to a different church, one with a strong teen program.

Indeed this was difficult for them, but, not wanting a repeat of Dan's suicide attempt, they eventually followed my instructions.

Dan's fourth session:

Dr. S.: Dan, do you see any connection between being the class clown and your unhappiness?

Dan: No.

Dr. S.: Do you know why you try to be the class clown?

Dan: No.

Dr. S.: Dan, I judge you to be extremely intelligent, but the way you're dealing with life is extremely stupid. (Dan gives his full attention but says nothing.) You want your friends to like you? (He nods.) You want to be liked? The way you go about it is to be a clown. But, there is more to it than that. You are one scared kid.

Dan: What do you mean?

Dr. S.: You're afraid of failure. You're afraid that if you put all your intelligence into your schoolwork and then fail—well you can't face that. You're terrified to work hard—to put everything you have into it and then possibly to fail, and to you that could only mean one thing. You're dumb. That scares you.

Dan: I am dumb.

Dr. S.: No! Damn it! No! Dan, no one wants to fail. It hurts to fail. You provide yourself with a convenient excuse. By clowning around and not doing your work, you avoid taking responsibility for your failure. It's a cop-out. In your mind, if you don't do the work, if you avoid the work and fail—then you have your excuse. Unfortunately, doing the things you're doing guarantees your failure, and the more you fail, the worse you feel about yourself. By avoiding the hard work, you indeed will keep failing. I bet that all during the time you spend cruising, clowning, or watching TV, you're worried about school. It never leaves you, that gnawing, nagging feeling that you're not doing what you should be doing.

Dan: I am miserable. I don't want to continue feeling this lousy. I just can't pull it together.

Dr. S.: Look Dan, I laid a lot on you today. I want to give you a homework assignment. I want you every day this week to think about what I said. That's all. Just think it over. OK?

Dan: OK.

Dan's fifth session:

Dr. S.: Did you do your homework?

Dan: Yes. Do you know something? I hate myself when I clown. I don't like me. I feel like an idiot.

Dr. S.: So this all adds up to feeling worse and worse and worse. You don't try, so you fail. The excuse for failing doesn't really work. Instead, the failing makes you feel miserable. Plus, you worry about school all the time. Then to top it off, you feel shame for being a buffoon. All these self-defeating behaviors add up to feeling depression, anxiety, worry, and shame. No wonder you feel so rotten.

Dan: It adds up.

Dr. S.: There's another thing we need to look at. Do you notice how you blame everyone else for your problems?

Dan: The other kids, the teachers, and my parents?

Dr. S.: Exactly. The kids are noisy. You can't concentrate. The teachers pick on you. Your parents stay on your case. Dan, if I had to put up with your behavior, I'd be on your case too. You are a pain in the neck to all of them. Your teachers and your parents are desperately trying to get through to you. They're frustrated. Are you hearing me? The day that they stop getting on your case is the day they really don't care about you. They think you have brains but that you're throwing it all away, and that frustrates them. I've been seeing your parents, and I know they love you. They're scared you're going to wind up a zero in life. They want you to be somebody. They are angry with you. They see you with all this talent and you're doing nothing with it.

Dan: (Crying) I don't know what to do.

Dr. S.: You have tried one solution. Death, the ultimate escape from responsibility. Dan, it is going to take two things: courage and self-discipline. That's all you need to know: courage and self-discipline. Do you realize that help is all around you? You have me, your parents, your teachers, and don't forget God. We can help you get started, but it's up to you to take responsibility. Your alternative is continuing to be miserable.

Dan: My school counselor says I have low self-esteem.

Dr. S.: Do you?

Dan: Yes, I hate me. I feel like a piece of sh——t.

Dr. S.: What is the only way you can change this low self-image?

Dan: I know what you are going to say, earn it!

Dr. S.: (I smile) You got me figured out, huh?

Dan's tenth session:

Dr. S.: How are you?

Dan: A lot better. I'm not clowning any more. My grades are coming up. But, I don't know. I can't explain it. Everyday is like (pause), I just don't know.

Dr. S.: Can I try? (He nods.) Empty. Nothing to look forward to. No fun.

Dan: I think so.

Dr. S.: What's happening at the new church with the other teens?

Dan: Nothing. I don't want to be a clown, so I just stay quiet.

Dr. S.: Did you ever think that maybe you're shy?

Dan: (Looking up surprised.) I never thought of it that way. I am! I really am! I never thought of that. I'm scared to open my mouth.

Dr. S.: Would you care to read a book about overcoming shyness and how to meet other kids?

Dan: Yes.

Dr. S.: OK, read it, and we'll talk about it and work on it. I might have some suggestions to add to it.

Dan's fourteenth session:

Dr. S.: Any progress?

Dan: Yes, lots. I'm following the stuff in the book. I'm trying to be warm and nice, and the other kids seem to like me. They're asking me to their parties. We went tubing down the river last week. I loved it.

Dr. S.: Dan, I want you to know I admire you. You listened. You had the courage to really try. That takes a lot of guts.

Dan: I feel like a feather. It's like a ton of bricks off my shoulders. Where do we go from here?

Dr. S.: We keep working until you feel sufficiently secure not to need me, but I'll always be here.

Notice that I was direct, honest, and straightforward with Dan. Teens pick up on honesty. Dan was in pain. Patients in pain want to cooperate. They want help to make the pain go away; therefore, they listen.

This chapter dealt with thoughts and beliefs. The next chapter focuses on some of the most important beliefs, called values. We'll talk about the most important values for your teen to learn.

Value Education

Values are beliefs about those things we cherish and hold as important. Values govern how we conduct ourselves and what we aspire to be. Values motivate us. They define who we are. They define what we believe to be right or wrong. They define our morality.

Most teenagers are thoroughly confused about what they value. In this chapter we're going to look at why teenagers are so confused and what we can do to help them.

WHY TEENS ARE CONFUSED
ABOUT VALUES

Does your teenager exasperate you? Are you upset because she cares little about school? Is she making poor grades? Are you upset that you are investing between $50,000 to $150,000 on her college education and your teen is barely passing her classes? Does it "drive you up the wall" when all that seems to interest her are members of the opposite sex? Do you scream at her for not helping with housework as she whiles away the hours in front of the TV or talking on the phone? Are you frustrated because your teen treats you with disrespect? Do you sometimes find yourself saying to her, "What is wrong with you? Why can't you get your head on straight?"

Unfortunately, "getting their heads on straight" is precisely the problem. What does "straight" mean? Today, teenagers are thoroughly confused because they are inundated with values that are contradictory, paradoxical, inconsistent, poorly defined, and thoroughly muddled. How can they develop a clear set of values when parents aren't home enough to teach them, when the extended family is no longer there, when parents don't communicate with them, when they are flooded with low values from the media, when schools teach nothing about values, and when the primary source of their value education is their peers?

Albert Ellis is one of the pioneers of modern cognitive psychology. One of his most important principles is the unknowingness of many of our beliefs and values. Either we are unaware of many of them, or we have never clearly articulated what they are. This chapter focuses on teaching values to our teens. But many adults have not clearly thought through what they value. They may be able to define a few of their basic values, but there are others that are beyond awareness or are undefined. For example, do you value education? Your immediate response is, "Of course I do." But, do you? Do you treasure learning itself? Is your life filled with serious reading about history, art, music, philosophy, theology, science, and so forth? Do you regularly go to museums, theaters, concerts, and historical places? Or do you sit in front of the television watching Jerry Springer? What values about education are you transmitting to your teenager? What is he observing in you as a role model? Is the conclusion he derives from you that education is a noxious thing one must get through in order to ultimately get a good job? If so, then it is not education you value—it's money and position. What exactly is your teen learning from you?

How can we teach our teenagers to have clear heads and solid values when we have not deliberately and consciously selected those values for ourselves that are important? How can we teach what we do not know? Do you get upset with your teen for violating something that to her and you is vague, unclear, and nonspecific in the first place? For example, do you get upset when she performs poorly in school? As previously pointed out, what value do you really convey about education? What has she been learning over many years by watching and listening to you?

Psychology and education have done little to help with value education for our teens. Not only do schools not teach values, it is against the law to teach values that may conflict with the political, ethnic, cultural, or religious beliefs of families. Cognitive psychology also has not focused on researching values that aid in healthy functioning. The disciplines that have grappled with values appear to be primarily philosophy and theology. Since few people read serious philosophy and theology, few have worked through and consciously decided their value systems. Some people who regularly attend houses of worship and study the scriptures may have done some sorting out of values, but, even then, there are many values that often haven't been carefully thought through.

Our goal is to define the ten most important values to teach our teenagers. Before doing that, it is essential to explore how values personally affect us.

GOD'S LITTLE WHISPER

Freud called it the "super ego," many call it our "conscience," Scott Peck calls it "unconscious imminence," but I prefer Harold Kushner's phrase: God whispers in our ear. To me this concept implies that somehow and in someway God has given a guidepost to keep our behaviors responsible and moral. This guidepost is our feelings. Whenever we do something wrong, we feel bad. When we do the right things, we feel good.

To define more clearly what good feelings are, it's useful to turn to the Bible. The term *happiness* appears rarely in some versions of the Bible, but the terms *peace, serenity, joy,* and *calm* appear hundreds of times. Happiness occurs when an occasional and special event happens in our lives, such as getting married, having a baby, or winning the lottery. We escalate to euphoria, also called happiness, for a short time and then return to where we originally were. Happiness is episodic, circumstantial, and fleeting. It isn't a lasting emotion. Joy and serenity, on the other hand, are more consistent feelings and can be sustained throughout most of our lives by practicing only one rule, to constantly live by our spiritual and moral values. Our feelings, therefore, are our guideposts or "God's little whisper," which are determined by the type of beliefs and values that govern the behaviors of our daily lives.

When we do the right things, we enjoy feelings of peace and serenity. When we don't do the right things, we are usually filled with pain. These feelings of pain may be guilt, shame, anxiety, depression, or anger. It's important to note that we take our feelings with us everywhere we go. We can feel serene when alone in a room, and we can feel pain in the middle of a party or in the loving arms of another. When we do the wrong things in the way we govern ourselves, there is no place to hide. Our pain will follow us everywhere. Dostoyevsky, in *Crime and Punishment*, wrote of the anguish of a young man after doing a terrible wrong. He could not escape his excruciating pain. His torment followed him everywhere.

Laura Schlessinger calls bad behaviors "stupid behaviors." She bluntly states that people often seek relief from pain by seeing a therapist. She states that their pain is the product of doing stupid things and that they should indeed feel bad. She believes that a therapist does a patient a disservice by trying to soothe the patient's pain and excusing his bad behavior. Only responsible and good behavior will alleviate such pain. The term *stupid behaviors* didn't originate with Laura Schlessinger. It was coined back in the 1950s. Two psychologists, Neal Miller and John Dollard, wrote a very influential book titled *Theories of Personality*. They wrote of the inner turmoil and anguish that coincides with stupid behavior. They pointed out that stupid behaviors are often neurotic attempts to stop one's pain, such as drinking or excessive eating. Neurotic behaviors or stupid behaviors only give temporary relief from the pain. Actually, in the long run, stupid behaviors add to the pain.

Alcoholics Anonymous (AA) introduced the twelve-step recovery program. The AA program is spiritually based. AA teaches a very important lesson: if one follows spiritual beliefs and the associated moral codes of conduct, then peace and serenity will ensue, helping combat the urge to drink. If an AA member violates this spiritual code of conduct, then inner turmoil results and along with it comes the urge to drink in order to stop the pain. This urge is called a "dry drunk," which means that by giving up spiritual commitment and by failing to practice ethical behavior the person is ripe to take a drink in order to try stopping the pain.

This is an equally important lesson for teenagers to learn. I give my students an example of this feeling or inner voice phenomenon. I ask them to tell me what they experience when an exam is getting close and they haven't studied or when a term paper is immediately due and they haven't done any work on it. I point out to them that neurotic and stupid attempts to block out the pain, such as drinking, drugging, or partying, don't really work. There's no place to hide. The pain follows them everywhere, and overall it is a rather unpleasant way to live their lives while in college. The only solution for them lies in doing what their values dictate, which is to get their work done. Only responsible behavior will stop the suffering.

I think it's a miracle that God built this system of checks and balances within us. Psychologists do not fully understand how this works. We don't know the neurophysiology or body chemistry of why we react in such opposite ways to either responsible or irresponsible conduct. Why do we have a conscience? Why is God's little whisper within us?

Our next task is to define those values that, when practiced, help our teens, and us too, to feel emotionally healthy and at peace.

I almost chose to call this chapter "Spiritual Values." The reason is that one definition of spirituality is to practice those moral and ethical beliefs that help give us peace of mind. Training your teenager to adopt and practice the following values will go a long way toward helping your teenager to have a peaceful, fulfilling, and joyful life.

THE TEN VALUES TO
TEACH YOUR TEEN

I'll state each value as opposite poles. One side is positive and produces feelings of peace, serenity, and joy. The other side is negative and produces ongoing feelings of pain. This pain takes many different forms. It may be guilt, depression, anxiety, fear, remorse, and so forth. Its profile depends on what "stupid behavior" was done to violate one's values. This pain will not go away until one changes to more responsible and moral conduct.

Value I: Honesty and Integrity versus Hypocrisy

Have you ever gone into a store and the clerk mistakenly gave you change for a $10.00 bill instead of the $1.00 bill you actually gave him? Did you give it back?

I remember in Sunday school one day many years ago, we were discussing Christian ethics in business. A member of the group, a wealthy business owner, was boasting about his ethical business practices, and someone asked him, "How much do you pay your secretary?" We knew the secretary, and we knew that, as a single mother of two, her life was a constant financial struggle. He replied, "Well, I pay her the going rate." I asked if the ethics of the situation was the "going rate" or a salary sufficient to keep her family comfortable? I asked which should rule—economics or doing what is ethically right?

Do you ever wonder why so many of us, including former U. S. presidents, admire Harry Truman? It is because he tried so hard to do the right thing, no matter the personal cost. Many of us envy such a trait, but few of us practice it.

Remember American industry in the 1970s where the prevailing management policy was to increase profits by decreasing the product? Remember the junk cars we produced? Did we ever do Japan a favor! One Japanese entrepreneur said, "The best thing America ever did for us was the Harvard model for the Master's Degree in Business Administration." Quality was Japan's business model. Greed was ours.

In the New Testament, Jesus detested hypocrisy probably more than any other human frailty. He stated this repeatedly. He actually preferred the company of beggars, thieves, and prostitutes to the hypocritical wealthy who used cunning, lying, and cheating to make a profit. He also denounced those who presented themselves as religious and pious but whose only real desires were for power and wealth.

Scott Peck in *The Road Less Traveled* points out the difference between white lies and black lies. A black lie is blatant, and you know when you are doing it. It isn't right to do this, but at least then you are not a hypocrite. But, a white lie is small, perhaps based on a slight omission, where you convince yourself that you are not really lying because after all it is so tiny. This is one form of hypocrisy.

The teaching of honesty and integrity is best accomplished in a family environment where these values are truly appreciated. This means that honesty and integrity are beliefs that are central to all family members and are practiced in every daily activity. What do you model for your children? What do you actually practice? Whatever they see you practicing is what they are learning. Modeling is the most powerful mechanism for teaching our young. A good rule to remember is *don't do anything you would never want your children to find out about.* Preaching honesty and integrity is far less effective than what your children observe. Believe me, they are always watching! It is essential that we teach teens the true meaning of doing the right thing even though they may know that they won't get caught doing the wrong thing. Doing the wrong thing results in personal pain even when we successfully fool others.

William

William was a sixteen-year-old patient. His parents, because of his chronic lying and stealing, brought him to me. They constantly preached honesty and integrity to him. They regularly attended church as a family.

It was evident from the beginning that William was very confused. In fact, he was angry. He thought his parents were "hypocritical horses' asses." He said his dad lied and cheated almost every day. His father often bought stolen goods for his auto supply store. On many occasions his dad sold poor quality, reconditioned tires, representing them as a house brand that was better than some of the top-of-the-line name brands. William said one day the ATM machine gave his dad $500.00 for a $50.00 withdrawal. The receipt represented only the $50.00 withdrawal. He watched to see if his dad returned the money, but all his dad did was gloat all day about his lucky break. He stated his mother often lied to friends and relatives when they called and asked her to help with some projects. Her lies were designed to get out of doing something she didn't want to do. She then prided herself for being clever.

In addition, William was concerned about his parents' drinking habits. Heavy cocktails after work were a daily ritual, and, when his parents' friends were over, everyone drank enormous amounts of alcohol. Yet, both of his parents would get furious if they smelled alcohol on William's breath. They'd chide him never to develop such a habit.

Therapy focused on William's taking responsibility for his own life. What kind of person did he wish to be? If he detested the hypocrisy of his parents, what did he want for himself? These things were his choices. He could design his life and his values. William wound up choosing well: he never wants to be like his parents.

Perhaps this saying from Proverbs (21:6) will help:

> A fortune made by a lying tongue is
> a fleeting vapor and a deadly snare.

Value 2: Self-Discipline versus Envy:

Self discipline applies to two areas of life: first is achieving important goals.

Did you ever hear someone say, "I could have been a doctor" or some such thing? I hear it from my adult patients a great deal. "I could have gone to college." "I could have been a great basketball star." On and on it goes. I feel sad when I hear this. The covert message is that the person realizes he or she had a talent but lacked the self-discipline needed to "make their dream come true."

Many of my students do not understand how much work college really requires. Often they try to get by doing as little as possible. I constantly advise my students, who are mostly psychology majors, how difficult it is to get into a graduate program in psychology. Sadly, they continue to calculate how to minimize their efforts barely to get by. Then as seniors they're amazed when their grades are not good enough to get them accepted into an advanced degree program. With a little more effort and work, they "could have" achieved their goal. But sadly most of them never do. After graduation they'll have to choose a less competitive career.

I recall my sons' karate school promotion ceremony, when both of them received their blue belts. Their instructor said to them, "Remember the good feelings you're having at this moment and all the hard work you put into getting here. Apply that principle to all aspects of your lives." I hope that message stuck.

I can spend my life envying successful authors. Right now the sun is out, and it is a magnificent day. But, if I wish to be an author, perhaps even a successful one, then I have to discipline myself, which means I must force myself to remain at my desk and work and not go outside and play in the sun. Believe me, this is an extremely hard thing for me to do. If I choose to be an author instead of envying other authors, then I have to make myself do whatever it takes. Self-discipline versus envy is a choice. Since you are reading this, you know what choice I have made. You also know that I am *forcing* myself to honor this commitment. I honestly can tell you that right now I am very tempted to go out the front door of my house and play. But I have made my choice, and I will carry it through.

Teach your teen, by both example and discussion, that if she truly desires to accomplish anything in life, it requires self-discipline. The alternate choice is envy, the "I could have been!" Teens have to learn that now is the time that they must make choices that will affect the course of their lives. Later can be too late.

At the turn of the twentieth century the eminent psychiatrist Alfred Adler introduced the concepts of inferiority and superiority. One way to ensure feelings of inferiority is to be passive and do nothing. To develop superiority, there are two roads, or choices we can make in life. One, the unhealthy road, is to seek superiority over others just like Hitler did. The second, the healthy road, is to seek superiority or mastery over oneself, to work hard at cultivating and realizing one's personal talents. Self-mastery takes hard work, sustained effort, and lots of self-discipline, but this is the only way to realize one's full potential. This road of self-mastery often means facing periods of marked discomfort, such as the anxiety associated with studying for an exam.

The second application of self-discipline is in mastery over one's behaviors and emotions.

I remember being taught in graduate school never to say to patients anything about self-control and self-discipline because we were taught that patients really wanted to get better, and statements about self-discipline would serve only to frustrate them. We were taught they were sick, and they couldn't help themselves. This was the old way in which therapy used to be practiced. Then Drs. Albert Ellis and Aaron Beck, our modern-day versions of Sigmund Freud, introduced cognitive therapy and began teaching a different ideology. They clearly stated that the only true path to emotional health is through hard work and self-discipline. Only by intentional and deliberate control of our thoughts, beliefs, and behaviors will we ever achieve emotional health. They taught that mastery over one's emotions requires mastery over one's own thinking and behavior. That is the core of the message throughout their books and the message I'm conveying now. Only through self-discipline can we achieve our life goal and sustain emotional well-being. Self-discipline in cognitive therapy means forcing oneself to exert conscious control over one's thoughts and behaviors. Only by practice and effort will healthier patterns of thinking and behaving become new habits.

Laura Schlessinger talks at great length about people who have low self-esteem. She says this usually results from engaging in stupid behaviors, such as avoiding hard work or having affairs, and that those who make these choices deserve to continue to feel badly. She feels they can choose to have the discipline to control their behaviors. Harsh as she may sometimes be, she is right.

When you put all these ideas together, self-discipline means two things:

1. Work hard to achieve your goals.
2. Work hard to master your thoughts, desires, beliefs, behaviors, and emotions.

There is no other way. Ellis admits that this is a stoical point of view, but it sure beats a lifetime of envy.

Value 3. Process versus End

Do you often hear yourself or others say:

If only I were finished with school.
If only I were married.
If only I were single.
If only I had money.
If only I had children.
If only the children were grown.

A very important lesson to teach your teens is to learn to love life *now*. Learn to love the journey or process of getting to your goals and not wait to feel good only when you reach your goal. There are two benefits for enjoying the *now*: one, feelings of peace and serenity, and, two, tomorrow is far away and you would miss the joy of today if your focus is exclusively long term. Let me explain these two concepts more clearly.

The concept of the *now* has pervaded philosophy, theology, and psychology for hundreds of years. The idea is that the only reality we have is in the present, or the now. If you discipline your mind to focus on the now, you will actually benefit by feeling good. Look at it this way. If you focus on the past, you may remember some of the good times, but most often we wind up focusing on the losses and hurts we endured. When you bring the pains of the past to the present, you will reexperience those pains now. Focusing on the future can be positive if our focus is on our goals. Focusing on the future can be equally painful if we focus on what might go wrong in the future, our fear that something terrible will happen. Think about the irony of this pattern of negative thinking. We worry that, if something goes wrong in the future, we might possibly suffer. But, by worrying now, we're guaranteeing that we suffer right now. Dumb isn't it? In a moment I'll use myself as an example to elucidate these concepts. Recalling past hurts usually produces feelings of sadness or depression. Focusing on possible future failures usually produces feelings of anxiety and worry and often leads to freezing up, that is, not performing.

Right now I am writing. I have books strewn all over my desk. The focus of my attention is only on what I wish to say. The result is that I am feeling quite peaceful and productive. I could choose instead to worry whether or not, in the future, this book will ever get published. I could also focus on the past about how difficult it was to get my other books published: that hurts. Instead, right now I choose to do the very best I can and zero in only on the content of my message. Thus, I am focused on what I am doing right now, and therefore I cannot be focused on the neurotic thoughts of either the past or the future, which would only serve to give me pain. The result of my intense focus is on the now, and therefore I feel calm, productive, and at peace. I have almost no extraneous thoughts that could result in personal emotional discomfort and in not getting my work done.

The focus of the now for teenagers should be their schoolwork. They can choose to relish and enjoy the process of their education and the marvelous feelings of personal growth that occur in each day of their schooling. Or they can think about tests they failed in the past and conclude, "What's the use!" This leads to feelings of depression and resignation. Or they can focus on possibly not passing coming exams, and also conclude, "What's the use!" Then they feel anxious in the present. If they decide to give in to "What's the use" and stop working, then they increase the chances that they will actually fail in the future. By focusing with all their might right now on their schoolwork, they increase the likelihood that they will do well on their exams. Isn't this a more intelligent strategy?

Besides *focusing* on the now, there is another aspect about the now. We must teach our young to *treasure the now*. Melody Beattie, in her book *Lessons of Love*, wrote about the death of her son. I read it twice and cried through every page. One of the most important lessons she learned is that today is a gift from God and we had better enjoy it right now because tomorrow may not come. I advise teens to focus on what they must do today and also focus on what blessings they have this very day. Our only true reality is today, and we'd better savor it.

The now for teenagers can be filled with marvelous joys. If they learn to love their education, then they can love the wonder of the content of their courses and the personal joy of growth as their world of knowledge and awareness expands. In addition to their education, the now for teenagers can be filled with so much fun. Friends, dating, parties, and football games can be a treasure of experiences they can relish. Attending to and appreciating all these good and wonderful things is a matter of disciplining their young minds to focus on what should be apparent to most, but often is not. The joys of life are spread before us at this very moment. Teach them that the now can be filled with excitement and joy if only they'd pay attention and treasure it.

Living in the now does not mean that teens have a license to go into a hedonistic frenzy. We must teach them to set positive goals for their future. They must learn that to achieve these goals, they must strive for it now, one day at a time. This is the most productive use of the now. And, they must also learn to savor and enjoy all the blessings that surround them in the now, because all that can be and should be treasured in a given moment can suddenly disappear and be gone forever, as did Melody Beattie's son.

Value 4. Personal Accomplishment and Simplicity versus Material Accumulation and a Life of Complexity

We live in a country with an abundance of material wealth. But are we enjoying these fruits? Recall earlier when I discussed our harried lifestyles. Is the stress placed on our bodies, on our emotional well-being, and on our families worth it? Henry David Thoreau wrote about the benefits of simplifying one's life. He wrote about placing more importance on peace and calm rather than on the complexities involved in a life focused on the accumulation of material wealth. Most of the world's religions stress the same point about leading a life of simplicity and forgoing a life devoted to material things. What do you want your children to learn? This is an important issue that has profound ramifications on the type of lives our children will have: it's a difficult decision to make. Society pulls us in one direction, while good sense pulls us in another.

Many years ago I practiced full-time in a wealthy bedroom community of a major city. I saw a lot of unhappiness. There were plenty of nice houses and cars, but there was also a lot of unhappiness. It seemed that almost everybody in the community was hustling for a buck, and what they often had to do to accumulate money was absurd. In fact, I learned that many of these people did not have much accumulated wealth. They spent every penny to look as if they had money, but since I knew their secrets, I knew differently. Let's look at a case to amplify my meaning.

Susan

Susan was extremely attractive. She was thirty-six years old. She wore expensive clothing, and she drove a very expensive car. Her stated reason for seeing me was depression. It did not take long for her to reveal that her husband was physically and mentally abusive. In fact, she brought in tape recordings graphically revealing the horror of the abuse. Susan did not work. Her days were generally aimless since she had a full-time maid and her two teenage sons were quite self-sufficient.

Susan's husband had no idea that she was coming for therapy. I tried in vain to get her to invite him to see me, but she was so afraid of recrimination that she remained silent. She told me that her husband, age forty-four, owned five successful businesses. He worked constantly. He was worried constantly. If he was not at work, he was at home on the phone talking about business. Frequently, on weekends he had to fly out of town to oversee one of his businesses. If he stayed in town on a weekend, she said that he would stay wrapped in a blanket, exhausted and barely able to function. He was nervous every single day. She described him as a walking time bomb. It didn't take much for her to be the target of his pent-up anxiety and wrath. She tiptoed around the house afraid of triggering an outburst of his rage.

She desperately wanted to leave him, but, unfortunately, she was so dependent on him (codependent) that she never became able to do this. Since he checked every penny she spent, she had developed a plan of writing checks for more than the grocery bill in order to receive cash. She had secretly accumulated over thirty thousand dollars from this cash, planning to use the money to break away from him.

She often told me that if he ever abused one of her sons she would definitely leave him. Of course this happened. She even brought in a recording of him kicking his son in the spine while at the top of the stairs, which resulted in his son's tumbling all the way down. A trip to the emergency room revealed no broken bones. Sadly, that was not enough for her to leave.

I urged Susan to go to school to earn a degree so that eventually she could leave and support herself. She said she could not give up her beautiful home, the expensive clothing, or the opulent lifestyle. She was living in hell, a luxurious hell for sure. What did anyone in this family have? Her husband was exhausted, tired, often deeply depressed, explosive, and abusive to his wife and sons. At one point, while she was still a patient, her husband had to undergo quadruple bypass surgery for clogged arteries. It was obvious his life span was going to be shortened. Both he and Susan were slaves to material things, and at what a cost!

Why do people live this way? The odd part of it is that a lot of us do. In my practice, Susan's was not an isolated case. I have had numerous cases of people doing bad things to hustle for money. I have had some that embezzled from their father's businesses even though they were receiving lucrative salaries. I have had adult brothers steal from their sisters' bank accounts. I have had family members spend years in litigation with each other to accumulate more wealth. I have numerous patients who required bypass surgery because of the effect of years of stress on their cardiovascular systems, all in the name of gathering wealth. I discuss these kinds of cases as a springboard for teaching teens what they may be facing if they do not learn other more important values than the lust for money.

There is a strange paradox about living a stressed life for the goal of opulence. Often people do not just accumulate material things for the things themselves. They accumulate them as symbols of their success, of their prowess, and of their intelligence. They want respect, adulation, prestige, and esteem. As Eric Fromm puts it, they just want to be loved. I know that sounds a bit bizarre, but consider it. Humanistically oriented psychologists such as Eric Fromm, Carl Rogers, and Abraham Maslow have written about how profound our need to be loved is. By wanting love so desperately, people are sometimes willing to destroy others whom they love or even destroy themselves in the frantic scramble to get it. What a strange paradox! We are willing to destroy the very people we love in order to get love from them.

I have a simple and practical philosophy. It is wise to passionately pursue in life those endeavors that, to an individual, are meaningful, fulfilling, and joyous. If wealth comes along the way, fine. If one has to live in torment to accumulate the wealth, then the heck with it! All one needs is reasonable comfort, not affluence. Seek neither the external desires of prestige, power, nor adulation. Instead seek fulfillment, peace, serenity, and joy from within. We all want to be loved, but seek to be loved as a person and not as a symbol of power or success.

Many of us are curious about the Amish, and so am I. I have several paintings with Amish themes in my home. One of my favorites is of a lone Amish man driving his horse and wagon in a gentle snowstorm. I often think about how many of us are enamored by their calm and serene lifestyle. Perhaps we are curious about the peace their simple world seems to have, while our world of material comforts is fraught with excessive stresses. We long for what the Amish have. They live simply, work hard, and have peace. They are surrounded by family and friends in a marvelous bond of love and support. We yearn for these things, but can we ever release the stranglehold our materialistic values have over us?

Sometimes when I have difficulty sleeping I will read Thoreau's *Walden*. I read it to capture Thoreau's vivid descriptions of his uncluttered life as he sits quietly by the pond and savors the peace of nature. To him this was a way to connect with God. As I read this, I can feel the serenity he portrays wash over me and I can then nod off into blissful slumber.

I advise teens to passionately pursue the work they love. If the money comes fairly easily along the way, fine; if it doesn't, then live comfortably and focus on and enjoy the blessings of each day.

It is written in the Bible:

> Do not wear yourself out
> to get rich; have the wisdom
> to show restraint (Proverbs 23.4).

It is doing the work we love that will give us joy, not the material things we collect because of it. It is the love of family that gives warmth, not the expensive symbols with which we surround ourselves.

Tom

When I was growing up in New York City, I had a friend, Tom, who owned a gas station. Sometimes when I was tired of studying, I would walk a few blocks to his garage. While he was working we would chat. Tom's two brothers were attorneys, and his father was a judge. Of course, he had been pressured to follow in the family tradition, but he refused. His love was working on cars.

I enjoyed watching Tom while we talked. He was a massive fellow, square-jawed, and he looked as if he could crush rocks with his bare hands. He was always dirty. But I was fascinated by the look of joy on his face when he was intently working on a car. He loved his work. He told me this hundreds of times. I particularly liked Tom because he had a strong sense of integrity and honesty. Everyone in the neighborhood knew that they could leave their car with him, and, if they requested an unnecessary repair, he would tell them. He never padded a job. In turn, if something needed fixing, everybody gave him carte blanche to fix it, even without calling for permission. We all trusted him. He always charged a fair rate for his work.

I watched Tom's business grow over the years. He hired additional mechanics but always made certain that they maintained the quality of the work. He expanded the size of the garage to the limits the property would allow. Tom wound up with an income probably greater than either of his brothers. His success came from the love of his work and from his integrity. As far as I could tell, Tom was a happy man and most likely would still have been even if he were not making such a good income.

Plato taught about the contemplative life, as filled with learning and pondering and as an idyllic lifestyle. I think that is a bit lofty and snobbish. I prefer Albert Ellis's ideas about what he calls "Industrious Occupation."

"Industrious Occupation" means that we should find the work we love and devote ourselves passionately to immersing ourselves in it. Tom understood that secret. Former nun Karen Armstrong in her books, *The History of God* and *The Future of God*, talks about a total immersion in one's work as being a way of praying and giving praise to God. St. Benedict also wrote, "to work is to pray." I like that idea.

When we are industriously and deeply absorbed in productive activity, our brain focuses on our labors; therefore, our thoughts cannot drift to the neurotic nonsense, which makes people crazy. This is one healthy way to focus on the now. We can't think two thoughts at the same time. For example, I observe some of my colleagues continually upset over what the college president did or did not do, over something another colleague did, or over some decision of some committee, and on and on. Think how much better their lives would be if they spent their time and energy on the productive pursuit of their craft. They would be considerably more content with life, more productive in their jobs, and probably even enjoy being more successful. Instead, they choose to squabble, spread rumors, and worry. There are issues in the running of any college with which to be concerned, but some faculty choose to exclusively focus on problems and trouble.

Remember the values of enjoying the process and of focusing on the now. Industrious occupation combines both of these. If one focuses on the work one loves, the mind stays on productive things and stays in the present. Thoughts won't drift in negative directions. There is a sense of accomplishment. The soul becomes filled with peace and joy. Is this perhaps the secret meaning of life?

I hope teenagers discover the things they love and pursue them passionately. My advice to them is to keep their lives simple and love to learn and grow. I hope you teach these lessons to your teen. Help them get their lives started in a sensible way.

When I was in college I recall a brief conference with my advisor. I was confused about what career path to take. Dramatically opening the college catalog, he said to me, "Find what you love to do. Get better at it than anyone else. And don't worry about the money, it will come."

Value 5: Long-Term Goals versus Short-Term Pleasures

Teenagers often have difficulty envisioning what they would like to be doing when they are adults. This really isn't difficult to understand. One doesn't understand something until one is actually in it. Some teens may question marriage because they see most marriages failing. Some question having children. Often they are concerned about the demands of a career and having children at the same time. Sometimes the turmoil they personally experienced in their own homes while growing up may weigh against choosing to have children. Teenagers often question job and career goals because they may see work as nothing more than unfulfilling drudgery. Making a career choice is a hard decision.

I try to instill in my students and teenage patients the notion that they can design the way they would ideally like their life to be and that they can be responsible for making it happen. They can learn that marriages do not have to fail if they and a prospective partner agree on all the values necessary to make a marriage work before and not after getting married. It is essential to decide one's values even before meeting someone. That is what this chapter is about. They can then learn that searching for a partner involves finding someone who has similar values, thus increasing the likelihood of a successful marriage. They can learn that having children is a joy if their marriage is good. With careful planning, couples can make certain their children have ample time, attention, and nurturance. But both marriage partners must have as a premium value the care of their children.

Career choices for teens can be narrowed down if they discover those industrious activities for which they have developed a passion. A good career involves doing what one loves and working hard to get good at it. Thomas Moore indicates that loving one's work is an expression of spirituality and the soul.

Education, career, marriage, and children are long-term goals. Ask yourself the following questions as an aid in teaching your teen the importance of sustained, long-term goals and effort:

1. Are you giving them everything they want without their earning it? Do you overwhelm them with material riches because you don't want them to feel deprived? This is an excellent way to teach them not to plan or think. It's also an excellent way to train them in helplessness and dependency.
2. Have you provided them with an enriched cultural environment and all types of exciting experiences, such as trips to historical sites, visits to museums, and attendance at theaters and concerts?

3. Do you make education, learning, reading, and discovery important values?
4. Do you actively reinforce their academic efforts? Do you show a daily interest in their schoolwork, their readings, and their creative efforts?
5. Or, do you sit in front of the TV every night as a couch potato? This is an excellent way to model a nonindustrious lifestyle.

If you want your teen to learn the importance of long-term goals and sustained effort, then it is essential to actively nurture their efforts, provide an enriched cultural environment, be a good role model, and make certain that your marriage and their family are safe and secure.

Teenagers will never learn the meaning of sustained effort for long-term goals if we give them everything with no effort on their part, if we do not attend to and reinforce their hard efforts, if we fail to make learning an important value, and if we're poor role models.

The deciding of long-term goals that are of personal importance to a teenager creates meaningfulness in their lives. Short-term pleasures are quickly gone, and, once gone, they are replaced with an empty void. Emptiness happens when there is no meaningful purpose in life, the loss of what is called "essence" by philosophers. I have yet to see a happy person that is a hedonist. It is good to have fun, and teenagers should have fun. I not only do not argue against teens having fun, I also encourage it. I like to define *fun* as *a break from industrious enterprise while on the road to long-term accomplishments*. Fun, as an exclusive end by itself, does not bring joy.

I love the writings of Rod Serling, and I recall one of his stories of an evil man who dies. When this man awakens, he does not know where he is. Soon he discovers that he is in a place where his every wish and desire is instantly fulfilled. At first this is a "wonderful dream come true." But, as each day passes he becomes more bored, aimless, agitated, and irritable. He increasingly grows more and more miserable. Finally, he inquires why heaven is like this, and, of course, he discovers that he is actually in hell.

Things are precious to us when it takes time, planning, and effort to obtain them. This is an important lesson for teens to learn. Recall our discussion about the process toward the end, and our talk about industrious occupation. Are you beginning to understand how those values interconnect? Immersing oneself in one's endeavors and enjoying the peace that focusing on this gives us is one of the secrets of inner joy. Employing our minds on meaningful endeavors keeps them off the everyday neurotic annoyances that can make us miserable. The daily focus on an industrious passion brings peace and joy during the journey, then one day we get the extra special prize of achieving the goal we aimed for.

Try to teach that it is the journey itself that helps keep us emotionally and spiritually healthy, and that when we finally reach a particular goal it is added to an already joyous life.

Jane, the Would-Be Psychologist

One day, Jane walked into my office. She politely asked, "Dr. Stein, can I talk to you?" I gladly respond with an "Of course." I have known Jane for several years. Jane announces that she had decided to become a clinical psychologist. "Jane," I ask, "What is your GPA?" She says 2.6. However, now that she is a senior, she tells me that she has decided to begin making all As. I think to myself how mystifying it is that students miraculously believe they can suddenly make straight As after years of mediocre performance and bad habits. I sadly say, "Jane, do you realize that your GPA will probably be too low for any accredited doctoral program?" Jane sadly replies, "I guess I should have taken college more seriously." I quietly nod, thinking about how she may have had a chance at a psychology career if her parents had groomed her to make more mature decisions and commitments to long-term goals earlier in her life.

This is a typical conversation with an overwhelming majority of my students. The days of partying and ignoring long-term aspirations finally have a price ticket. Jane cannot achieve what she finally discovered could possibly have been her life passion. Her decision came too late. I hope Jane can find a new goal that she can realistically strive for, one that will be fulfilling for her. She could have spent her four years in college deeply immersed in psychology courses. Her studies could have been a joy in themselves, culminating in getting into a graduate program. She would still have had ample time to party. For Jane, being a psychologist will not become a reality.

Perseverance is crucial for achieving long-term goals. Teens must learn that goal-directed and tenacious hard work is necessary over a long period of time if they are ever to achieve anything. The alternative is aimless drifting to just get the years of their lives over with. I feel so sad when I see this type of chaotic, aimless existence in the young. Philosopher Jean Paul Sartre, and other existentialist philosophers, wisely advised us to deliberately create meaning in our lives, which they called "essence," as opposed to empty lives of mere existence. I hope your teen can understand this.

Value 6. Freedom versus Slavery

What does the value of slavery versus freedom have to do with teens? Everything. There are many ways to be slaves, and sadly many teens are right in the middle of some of them. God gave us souls and with them the wonderful power of free will. Free will means exercising choices. We choose our values. We choose our behaviors. We choose what we wish to become. All of life means making these free choices and then having the power of self-discipline to work toward making these choices become realities.

Ricky

I am seeing a woman, age forty-seven, who is in torment because her teenage son, Ricky, is in jail. Originally, he was arrested for possession of enough ounces of heroin to convict him for "intent to sell." He was sentenced to five years but was given probation instead. Later he was arrested once again for possession, but this time with only a small amount. But he had violated his probation, so he went back to jail to finish the five-year sentence.

This nineteen-year-old is a heroin addict. His recorded IQ is 144. He used to excel at mathematics and science. God knows what he could have been. His mother believes he must have been doing other drugs or inhalants because he has sustained brain damage; consequently, his intellectual functioning is considerably reduced. He probably has lost the intellectual capacity ever to be a scientist. As an addict he can no longer be totally free to choose his life's course.

When people become addicted, they give up their freedom. They become slaves. They lose their free will. And addictions come in many forms. We have no way to detect which teenagers have addiction potential. There are no psychological tests that can uncover who may become addicts. There are no medical tests to uncover addictive tendencies. The only way we can find out is when a teen experiments with something addicting and then becomes addicted.

There are two types of addictions. Substance addictions, the type with which we are most familiar, are to chemicals such as pot, heroin, cocaine, amphetamines, and alcohol. The second type is called process addictions, which are addictions to behaviors, such as sex, gambling, eating, and partying.

Stopping an addiction of any sort is extremely difficult. I work tirelessly to get physicians to stop prescribing Ritalin, other stimulants, tranquilizers, or any other mood-altering drug to teenagers or children. These drugs can trigger an addiction in some children that may be impossible to reverse. Ritalin is a stimulant that is similar to cocaine. It terrifies me what doctors are so readily doing to our children. It is so irresponsible. It makes my blood boil. How can we fight the drug problem in this country at the same time that doctors are giving these drugs to children and teenagers?

Educating teenagers about drug addictions is crucial. They tend to think of addiction as physical addiction. Not true. Few drugs are actually physically addicting. The majority of drugs that young people become addicted to are psychologically addicting. I do not want teens or parents to underestimate the power of psychological addiction; I have had young peoples' lives totally destroyed because of this. The power of psychological addiction is terrifying.

Psychological addiction is defined by two reinforcing properties of drugs, and either property can make a person an addict. The first property is "getting high," which is another term for euphoria. The second property is the ability to escape from worries and problems and to experience a sense of relaxation, in other words, to escape pain. The combined euphoric and escape power of drugs can be so potent for some personalities that, once they get into them, they cannot stop. They are slaves with no free will. When teenagers get addicted, they relinquish every value they have. Everything they cherish means nothing to them. They will behave like cornered rats.

Did you know that when heroin addicts become so physically tolerant to the drug that they can no longer get a psychological high, they will deliberately go through physical withdrawal just to start getting high again. They will do this knowing what hell physical withdrawal is. Heroin is highly physically *and* psychologically addicting. But it is the psychological addiction that is most important. Physical addiction is defined by the occurrence of strong physical withdrawal symptoms, such as nausea, vomiting, diarrhea, severe chills, severe stomach pains, and muscle contractions, just to name a few. Addicts will go through the hell of physical withdrawal for several weeks just to start getting high all over again, which is the psychological addiction.

Nick

Nick is sixteen. He is addicted to pot and cocaine. Before he got started, he played high school baseball. He was considered so good that several major colleges were interested in him. Once hooked on drugs, his body became weak, he quit going to practice, he started failing his courses, and he stole anything he could from his mother or anybody else to feed his habit. He would cry in my office, begging for help to stop. Since hospital-based programs were currently only allowing four days for detoxification, they would not be of much help. Nick really did want to stop. He was reluctant to go to AA meetings. He missed his appointments constantly. His will was gone. Whether or not he will ever overcome this, I honestly do not know.

Remember I said that teenagers could also become addicted to behaviors, such as sex and partying. These process addictions produce a euphoric high in the form of a thrill. Engaging in forbidden behaviors gives the teen an adrenaline rush—the euphoric high. The obsession with the behavior also provides a brief escape from everyday stresses, which is the second component for psychological addictions.

Angela

Angela was an eighteen-year-old college student. She was addicted to sex. Almost every night she would go to a neighboring all-male school and have sex with several guys at the same time; this is referred to as a "gang bang." On some occasions when the boys finished with her, they urinated on her. It was terrible. She subjected herself to humiliation and to the obvious risk of life-threatening disease, but she could not stop. What bothered me considerably were the boys who willingly participated in this. Their low values and their risk of disease did not seem to bother them either. I tried to help Angela, but the last time I saw her was when she dropped out of college.

Why did Angela do this? She obsessed about the sex throughout each day. It gave her an excitement she just could not contain. Her frenzy would build until the nighttime when she would complete the act. After each incident, she would be deeply depressed and remorseful, but each night she would do it again.

As her grades declined, the obsession became increasingly more important. The excitement and the mental escape from the escalating difficulties of her everyday life became so powerful that she lost all sense of control. The worse her life got, the worse the addiction got. It became a nonstop downward spiral. Her self-loathing and depression progressively got worse. She was living in hell. She was a slave. She was an addict. Her free will was gone.

I also have seen many teens, including college students, addicted to partying. Every night they seek out the high or euphoria of the party atmosphere, and in addition, they temporarily escape the stress of schoolwork. They escape the ardor of study and hard work. As with any addiction, functioning and performance decline. Grades fall. Life becomes more painful, and the addiction gets worse. There is no official diagnosis for this, but it is important that teens reflect on this issue. The only way not to be an addict is for a teen to avoid ever starting an addicting cycle. The best prevention is for the teen to build a strong value system that will prevent him from getting into drugs or wild behaviors in the first place.

I try to tell teens that there is absolutely no happiness in any of these addictions. It is filled with failure, self-loathing, guilt, and depression. The brief escape from worry with each addictive episode only brings more and more misery. Once one is addicted, free will and free choices are gone, and then slavery takes its place.

Value 7: Good Self-Esteem versus Poor Self-Esteem

Self-esteem, or the quality one places on oneself, is developed in five ways. The first source involves the way a teenager has been consistently treated by adults. If he has been treated with love and affirmation, then a positive self-image results. If, on the other hand, he has been treated poorly, such as constantly being yelled at, having derogatory remarks consistently made toward him, such as being called lazy, stupid, or fat, then expect him to develop a low self-image.

The second source is how one has been treated by peers. If they've been called names or excluded from activities, a low self-image can result. I am enraged at the epidemic of teasing, taunting, and bullying in this country.

Parental neglect provides a third venue for poor self-esteem. Recall our discussion about de jure and de facto neglect. Either form of neglect sends a message that "you are not worth caring about." It is easy to understand how children, under these conditions, can develop poor self-esteem.

The fourth source is more difficult to understand. If a child, during her early years, develops a habit of "poor me" verbalizations, which gains attention from adults, then eventually she'll internalize what she has been saying. Poor me's consist of "you don't love me. No one loves me. I can't do anything right. I'm stupid," and so forth. After years of repetitively saying these statements, she'll begin to believe them.

The fifth source of self-esteem is particularly important to a teen. The fourth source depends on his own behavior and accomplishments. Here a teenager is in control. He can determine this part of his self-image. Engaging in moral conduct and hard-earned accomplishments requires dedication, self-discipline, and perseverance. If a teen does these he will probably enjoy good self-esteem. If, on the other hand, he violates decent conduct and does nothing with his life, then low self-esteem will result. Laura Schlessinger would probably say he would then deserve to have low self-esteem. She'd probably say that if he wanted to reverse his low image, he'd have to earn it. I tend to agree.

A teen has a choice. He can drown in a sea of self-pity or he can work with all his heart and soul to engage in those behaviors and accomplishments that will *earn* him a positive self-image. Some teens have a history of bad treatment at the hands of others and indeed that is sad. But feeling sorry for them accomplishes nothing. As attorney Alan Dershowitz would say, "the abuse excuse is a cop out." If teens want to feel good about themselves, then they'll have to do it the old fashioned way and *earn it*.

Value 8: Quiet versus Overstimulation

Last night, while I was jogging, a teenager driving a car raced past me. The car window was open and the radio was blasting rap music. I was in a reflective mood and was enjoying the peace and quiet. The weather was mild, the wind was gentle, and there was a sweet fragrance in the air. As his car zoomed past, I could not help thinking about his missing the beauty that God was laying out before him. Maybe it was me who was missing the "beauty" of his music.

I bet you often hear your teen say, "I'm bored!" You look at them, probably quizzically thinking, "Six of your friends just left. You spent the day at the video arcade. You came home and I ordered pizza for everyone. All seven of you watched a video movie about two teenagers brutally knifing people to death. You then sat around and talked for two hours while, of course, your music was blasting. Within five minutes after your friends left, you're bored?!"

Is your teen so addicted to stimulation that she finds even a few minutes of quiet boring? It is important for our teenagers to be able to enjoy daily periods of peace and quiet. As Thomas Moore and Deepak Chopra claim, quiet time is healthy for the soul. It is time for meditation, reflection, contemplation, and prayer. Daily periods devoted to rest and renewal are essential for both physical and emotional health. Let me review what you can teach your teenager and what you, as an example for your teen, may wish to adopt for yourself.

First, quiet time keeps us physically alive. A physician friend of mine had a heart attack and died at the age of fifty-six. He rarely took time for rest, relaxation, and pure quiet. His life was filled with overstimulation and stress. There were many occasions when he told me how tired he was.

I am often asked to speak to professional groups about the topic of stress. This is the most commonly requested topic I get from professional groups, including physicians. I usually begin my presentation by telling them that what I am going to say is opposite from what their monthly speakers present. Usually they hear about time management; increasing the number of patients, or clients; about improving office efficiency and the bottom line of how to maximize profits. Instead,

I tell them that I prefer to instruct them on how to stay alive. Professionals in highly stressed jobs such as medicine, dentistry, law, and management generally have a much higher divorce rate, a very high rate of suicide, and a very high rate of alcohol and drug abuse and die younger than the general population. Do you know that physicians die at an average age of fifty-eight? The average life span is seventy-three for men and seventy-eight for women. What is it that kills professionals? Part of the answer can be found in the writings of Deepak Chopra, who as an endocrinologist has been concerned about the effects of stress on the immune system.

Chopra talks about spiritual issues from a Hindu perspective, and he emphasizes how crucial quiet and meditation are to a healthy body and mind. My physician friend who died worked enormous hours, beginning from his first day in medical school. On his days off, he worked as a Boy Scout leader. He also gave much of his time to his church as a lay leader. He had so adapted to this helter-skelter, overstimulated lifestyle that he failed to notice what all this was doing to his body. Excessive stimulation is stress, and it is a killer. It killed my friend. He failed to regularly schedule daily time for absolute quiet and rest in order to let his body recuperate from the pounding of daily stress.

One of my closest friends teaches at a medical school. He had a history of severe high blood pressure that required large amounts of medication to keep it under control. However, the medication rendered him infertile, which many years ago was preventing he and his wife from having children. One evening he called me and asked what I thought about his taking a course in meditation as an attempt to control his blood pressure without the medication. I told him that for some people it worked well and for others it did not, but I thought it was certainly worth a try. He took the course. After that, he began closing his laboratory door two or three times each day. The students knew not to disturb him because he was doing his meditation. He has done this faithfully for many years. He never had to go back on the medications, and he now has two beautiful adult daughters.

I deeply believe that the time to begin preventing the ravages of stress on our bodies is in our youth. It is important that teens learn that daily quiet time is essential for physical health and longevity. The body must remain as calm as possible each and every day. One important way to achieve calm is simply to shut off the mind and let our spirit rest.

Hopefully your teen can also learn that quiet time is equally essential for spiritual and emotional health. For thousands of years, most Eastern and Western religions have strongly emphasized how crucial meditation is for our spirituality. They see meditation as an important tool for connecting with God. In my faith as a Christian I practice contemplative prayer. I believe that in this way, as I stated earlier, God whispers to me. When I am quiet, I try to listen to His directions. My quiet prayer calms all my senses and protects me from an overwhelmingly stressed-out and overstimulated environment.

Teenagers desperately need this quiet time. Television, video games, blasting radios, and screeching cars give them no peace. Too many teenagers stay in a constant state of inner upheaval. It is OK for a teen to be a teen. Music, TV, radio, and cars are a part of their culture. I am not condemning that, but they also need to learn about how wonderful inner peace and harmony can be. Formal meditation and/or contemplative prayer are rather lofty and may not be particularly attractive to teens. But, perhaps your teen can learn simply to take time for a daily quiet walk.

I grew up in crowded New York where everyone frequently has to walk to his or her destination. The streets were always crowded with walkers. Now that I live in a beautiful place with grass and trees, and birds and squirrels, I never see a teenager outside taking a quiet walk. I see some adults, but no teens. I suspect that they are either glued to the TV, playing video games, or talking on the phone.

Psychology has a variety of ways other than meditation for teaching people ways to calm themselves. These methods are employed for dealing with daily stresses and for slowing down the physiological system. These techniques include progressive muscle relaxation, imaginal relaxation, biofeedback, and thought stoppage. However, quiet meditation and walking can achieve equal or even better results in a more enjoyable fashion.

Encourage your teenager to try a daily quiet walk for one week. Even as little as twenty minutes a day is sufficient. Go with her. Try not to talk. Instead focus on the air, the sounds, and the smells. Both of you try to get in touch with your bodies and minds. See if both of you can discover how good peace and tranquility can feel. If your teen likes this, perhaps she would be willing to extend this to a regular daily practice for the rest of her life.

As I mentioned earlier in the book, when I discussed family time, we overprogram our teens. In our zeal to educate them and to help them develop their potential talents, we schedule them into too many activities, such as sports, music lessons, and church activities. Part of being a kid is to simply be a kid. In other words, teenagers need time to relax and have time to just be a kid. They have to have time off from commitments. They have to learn the importance of a healthy balance between work, play, and rest. If we overprogram them, this indoctrinates teens into living the rest of their lives filled excessively with activities and overstimulation. They lose the capacity by adulthood to "take it easy" and "have quiet time." They can become addicted to overstimulation.

Be sensible in helping your teen find a healthy balance between industrious occupation and rest. A good goal for your teen is to ultimately expand his quiet time to at least one hour each day and perhaps even more hours on weekends. Just as the body needs exercise, the soul needs rest.

Value 9. Real Love versus in Love

Teenagers love to be in love. They live for their boyfriend or girlfriend. Being in love creates an incredible high, possibly even a greater high than any drug can produce. They love it. To be honest, so do adults. It does feel wonderful, and I am glad God gave us this capacity. Being in love releases powerful hormones, such as endorphins, that give a sense of euphoria. But it is only a temporary state that is essential for initiating a relationship. As Scott Peck says, "The work of real love is when you don't feel it."

For over twenty-five years, I have been leading divorce recovery groups, currently those at two churches. In helping group members understand what went wrong and how it might be possible to avoid repeating their mistakes, I often ask them the question, "When does divorce begin?" My answer often surprises them, "It begins when we fall in love." It's typical for group members to react as if I'm crazy. But hear me out.

Have you ever tried reasoning with someone when he or she is in the "in love" stage of a relationship? You can have a more sensible conversation with a wall than with someone in love. Think about it. Just about every marriage begins with a couple meeting and falling in love. Yet the divorce rate is between 50 and 60 percent. Less than 6 percent of couples that stay together report being happy. That means that about 94 percent of couples who fall in love eventually wind up out of love and unhappy.

We call the "in love" initial stage of a relationship different things. Terms such as *in love, in lust,* and *infatuation* are common. I prefer to call it the *in hormonal stage* because that is exactly what is happening. God programmed us to fall into this stage only to begin a relationship. Eventually, the hormones subside. We wake up one day and that beautiful and delicious feeling is gone. You know how the song by the Righteous Brothers goes, "You've lost that loving feeling and it's gone, gone, gone, gone. . . ." When the feeling goes, then what? Usually our answer is divorce or live the rest of our lives in a miserable relationship. It does not have to be this way. It can work out well, but the time to begin learning about love is when we are teenagers. Yes. I believe this deeply. Most of us only begin to understand love when it is too late: when in adult life our relationships fall apart. Only when there is pain do we begin to try to wrestle with the meaning of love. It is best if teens are given some sobering information about love early in their lives. Early knowledge may actually increase their chances for a truly successful relationship.

When we fall in love, it is usually because of a few initial and superficial traits, such as how attractive the other person is or how rich she is. Once the "in love" process is triggered, our hormones explode and our thinking, perceptions, and behaviors become very distorted. When we fall in love, I often say, in an exaggerated fashion, our IQs drop to about five.

Teenagers are capable of falling more deeply in love than adults. I take it very seriously when a teen tells me he is in love. A teen's mind is less cluttered with a history of painful failures, or with a life of experiences, or with information from reading. Their love is more pure, more innocent, and more powerful than that of adults. Remember how old Romeo and Juliet were? The story of Romeo and Juliet had been written numerous times before Shakespeare wrote his version. He deliberately portrayed the star-crossed lovers as very young teenagers to heighten the blindness, innocence, and hysteria of their relationship. It was the custom at the time.

Once we fall in love, we release hormones that can really play tricks on our perceptions. We perceive the other person as perfect. Either we see her as having no flaws, or, if we do see her flaws, we brush these aside because we don't want anything to contradict or spoil our delicious euphoria. Did you ever ask a friend to describe someone they've fallen in love with? The answer, if it comes from a young woman, usually sounds as if the love of her life is a perfect blend of Brad Pitt, George Clooney, and Tom Cruise all rolled into one. And you are thinking, "Are they nuts?" You see it completely differently. You are perhaps objective and clear-headed. You are hormone free. But, because you are being kind, you say nothing.

In addition to perceptual distortions, when we fall in love, we put our best behaviors forward. We dress carefully, we act thoughtfully, and we say sweet, tender, and wonderful things to each other. Neither party acts as his or her true self. When the hormonal stage abruptly ends, our perceptions clear up, our behaviors return to normal, and we suddenly feel disillusioned. If this phenomenon happens after ten years of marriage and two children, the consequences can be painful and disastrous.

Eric Fromm, a writer in psychology, calls in love "immature love," and he calls real love "mature love." That is a pretty good way to see it. The Greeks used the term *eros* for passionate love and *agape* for nonpassionate love. The formula for having successful relationships generally involves combining love, or the heart and hormones, with real love, or the mind and reason. It is a hard lesson to learn and even harder to practice because, once those hormones take over, it feels so good and it is easy to lose control.

I believe in teaching the realities of love to teenagers, and I also believe that the teen years are the best time to help them understand preventative solutions for failing relationships. Here are some of the points I cover with my teenaged patients and with my college students:

1. Real love begins by sorting out who you are and what you want from another person long before ever getting into a relationship. Defining who you are is deciding what your values are. Then what you want in another person, when you meet him or her, is to learn what his or her values are "before" letting yourself magically fall in love. Passion is important, but deciding on a lifetime contract with another person based solely on emotions is stupid. Real love means exploring each other's values, beliefs, and conduct before letting the passions loose.

2. It is important to consider how you plan to handle your relationship when the hormones subside. Do you plan to work at making a transition from the intensity of the in love stage to a warmer and more intimate companionate love? Companionate love is a deep friendship. It involves working at being a good soul mate, and it also involves the partner having the same commitment. It is best to know these beliefs or values in each other before falling in love. The only way to do this is through open dialogue, which isn't easy to do. This is perhaps the best way for making a transition to mature love.

3. Real love begins by working early in life, as a teen, at the self-development of the kinds of values that are deep, meaningful, and lasting. For a teen, this takes considerable dedication and effort so that she can become the kind of person that will be ready for a long-lasting relationship. These ingredients are necessary to avoid the tragedies of broken homes later in life. I ask my students and my teen patients to think about the effects a broken relationship will have on the children they hope to someday have. If their parents are divorced or are in a miserable relationship, I ask them to reflect on what this situation is doing to them. I tell teens that if you want children and you do not want them to suffer, you had better work out these issues now! Naiveté can have a painful "price ticket" later in life.

4. Barbara DeAngelis, in her books on relationships, advises couples to date a very long time and seriously probe how compatible they are by asking

lots of penetrating questions. Getting to know the other person is crucial before making a commitment. I think of the issue of getting to know the other person as searching for a spiritual partner because marriage means a joining of souls. Know what values both of you have about family, children, fidelity, commitment, God, money, integrity, and so forth. By dating a long time, the hormones may subside sufficiently to allow you to see each other more accurately. Teach your teen not to trust his perceptions in the early stages of a relationship. Be patient. It takes a very long time to know someone else.

Tanya

Tanya was fourteen when I first started seeing her. She was a headstrong and rebellious young girl. It was immediately clear that she was not going to listen to reason. Tanya had fallen passionately in love with Tony. She described him as sensitive, loving, responsible, and tender. Tony was sixteen. Tanya's mother saw Tony as one of the biggest losers she ever met. I met Tony and must confess I thought the mother was quite accurate. But, Tanya was in love. She deliberately got pregnant in order not to lose Tony. He also gave her herpes. By the time Tanya was sixteen she was living in hell.

Tony lost one job after another. When they had any money, they lived in a trailer. When they were broke, which was often, they lived with friends, if they could find any that would take them in. Tanya's mother gave them money when she could in order to be sure that they and the baby had food. Tony and Tanya fought constantly, and sometimes they would exchange blows. Tony began drinking and coming home late. Tanya constantly stayed depressed and lonely most of the time. This is still the situation as of this writing. Sad, isn't it? Early education about love might have prevented this horror for them and their child.

Value 10: Love versus Sex:

More than half our teenagers have had sex before graduating high school and almost 80 percent have had sex before leaving college. Studies, plus my personal discussions with teens, seem to support the idea that, while teens are having sex, few are promiscuous. Usually they are "going with someone" and view sex as a normal and integral part of their relationship. I am not saying this is a good thing: that is just the way they see it.

I remember in my youth my outrage when an "older person" on television espoused the evils of rock and roll and the devil drug marijuana. I thought what nerds they were. As an adult, a father, and a therapist, I feel quite differently. I like rock and roll, but the content of some of the lyrics exceeds decent standards and is pure filth. Some of the music is about violence, but much of it is about sex. TV shows, movies, and advertisements are blatantly filled with sexual content. This stuff strongly influences teenagers. The media hype confuses teenagers about the differences between sex and love. Add the prevalence of drugs within the youth culture, and the problems over sex are severely multiplied. Put pot, alcohol, or other drugs together with teenagers at a party and ask yourself if, while under the influence, they are going to restrain their sexuality.

I, myself, did not truly understand the spiritual meaning of sex until I witnessed the birth of my children. How could anyone escape the profound miracle of life that God gives us when witnessing the birth of our children? Watching them grow, to me, is also a miracle. Teens need to learn that there is a sacred side to sex, namely, the creation of life. Sex education must include learning the spiritual values that should be associated with sex. Think about how difficult it is for teens to learn how sacred sex is and that it is an expression of deep and mature love between mature people. What confusing values are they being presented when gratuitous sex is part of their daily media diet, and when the issues of the creation of life are becoming increasingly confused with the issues of birth control, artificial insemination, and surrogate mothering? Sex has become an all too casual value. It is losing its sacred side: the creation of life and the expression of deep love between two mature individuals.

God gave our teens a powerful sex drive, but He gave us the responsibility of educating them in their values to help control this drive. We must gently teach them that through God's love we have the gift of loving and respecting our soul mate and the miraculous creation of life. It is a spiritual and sacred decision that can involve the creation of life. Such a decision should not be made emotionally, while passions are out of control, or when under the influence of chemicals.

Teens can be taught that, if they truly love their current boyfriend or girlfriend, then they will respect them and not use them as an object for personal gratification. Using someone is not love. I do not know if teens in general will be receptive to these values, but, if we, as parents, at least try, perhaps we can reach some of them. The Hugh Hefners and Timothy Learys of this world, I believe, never fully understood the impact the values they preached would have on the minds of the very young and the very immature.

Teens are not ready to handle the intense and powerful complexities of two people having sex. I often have to deal with teens after an unexpected pregnancy becomes a reality. The choices a teen then faces are a nightmare. Having the baby is one option. Taking care of an infant means the loss of a teen's youth. It is an awesome responsibility that brings to a close the teenage years and plunges teens into an early adult life. Abortion is a choice I do not counsel. I have rarely known a teen who did not suffer terribly after choosing to end a life. It is a scar that never heals. It is a terrible secret to live with. The third choice of giving a baby up for adoption is also fraught with a lifetime of painful doubts. It is a difficult thing never again to know what has happened to your child. Each choice brings with it personal torment that teens must face as distinct possibilities as a consequence of recklessly choosing to have sex. I wish every teen could see a video of what unfolds when a teen tells me they are pregnant. Not only is it difficult for them to tell me, it is even harder to tell their parents and even harder to deal with the issues we just discussed. This can be a teenager's worst nightmare.

So far I have said nothing about sexually transmitted diseases. Teens turn off and tune out lectures on that stuff. I have found that if they do practice safe sex by using condoms, they often conclude by the third time after initially having sex that everything is safe and it is henceforth OK to no longer require the condom. I call this the third time rule: it is almost universal.

I deal with the harsh realities of human weaknesses. I deal with teenage patients and students seeking consolation after either becoming pregnant or contracting a sexually transmitted disease (STD). The fear and the grief I witness are both heartbreaking and profound. If teens could only see that these things are very real and perhaps appreciate the terror involved, maybe they would more readily appreciate the consequences of their acts.

If you agree with my position, it is important not to lecture. Nothing triggers an oppositional attitude in a teenager more than a lecture. A teen church, synagogue, or mosque group can help by surrounding them with peers who may have more conservative values about sex. This is all the more reason to get them into such a group. Houses of worship can also serve as places for discussion and guidance over sexual issues. Teens must ponder this decision before it is too late. Express your hope to them that they will think about these issues. Then hope information and intelligence will override their desires.

In the next chapter we'll look at the value that is central to the teen years— valuing education. We'll learn that there is much more than merely getting a good job that makes a teenager's investment in her own education so important.

12 | Valuing Education

Chapter 11 explored value education, which is teaching teens values. In this chapter, we'll explore education as an important value in itself, or valuing education.

The work of the teen years is education. It is one of the most crucial endeavors in preparation for adulthood. Because it is such an important value, it deserves a chapter solely to explore issues surrounding the educating of our teens. We'll look at why many teenagers don't like school, what can be done to instill a love for learning, the pros and cons about sending your teen to college, and the importance of instilling a love for reading as a key ingredient in valuing education. The next chapter will focus more in-depth on college issues.

SCHOOL ISN'T ATTRACTIVE FOR MANY TEENAGERS

Many of my teenage patients "hate" school. Well, I should be accurate; many may like attending school to be with friends, but too many hate schoolwork. Does this surprise you? Would it surprise you if I told you that many of my college students don't particularly like schoolwork either?

Lucas

Lucas was sixteen when he entered therapy. He was a handsome young man. His grades, which consisted of one or two Cs, numerous Ds, and a few Fs were barely sufficient for his yearly school promotion. His mother and father were divorced. His mother ran away with another man when Lucas was ten, and she rarely visited or called him. Lucas's father was an electrician. He was an honest, hard-working man. He and Lucas were extremely close, spending as much time together as possible hunting, fishing, and camping. Lucas was an only child.

When Lucas entered therapy, he did not represent a rebellious profile. He was soft-spoken and very polite. I judged Lucas to be extremely bright. He stated that he liked being with his friends at school but that he hated his classes. He pointed out that the subjects were boring and often wondered why they had to know "all that stuff."

Lucas turned out to be a successful case. Using the techniques I will soon discuss, his grades rose. However, it was my work with his father that yielded the most meaningful changes in Lucas. I will shortly reveal what changes his father had to make in order to change Lucas's attitude. Lucas is now a college graduate.

There are several elements in this case that highlight why teenagers don't value education. Lucas's father wanted his son to get a good education, but he did nothing to foster a love for learning. This is a very common pattern.

THE WRONG MESSAGE

The cliché "get a good education to get a good job" sends a very misleading message. It says that getting through school is a roadblock along the journey to what is really valued—making money. It says nothing about the value of the journey itself: one of our greatest mistakes.

Education must be one of our supreme values. It must be something we revere and cherish. We must demonstrate it. Did Lucas's father ever take him to a museum? I realize his dad worked as an electrician and only had a high school education. But, many blue-collar workers worship learning. When I grew up in New York, my barber loved opera and art. He visited the art museums regularly. It may surprise you, and it is quite true, that he even corresponded with Albert Einstein. He wanted to know how Einstein felt about God. One day he wrote Einstein; within a few weeks he received a lengthy response. Not wanting to burden Einstein, he kept his correspondences short and infrequent, but each time that he did write, Einstein graciously responded. I read these letters. Einstein took the time and energy to correspond with an ordinary man. Einstein understood this simple barber's devotion to and reverence for the world of ideas.

My family was also blue collar and uneducated. However, many of my extended family dedicated themselves to instilling in me the importance of education and a love for learning. The love for learning, the worship of knowledge, and the reverence for books surrounded me. Lucas did not have that. Why should Lucas care about education if all it represented to him was a hurdle to jump over in order to eventually make money? How sad it is that many parents do not understand that it is the journey itself that is the joy.

> How much better to get wisdom than gold,
> to choose understanding rather than silver! (Proverbs 16:16)

EDUCATION AS A FAMILY VALUE

Valuing education will not take root with your teen unless you actively demonstrate that learning is important to you. There are a number of things you can do with your teen that will help.

Take your teen on short educational trips. Visit museums, college campuses, and historical places.

Make learning about nature important and fun. Take trips to scenic places. Go camping and teach your teenager camping skills. Go hiking. Get up early to watch the sun rise. Buy a telescope and scan the heavens. Have your teen help plant flowers and shrubs. Visit planetariums.

Show an enthusiastic interest in his schoolwork. Talk with him every day about his day in school. Show your pleasure when he gets a good grade.

Demonstrate your love for music. I love rock, pop, and classical music. Therefore, I take my children to the milder forms of rock concerts as well as to the symphony. I've found that teenagers often don't like classical music until they attend a live concert and then amazingly the beauty of the music, for them, comes alive.

Take your teen to plays. Many communities have free outdoor presentations (also concerts) during the summer. Go as a family. You'll have fun too.

HOW SCHOOLS AND POLITICIANS ARE CONTRIBUTING TO TEENS' DISDAIN FOR LEARNING

Our school systems, from kindergarten through college, are increasingly becoming a mess. And much of the blame can be directed toward our politicians, and their cliché-laden policies.

I don't like complaining without offering solutions. I believe that politicians can "have their cake and eat it too." How's that for a cliché? There are ways politicians can change policies in meaningful ways, resulting in improving the educational environment; help children to enjoy school; get many children off dangerous medications; make life easier for teachers and parents; and win votes, all at the same time.

What Mistakes Politicians Are Making

Many politicians express concern that schoolchildren in the United States are academically behind children from other countries. They often cite France, Germany, Spain, and Japan as producing students of higher educational achievement. They also often campaign on the cliché "back to basics," which means an ever-increasing academic day of reading, writing, and mathematics, and less and less emphasis on fun things, such as music, art, physical education, free play, and healthy exercise. Teachers are reporting a decrease in art supplies, musical instruments, creative play equipment, and anything that may be construed as fun to children. Consequently the school day is becoming increasingly dull, dull, dull!

Don't confuse basics with fundamentals. Basics refer to subjects, while fundamentals refer to skills. Skills can be taught in more fun and inventive ways by incorporating them in the arts, music, and physical health activities. Instead politicians are emphasizing more and more school hours focused on academic subjects.

The results of political posturing has also been to accelerate school subjects, by introducing advanced academic material in kindergarten, material that used to be taught in first, second, and even the third grades. Children are being pushed harder and harder to excel academically earlier and earlier. By the time children reach the second or third grade, they are either burned out on school and bored, or didn't attend to the teaching of skills and therefore failed to learn many important fundamentals. Once fundamentals are not learned well, the child will fall further and further behind, making school even less pleasant. Failure to learn fundamentals, as stated earlier, is the main cause of learning disabilities, which often co-occur with attentional problems.

Politicians have insisted that a system of S.O.L.s, Standards of Learning tests, be administered to children beginning in the third grade in order to establish assessment guidelines for children. S.O.L.s aren't necessarily a bad thing, and I am not opposed to them. However, test scores have been used to gauge whether or not teachers, assistant principals, principals, and school superintendents are doing their part to make certain that children perform well. Tying scores to teacher and administrator survival has created a paranoid environment for them, and a miserable classroom atmosphere for children. It is because of these tests that children are being pressured from kindergarten to learn quickly, and learn a lot, because teachers and administrators may lose pay raises or even their positions. Classrooms have become bastions of pressure. Education has been made more banal than ever because teachers "teach to the test," which means pressuring young children to memorize previous test items and more and more academic material. School has become a survival camp, which neither the teachers nor the students any longer enjoy.

"Back to basics" can also mean treating all students as if they were going to college. Woe to the student who is vocationally inclined, because for them there is little available. All students are subsumed under curricula that are intended as preparation for admission to college. Course content has therefore become elitist, and more and more academic. This philosophy adds to the decline of fun, hands-on activities. Since about 60 percent of high school graduates do not go to college, it appears that the needs of the majority are not being met.

By the time a child reaches the teen years he has deeply learned to hate the drudgery of dry, meaningless schoolwork. They have been so thoroughly conditioned to hold learning in contempt, by the time they are thirteen there is little chance of reversing their attitude.

COLLEGE IS NOT FOR EVERYONE

I see public education, grades kindergarten through twelve, as having become excessively elitist, pushing all students as if they were going to college, and the needs of non-college-bound students are often not being met.

Tony

Tony is a common example of too many of my cases. As a sixteen-year-old, he attended high school in a neighboring county. He emphatically stated that he hated school and that he found most of it boring. His reading scores on national tests fell between the twenty-fifth and thirty-fifth percentiles, yet my personal judgment was that he was extremely bright.

I remember his stating one day, "Why should I give a sh——t about pronouns and adverbs, or about farm parity pricing in the 1930s. All we study is this war and that war. Dr. Stein, please tell me when the hell I'm ever going to use algebra, geometry, and trigonometry. Who gives a damn! Did you ever have to dissect a frog? Why should the guts of a frog interest me? Most of the books we read in literature class just seem like a pile of crap to me. Don't worry, I'll get my degree. I know you can't get a decent job without it, and I know the military won't even take me. I just want to get done with it."

Tony and I had an excellent relationship. I was glad he could openly state to me what he felt. Like most of my teen cases, Tony did not want to go to college. Tony could take a car apart and put it back together blindfolded: this is a literal fact. He constantly fixed neighbors' cars in order to earn a little spending money, and he loved doing it.

Tony was a nice kid, obedient and never in any trouble, but he hated school, and I believe deservedly so. Tony is right, and we are wrong! Our curricula are losing the majority of our teens. Why should they like school? To them it is meaningless and boring. They believe it has no relevance to their lives. Very little imagination has been put into our courses and curricula to meet the needs of our Tonys, who actually comprise the majority of our students. Most young people don't desire to go to college, but our school systems are almost exclusively designed for the college bound.

Politicians often say, "return to fundamentals and excellence in education." What about the terms *realistic, relevant,* and *pragmatic?* We tell our young people that school prepares them for life. I don't see where it does. Little of what we teach helps us to buy a house, be parents, be a smart consumer, communicate well with others, fix a light switch, repair a car, or be a good marriage partner.

I love higher education. But for Tony, this type of material is inappropriate. He hates it. He will never grow to like it. And, it is time we acknowledge that fact. With a little imagination we can develop courses that fit Tony's needs and train him in the skills he will truly need for life. Some exposure to the arts, literature, and the sciences can be enriching for Tony, but the balance of his courses should be pragmatic.

Let me share some of my ideas about courses I would like to see being taught:

1. Consumer economics courses, including:
     How to buy a house
     How to prepare personal taxes
     How to manage a family budget
     Wise purchasing and comparative shopping
     Understanding life insurance
     How to buy a car
2. Trade courses, such as:
     House repairs, or even house building

    Electrical repairs and maintenance
    Car repairing
    Carpentry
    Brick laying
3. Courses in parenting skills
4. Small business management courses
5. Dealing with human problems
    Marriage and relationship issues
    Communication skills
    Social skills
6. Courses that present true and accurate information instead of sugar-coated, watered-down versions that we teach (I find accurate history to be so much more exciting and interesting.)
7. Courses that deal, in depth, with drugs and alcohol

One can incorporate the basic skills of reading, writing, and arithmetic within the context of these more life-relevant courses. Material that is relevant and interesting can help reach many of the teenagers we are losing. Getting educators and politicians to change the way they envision education is usually fraught with frustration.

Many years ago we had a track system in high schools. One track was geared for the college bound, the other was designed for those students who wanted to work and learn a trade. Students on one track had room in their schedules to take elective courses from the other tracks. We need to return to that. The two tracks can overlap, allowing students to customize their courses to meet their own particular needs and desires. Some students may wish to take college-bound courses, and flexible curricula can allow for that. In education, we call this "individualization."

READING

It is doubtful that a teenager will love her education if she does not love to read.

Dr. Stein

Let me share with you a part of my personal life. I have learned an important lesson in life, one that you may already know. Often when I thought something was an adversity in my life it turned out to be a blessing.

While in college I spent between three to seven hours a day on the New York City subway. I desperately wished I could attend a picturesque dormitory college, but that just was not the case. My family was poor, and therefore I had to live at home and work, which necessitated the subway as my only means of transportation. It was noisy, dirty, and often crowded. In order to block out the environment, I read. I read more books riding the subway than I did for college. I deliberately chose not to read my textbooks while on the subway. I believed that in order to give my texts my full concentration, the quiet of my home was necessary. I look back and realize how precious that time on the subway turned out to be. There was nothing else I could do except read. I therefore read voraciously. Sometimes I would get so immersed in a book that I would miss my stop. The subway helped make reading a passion for me.

Suggestions for Instilling a Love for Reading

The love of reading is the most fundamental requirement for doing well in school. It is best to instill this love for reading when your children are young. However, this can still be done with teenagers. The crucial component in helping your teen want to read is to help her discover that reading is *fun*. She can learn to value and cherish reading. Here are some helpful hints:

1. Help your teen select reading material that ranges in difficulty from her current reading level to an easier one, as determined on her yearly national tests. It is not fun to read if you trip over every other word. If reading is made easy, she will enjoy it more and therefore read more. The more she reads, the more her reading scores will improve. The practice of reading itself improves the skills of reading. In education this technically is called "experiential reading." As her skills improve, she will escalate to higher levels of reading choices.

2. Let her choose topics she enjoys. Focus on her areas of interest. If a teenage girl says she wants to be a model, and almost all of them do, then ask her if she has ever read anything about modeling. She may also want to read books or magazines about exercise, health, and nutrition. If a boy loves sports, then let him read biographies about famous athletes, or books on improving performance. If your teen likes romance novels, then, with some careful screening, let them read romance books. Even comic books are OK, but again screen out the risqué and violent ones.

3. At bedtime, if she is not sleepy, give her permission to stay up later, but only if she reads: no games, drawing, or other alternatives. If you later find

her under the cover reading by flashlight, then smile because you have won. Quietly back out of the room and leave her alone.

4. Take her to the library and the bookstores frequently.
5. Let your teen subscribe to magazines, with your approval of course. It means a great deal to him when his subscription arrives in his name.
6. Shut off the TV. If you want him to read, then you must also read. Set aside at least one hour for a nightly ritual of quiet time and reading. Reading time can be family time.
7. If he is willing, discuss his readings with him. Show an avid interest. Don't use these moments to pressure him. Simply be a good listener.
8. Leave lots of magazines around the house, especially in the bathrooms.

Valuing education is the last of the values we'll cover. There are many more values of importance and perhaps you have some that you favor. Because of limited space, I covered those that may help most with your teen.

BULLYING, TEASING, AND TAUNTING

Before ending this chapter, I must address the epidemic of bullying, teasing, and taunting that is inundating our schools. Not only is it rampant, it is vicious. It appears that once a particular teen is targeted for taunting, it becomes merciless. I have to deal with teenagers who are deeply depressed, and even suicidal because they've been targeted. It is the lack of values that lies at the core of so many teens being ruthlessly and insensitively cruel to other teens. It is the same lack of values that cause them to hate schoolwork and disrupt their classes, now called attention deficit disorder/attention deficit hyperactive disorder (ADD/ADHD), and to be cruel to their parents, now called oppositional defiant disorder (ODD). Neither parents nor school officials seem to be doing anything constructive and substantive to combat this problem.

I consult with the Virginia State Police, and therefore I talk to many school-based police officers. They tell me that the teasing and taunting are beyond the imagination in the depths of their cruelty. However, children getting beat up is equally as rampant, but administrators do not criminally prosecute the teens responsible, because it would show up as a bad statistic on the computer records now available to the public. The police tell me that many do get prosecuted, but the ones reported barely scratch the surface about what is really going on. Many states have passed laws requiring schools to teach values, character education, and sensitivity training, but few are enforcing them. They state that there is no time because of the S.O.L. tests.

In the next chapter we'll continue our discussion about education, but we'll focus on college. Is your teen college material? Is it worth investing a fortune in a college education? Should you wait until he matures? And, if you decide to send him to college, what inside information do you need to know about colleges themselves that no one is telling you, before you invest most of your life savings? The next chapter will help with making all of these decisions.

13 Choosing a College–What You Need to Know and What They Aren't Telling You

The issue of whether or not to send your teen to college demands more in-depth discussion. The economics of sending your teen to college is crucial. College expenses are enormous. This is true for both private and state-funded institutions. Tuition in the private colleges can easily exceed thirty thousand dollars a year. State-funded colleges often charge more than twelve thousand a year for room, board, and tuition. Supplementation with tax money makes up the difference. These expenses are escalating every year. Is your teen worthy of this gigantic investment? Is she academic material that merits a fifty to two hundred thousand-dollar, four-year investment?

Computers and technology in the classrooms are adding enormously to college costs. Colleges are increasingly requiring students to have their own computers. This means that colleges must upgrade the entire electrical and telephone capabilities of their campuses. Computer support services have to be enormously expanded. The dollar amounts are huge. This is being reflected in considerably higher costs for you to send your youngster to college—and don't forget you must buy the laptop.

State colleges across the country are steadily increasing in physical size as well as in the number of students admitted. You are paying a substantial part of their expenses through your taxes. In fact, your tax dollars are scholarship money for these students. Did you ever think of this in these terms? Many of these students are plainly not college material, yet we are giving them our tax money. I went to a public institution, and I thank the good Lord it was there, but it was extremely difficult to get in and extremely difficult to stay in. My fellow students and I worked very hard. I had to earn every penny of the taxpayers' support I was receiving. Today hard work happens in only a few of the more prestigious state colleges. Some states, such as North Carolina, Florida, and New York, require academic

209

excellence for admission to a state school. Their academic standards are high, thus making it difficult for students to stay in. However, in many states the politicians, eager to get votes and please everyone, are allowing the expansion of state schools to such an extent that very poor academic students are, by necessity, accepted. Then the schools must offer remedial services to help marginal students stay in. This is called "retention." "Why?" I ask. It is your money; you decide.

Alternative programs are presently available, and even newer concepts in higher education are being developed, to reduce costs. Colleges are developing distance learning programs where a professor's on-campus lecture, in front of a live class, is televised to distant off-campus sites. This is an excellent and less expensive alternative for the student who may be a slow starter or for the older, nontraditional student, such as a working adult. In this way students can live at home, register for fewer credits, and perhaps hold a job. However, I see one major drawback. It does reduce the personal impact of the dynamic professor, but there are no perfect solutions. Videotape classes are also becoming popular. Class tapes are mailed to the student's home, where the student follows the same requirements as the on-campus students. However, they loose the advantage of live discussion. Designated local proctors administer exams. This is also an excellent alternative for the working adult with family responsibilities.

Community colleges are a far less expensive alternative for the marginal student, but the quality of these schools varies considerably. Some are what I call A factories, where they make courses easy and give As away, while others maintain fairly high standards. Since these are generally commuter schools, their operating expenses are considerably reduced. They don't have expenses for residence halls, food service, large maintenance staff, security police, and many other services that four-year colleges require. Thus, tuition is lower and there are no room and board expenses.

If you still desire for your teenager to go to a traditional residential four-year college even though he is a marginal student, then tell him that he will attend only on a semester by semester basis. Contract with him that if he maintains relatively strong grades, such as a B average, you will continue supporting him for another semester. If you discover, however, that he is not deeply invested in his college work, that he has a "party hearty" mentality, and that he is only getting by with mostly Cs or lower, then require him to withdraw from school, live on his own with no support from you, and work. I feel that you should not resume paying college expenses for a minimum of one year, and, after that, make it his responsibility to convince you that he is ready and worthy of your investing in his returning to school. Again, let him know that if he returns he will still be monitored on a semester by semester basis. Another poor semester and back out he goes for at least another year.

COLLEGE ISSUES

I am also concerned about our college students. Higher education is intended to take young minds to the pinnacles of human thought. It is designed for the young to begin mastering the concepts developed by the greatest thinkers, the greatest writers; the most important ideas in science and mathematics; the wonders of great art, music, and theater. To endeavor to master the highest levels of human thought, a young person must value education and learning with a passion. Sadly, many college students do not.

At the beginning of every semester, I endeavor to inculcate a love for education in my students. I try to teach them the joy of understanding a concept developed by great thinkers. Each conquest of knowledge is a marvelous growth experience. It is not something to be memorized, spit out just to pass exams, and forgotten "in order to ultimately get a good job." Our intellect separates us from animals. God gave it to us. It is our responsibility and joy to feed our minds and enjoy the feelings that accompany an expanding foundation of knowledge. Indeed, it is hard work, but it can be such exciting work.

During Christmas, several years ago, I took my sons to New York City. We exhausted ourselves trying to take in as many of the sites as we could. When we were in the American Museum of Natural History, and while we were sitting by the early American exhibits, I asked them to look around and think of all the people who were responsible for putting the exhibits together. I asked them to tell me what kind of knowledge these experts had to have; what professions were represented, such as archeologists, biologists, anthropologists, historians; and on and on. We talked about the actual work these people did, such as climbing mountains, exploring forests, digging in the earth, diving in oceans, and exploring caves. They were discovering that learning itself could be exciting and fun.

I had a special trick that I used when I went to college. I went to the City University of New York where competition for admission was fierce. We had a long list of eminent professors. I truly believe I received the highest quality education. My special trick was to keep a record on many of the professors. We did not have a system of student evaluation in those days, plus the college was enormous. It was difficult to know any information about the professors before I registered for courses. Therefore, before a semester began, I would stand in front of the posted lists of which professors were teaching the courses I needed. As older students came by, I would ask them to rate the professors as poor, fair, good, or excellent, and I recorded tally marks. Most of these students willingly filled me in. When I would register, I always chose the professors rated as excellent even though some of them had reputations as rather tough graders. I discovered that excellent professors made their courses come alive for me. They ignited a magic fire in me. By practicing this little trick, I learned to love the journey of my education. I had classes where professors received standing ovations at the end of the semester. To make matters more exciting, many of my fellow students felt the same way about their education as I did. They loved to challenge the professors. They would debate with them. Often there was an enlivened exchange of points of view. And the professors, in turn, also conveyed their enthusiasm for having such committed students. They seemed to relish such sincere interest.

One semester, a girl I was dating convinced me to register for the easy professors, the ones that gave As away. I found out why they gave away As. As teachers, they stunk! If they didn't give lots of As no one would take their classes. I maintained my grades, but I hated that semester and I never did that again.

Parents, if your teen is college bound, share this little trick with them. Perhaps registering for wonderful fiery professors will, as it did for me, ignite their desire and thirst for learning.

Now as a professor I begin each semester trying to ignite such a fire in my students. When I first meet them, I discuss an interesting point of view. I tell them that all of their professors and I want to teach them how to have fun. Since they are typically party animals, they look at me as if I have gone nuts. I tell them that they can continue the college "party hearty" tradition, but they can add more to it. By expanding their knowledge and understanding in all of their courses, they can learn to love and savor many new things, such as the exciting worlds of art, literature, music, theater, science, history, philosophy, and so forth. If they give it a chance, they may discover new avenues of fun they previously never considered. I do reach some of them, and for that I am grateful.

Curiously, one of the places I never visited as a teen was a college campus. If your teen is clearly college bound then take him to visit numerous campuses. Free tours can be easily arranged. Most campuses are quite beautiful. This can help make the idea of college more concrete and real. Perhaps, the desire to live for a few years in such a beautiful setting will motivate their desire to have college as a goal and to perform better in school. It is worth a try.

WHAT YOU NEED TO KNOW
ABOUT THE COLLEGE

Sending a child to college is the greatest expense that most parents ever have to make. Think about it. Even when we purchase a house, we eventually get a return, and even a profit, on our investment. But a college education costs a great deal of money, none of which we get back. Why do we invest so much in our children? I think the answer is obvious. We love them, and we want them to get the best education possible *and* become competitive in the postcollege, or postgraduate school, economic market. We want to give them a solid start in life's journey. But, how do we go about selecting the right school? I know that many readers believe that selecting a college is indeed very difficult. It is difficult when parents have to wade through mountains of information trying to make the best possible choices, but the task becomes even more formidable when parents cannot rely on the information made available to them.

Colleges now see themselves as businesses, and they have rapidly been learning to market themselves by making themselves look better than they actually are. It is not dissimilar to the corporate scandals currently making news headlines. Corporations are tampering with balance sheets to make them look better and healthier than they actually are. Each week new accounting tricks and gymnastics are being uncovered, and sadly similar practices are going on in higher education. This section gives parents some idea of the paper juggling shenanigans that are being used by some colleges and universities to make them look better than they actually are. We'll explore what questions to ask in order to get a better handle on prospective institutions that you may be considering for your child. After all, it is your child's intellectual development that is at stake.

Especially important are the state- and public-supported institutions, into which our tax dollars are being poured. Lots of tax dollars. Every youngster who attends a state school is, as I stated, in a sense, on a scholarship, because their expenses are supplemented by tax dollars. That is why the tuition at state schools is generally lower than private schools. Are we getting our tax dollars-worth from state schools or are we being duped? In some states we are indeed getting every penny's worth, but in others we are being drastically cheated out of hundreds of millions of our tax dollars, and this chapter will show you how.

Marketing Professionals—PR for Colleges

Most colleges, as I stated, view themselves as businesses. They therefore now retain an army of professional marketers. I call them masters of disguise. These are PR professionals whose sole purpose is to make the institution look fantastic, and they are darn good at it. Some of them can make a slum look like a resort.

My first piece of advice is don't believe any colleges' beautifully colored glossy brochures. You must visit the campuses and see for yourself. There is no other way. Much of the information given is slanted to make the schools look good, very good. This section is intended to help you gather the right information and demand answers for some of the most pertinent questions.

SAT Scores

Many schools present themselves as having excellent admission standards, claiming to have solid admission SAT averages, such as an approximate combined verbal and math score of 1080. For parents who aren't familiar with interpreting the scores, the range for verbal is between 200 and 800, and the same for math. The two scores are then combined. Separate math and verbal scores of 500, and a combined score of 1000 are right at the fiftieth percentile for the nation. This means that a student with a combined score of 1000 ranked right in the middle nationally. Schools with an average entrance score around 1000 are admitting that half their students are below average—some can barely sign their names.

Some state schools have SAT averages close to 1000, while in others the *minimum* scores to even be considered for admission are 1000, 1100, or even 1200. In states with higher standards for public institutions the prevailing philosophy is, *"We aren't investing state tax dollars in those students who are weak in educational skills. They may attend the community colleges for remediation, or they can go to the expensive private schools. But tax dollars will not be poured into backing marginal students!"* Why some states support below average students with tax dollars is beyond me. Why not let the community colleges, which are considerably cheaper to operate, absorb them?

Therefore, the first question to ask when looking at schools is, "What is the *minimum* SAT score needed for admission consideration?" The stronger schools will readily tell you. The weaker schools will try to get you to focus on the average scores.

There is an additional potentially hidden problem with SAT scores, one about which the public is hardly ever informed. A correction factor is sometimes automatically added to the scores of minority candidates. This is a form of affirmative action. I take exception with this tactic when the public and families seeking admission for their child aren't told. If this information is clearly made available, then so be it. All I ask for is truthful disclosure.

Major Field Achievement Tests—MFATs

Some colleges administer what are called exit exams. These are comprehensive review tests given for the different majors in the senior year of college. On the surface they seem sensible, but in reality they are misadministered and mishandled. One of the favorite tests used is the Major Field Achievement Test, MFAT. Test scores are based on percentiles compared to other schools in the nation that also administer the test.

If we probe a bit more deeply we begin to discover how these tests are growing as a marketing tool. Generally, only the weaker schools use the test, and therefore weaker schools are compared to other weaker schools, making a school that performs well seem better than it actually is. Schools may present a particular department, such as Psychology, nationally scoring perhaps in the ninety-fifth percentile. This is a misrepresentation, since the test scores were only compared to those of other weak schools. Therefore, they placed in the ninety-fifth percentile when compared to other weak schools. Unfortunately, parents aren't told about this practice.

New, even more underhanded practices are developing with these tests. Test items tend to be repeated every few years. Some departments, in the guise of review courses, actually rehearse with the students previous test items for the entire semester prior to taking the test. The students thus take the test already knowing all the answers. Oddly, many of these same schools pride themselves on having an honor code. It pains me to think that some professors actually equate this nonsense with higher education. This is in reality a form of cheating and does not represent true and meaningful higher education standards in any manner or form. It deludes students and parents into believing that they are performing better than they really are. I know many students who have done well on these tests who cannot accurately answer more thought-provoking open-ended questions. Let me give an example. The test may ask who founded classical conditioning. The student, having memorized that it was Ivan Pavlov chooses the correct answer. However, if I ask that same student to explain classical conditioning to me, I usually get met with a blank stare or am given an answer that is not even remotely correct. The student has never mastered the concept. I would suggest that you ask if the school uses the MFAT, or an equivalent test, and if the answer is yes, look elsewhere for a college for your child. If the school also has a review course, ask if previous test items are reviewed, and again, if the answer is yes, look elsewhere.

By the way, I don't mind review courses; I do mind rote memorization of prior test items, which is known as teaching to the test. Higher education should require the understanding, digesting, deciphering, unraveling, and figuring out of the highest levels of human thought. This requires considerable sweat on the part of the learner, but the efforts are well worth it. What a wonderful feeling it is for a student to progressively rise to the thinking levels of the great masters.

This is prevented by rote test-item memorization courses, which are to me a violation of higher educational standards and an abomination.

Graduate School Admissions

One of the best barometers of a school is the percentage of students that go on for advanced degrees. Don't be fooled by the numbers that go on for master's degrees, which are often obtained at schools where it isn't all that difficult to gain admission. Ask instead, how many premed majors gain admission into medical school, or dental school? How many pre-law majors gain admission into law schools, and which ones, since there are D, C, B. and A level law schools; you want to know the entrance rate into A and B level schools. How many students get accepted into doctoral programs from the various disciplines?

If admissions to the more serious graduate programs are low, look elsewhere.

A Word about the Job Market after College

Colleges, and more specifically departments, often lie to students about their chosen major. They often indoctrinate incoming freshmen with how great a choice their major is and how marketable they will be after graduation. Let's explore this issue in more depth.

Students are often told that almost any liberal arts major is looked upon favorably in the corporate business world, majors such as psychology, history, sociology, political science, and so forth. Not so. There's a bit of history behind this. In the 1970s the U.S. corporate world had a philosophy that we can call "screw the customer," which meant to make the product cheaply and sell for the highest possible price. Because of this philosophy during the 1970s and 1980s the United States practically handed our markets over to foreign competitors, whose philosophy was to make quality products and sell at reasonable profits. Our policies were a disaster. Americans grew to distrust American products. After this period corporations turned away from business majors toward the liberal arts majors. However, things then got even worse. American companies discovered that liberal arts majors were poor at making business decisions. University business departments then regrouped and started emphasizing entrepreneurship, resulting in far better prepared business majors. Businesses now have returned to preferring the business majors and generally shun the liberal arts graduates.

There is a job market for liberal arts majors but it is rather mediocre, with relatively poor entry-level salaries and little chance for real advancement. For the most part liberal arts majors become schoolteachers, sell real estate, or work as bank tellers. They rarely work in the subject area for which they went to college. If they wish to focus on their major they must go on for a doctorate, which usually means that they will become college teachers, but few qualify for doctorates.

It is crucial that parents know the goals of their youngster before choosing a specific major. Make certain that your teen's goals are solid and realistic or else don't pay for it! Don't count on a college advisor to tell him or her the truth. If you and your child choose poorly, you will never recover the amount of money spent for their college education. The money would fare better if it were invested.

Party, Party, Party

Having fun in college is important. The college years are the last time period when a youngster is still protected by their parents. Students may view themselves as having complete freedom and total independence, but we know that this is an illusion. Parents pick up the tab, allowing their youngster an unburdened lifestyle in order to focus on studies. Ha! For too many youngsters this provides ample time and financial freedom to just "party hearty."

Too many young people do not know where to draw the line. Too many students lack the values, commitment, ambition, and motivation to focus on their academics, and for them college is a four-year all-expenses-paid country club vacation. And they get away with it. Many colleges, as we'll soon see, are so structured that they reinforce these shallow attitudes, and too many students are permitted to do little else other than party themselves to death.

I have many students who come to class completely unprepared, hung over, and conveying an attitude of utter contempt if I try to teach something serious. The last thing on the minds of these students is to get an education. Their theme song is "All I Want to Do Is Have Some Fun." They can't balance serious academic endeavor with fun. Instead, for too many, it's an exclusive diet of fun, fun, and more fun.

I am amazed at how many parents seem to be unaware of their youngster's grades. Twelve to fifty thousand dollars per year are spent on youngsters who are hardly learning anything and who are on all-expenses-paid four-year vacations. If a student is placed on academic probation, many parents don't question their darling, instead, the parents go to bat for them and challenge the school's right to dare to make academic demands.

Parents, wake up. Before sending your child to a college, walk around the campus during the week days and look for two things. How much partying do you observe on fraternity and sorority row? Then go to the library and see if it is full. If the library is empty and the frat and sorority houses are full, you'd better question what is going on at that school, and whether or not you want to invest your hard-earned dollars there.

It makes me angry when parents say, "He'll grow up. He's just late maturing, and I don't want to rob him of his chance for his future." If you have an immature child, a late developer, then send him or her to a community college for the first two years and let him or her mature there. It is a lot cheaper. Stop wasting the professors' time and your money.

Retention

Schools often contribute to the party hearty atmosphere and cater to the immaturity of students. The finances of many schools are based on head count. The more students they can hold onto, the more money that comes in. Sadly, too many state schools are funded with tax dollars in this same way. The result of this philosophy is to hold onto students at all cost. Poor students are provided with remedial services to keep them in the schools. Professors are brought to task if they give too many poor grades. Pressure is often exerted on tough professors to get in line with the school's financial agenda. The key word among administrators is *retention*. Retain students with every available resource. Don't require that the students work hard. Don't demand that they earn excellent grades. Dummy down the system so that marginal students can survive. Keep them wedded to the campus because the school needs the money. I ask parents to reflect on this for a moment. Is there any integrity in this? Do you want your child to be rewarded for mediocrity, or even for stupidity? Are these the kind of students you want performing brain surgery or building bridges? Do you value education? Or do you just give it lip service so that your youngster can get his or her degree and earn a good buck?

If young people are protected from meaningful consequences then many of them won't perform. They won't exert the sweat and effort required to become truly educated. The retention concept reinforces the party hearty campus environment and protects the young from consequences. As a psychologist and student of human behavior, I can tell you that when there is a perception of an absence of consequences most people will gravitate to the lowest level of functioning. Retention protects young people from consequences and allows them to function at their lowest.

If you hear the word *retention* when looking for a school, run to your next selection. If I send my child to a school and invest a fortune in his or her education, I want to know that I am getting my money's worth. I want to know that at the end of four years he or she is well educated!

Student Evaluations of Faculty

When the idea of students evaluating faculty began thirty years ago, I thought it had merit. I am now certain that it is dangerous. You, as parents, may be told that these evaluations are only part of the consideration for faculty tenure and promotion. Unfortunately, these evaluations have become sacrosanct, and form the central part of consideration for faculty security and advancement. Under these conditions faculty have relinquished cherished values about education. They have succumbed to watering down grades in order to gain favor with students, spoon-feeding to help students perform well on tests, and teaching to the test. Administrators tell faculty that the research shows there is no correlation between the grades professors give and student evaluations. I blindly accepted this until a few years ago when I investigated the research and found the opposite to be true. Most, not all, faculty who give away As and Bs get good evaluations, while the tough graders get poor evaluations. I love education. College or higher education is supposed to be about taking young minds to the highest levels of human thought, but since the start of faculty evaluations I've witnessed the quality of teaching sink lower, and lower, and lower.

When considering a college for your child, ask if this evaluation system is in place. If it is, ask why? You'll get the same pat answer I've gotten. Don't believe them; look up the research yourself. Many of the better colleges have done away with this system.

The Board of Visitors

Every college and university has an overseeing board, usually called the board of visitors, whose charge or mission is to make certain that the administration is doing its job in maintaining a healthy institution. The board typically is composed of lay appointees, who are usually prominent community members or political appointees. Boards usually have the final vote on major college policies. Unfortunately, here too camouflage, coverup, and misrepresentation are the order of the day. Boards are treated like royalty. When they are on campus they are wined and dined. The PR experts, under the watchful eye of the administration, usually orchestrate information presented to the board about the health of the college. Therefore, most negative information is screened and never brought to the board's attention. This screening process is often done with amazing finesse.

What can parents look for? Ask if the board meets anonymously with random faculty groups. If they do then they have access to what is really going on in the classrooms. If they don't then they are often clueless about what is going on at the college. Rarely do boards meet directly and under the safety of anonymity with the faculty. Therefore most college administrators have a license to get away with whatever they please.

Grades

There are two issues surrounding grades: first, what are the grade admission standards for a college, and second what are you child's grades?

Grade point average, GPA, is a better predictor of how well students will perform in college than their SAT scores. Therefore, knowing about GPA admission requirements is important. I suggest that parents know what *minimum* GPA is required for entrance to the school. Again, be careful when presented with averages. An admission standard of around a 3.0, or B average, looks good on paper, but it could mean that half the students admitted are marginal or even very poor quality students. If you want your money's worth for your child's education, then I suggest you ask what is the minimum GPA required in order to be even considered by the college. A minimum of 2.5, about a C, means the school has fairly decent standards, and of course, a minimum of 3.0, about a B, indicates a much stronger set of standards. Stronger admission standards mean a better peer influence surrounding your child.

The second consideration is to know your child's grades. I personally recommend that you not send your child to an expensive four-year college or university if his or her high school average grades are less than around a B. Save your money and send him or her to a community college for remedial work, to allow him or her time to mature, and to prove that he or she will take education seriously. If they pass this threefold litmus test for two years then it is safer for you to invest in a transfer to a four-year school.

I'm amazed, as I stated earlier, at how many parents do not know what grades their child is earning at college. I strongly suggest that if your child is not earning close to a B average, 3.0 GPA, that you yank him or her out of college and require that she or he live on her or his own for at least one year before being allowed to return to college. In addition, I also strongly recommend that you let the burden of proof be on his or her shoulders that he or she is motivated to do well in school and will justify the tremendous expense that you are making. If you aren't feeling satisfied with your youngster's presentation then let him or her continue to stay out until the burdens of living in the real world are sufficiently painful to motivate your child to get serious about school. You are not denying your child a college education; you are merely delaying it until you are convinced that your child is serious enough and mature enough for you to make the heavy investment.

If your personal agenda is for your child to just get a degree in order to get a good job, then I recommend you search for a college or university that does the opposite of everything you've just been taught. Invest your money in the lowest four-year college you can find, let your child have a mediocre career, and allow your child to remain immature, but don't come crying to me when your youngster is a middle-aged loser, with the shallowest of values. I consider it the *parent's fault*, which is something many of you detest hearing. Isn't it?

One Other Thing to Look For

If you visit the campus, ask to sit in on several classes. If you observe the professors ask reasonable questions only to be met with eyes downcast on notebooks, and few or no answers, then you are probably visiting a very poor quality school. If you observe a dynamic and lively exchange between professors and students, you are probably at the school that is best for your child.

14 | The Car

The supreme value for American teenagers is their love for "the car." So important is the issue of teenagers and cars that it deserves a separate chapter. I recently published two professional articles that solve the definition of the term *disease* in psychology and psychiatry, something that hasn't previously been successfully done. I can now claim fame to defining the term *insanity*—a teenager aggressively weaving a two-ton machine through heavy traffic, with his brain completely off. The term may further be extended to those adults who purchase said machine for said teenager, knowing that he or she has an extensive history of mindlessness, as evidenced by poor school grades, several traffic violations, oppositional/defiant behaviors within the home directed at said parents, evidence of periodic abuse of drugs and alcohol, and a total indifference for the rules of civilized society.

WHAT HAPPENED TO MY DAUGHTER, HEIDI

My daughter, Heidi, is now twenty-nine. When Heidi started the eighth grade, her school had a tradition of a gathering of all the students at a bonfire. Her Mom and I left her at the festivities at 8:00 p.m.

When we returned, every parent's nightmare unfolded. While driving into the parking lot, a teacher ran toward our car. Her first words were, "Heidi is all right, but she's been involved in an automobile accident!" "How could that be? She wasn't supposed to be in a car?" Being new, and wanting to fit in, Heidi, without permission, agreed to accept an invitation to a party. She got in the car of an unknown sixteen-year-old. She sat in the front passenger seat, and thank the good Lord, put on her seat belt. Showing off his driving prowess, the driver sped along a very dangerous winding road. He had not been drinking. However, on a sharp curve he lost complete control of the car, and spun out of control. Four teens, one was sitting on someone's lap, flew out of the car onto the road. One girl shot through the front window, and one very large football player shot through the rear window. Heidi and the driver were the only ones wearing seat-belts, but since airbags weren't required at that time, both suffered head trauma. No one was killed. Fortunately, there was no traffic from either direction. The football player suffered several arm fractures, and one of the girls suffered a se-vere head concussion, from which she eventually recovered completely.

It is so hard to describe what I felt that night. It was awful. We didn't disci-pline Heidi for her transgression, partly because we were so relieved that she was all right, and partly because she convinced us that she had learned a lesson she would never forget. She never did.

One of the darkest moments of that evening involved the driver's parents tell-ing us that the police swore he had not been speeding. This was immediately after I had had a conversation with the police, who told me that the skid marks indicated he had been speeding excessively. My immediate thoughts surrounded his parent's unethical behavior, and the danger they were once again putting their son in by protecting him from the consequences of his stupidity.

WHAT IS WRONG WITH
THE MINDS OF PARENTS?

I am not against teenagers driving, the responsible ones that is. I am against par-ents supporting and financing driving by teenagers who have a long and clear history of mindlessness and recklessness. Let's take a look at the issues:

1. No teenager should be driving who does not have at least a B grade point average. Poor grades are a good index to alert parents that a teen is not responsible, and should not be the captain commanding a dangerous ma-chine. I don't believe that being allowed to drive should be a reward for one or two semesters of good grades. Instead, I believe that a teenager who has a long and steady history of good school performance deserves a chance for the right to drive.

2. Teenagers have little reason to be driving or "cruising" during the week. I'm certain that you see many teens out during the week, weaving and bob-

bing aimlessly through traffic, and usually with a pack of friends. If a teen is properly doing his homework, has responsibilities for one major chore each evening, has dinner with his family every night, participates in a team sport, and is required to do some recreational reading, there should be "no time" left for cruising and aimless socializing. Parents, you are the boss! This book has given you the tools to assume command. Now be the boss and put a stop to this unnecessary practice.

3. It is poor judgment to allow a teenager who is failing in school to drive to a job in order to afford having his or her own car! A failing teen should have neither a job nor a car. Please spare telling me that jobs teach teens a sense of responsibility. Teenagers have two primary responsibilities, school and family. Job responsibilities are not even a close third.

4. Every day and night, I see countless teenagers driving very expensive souped-up, pickup trucks, jeeps, and other high-risk performance vehicles. Any parent who can't figure out that these vehicles are intended for showing off, speeding, and aggressive and reckless driving does not have a whit of good sense! It is time that we parents took these risky vehicles away from children! By the way, some of these children are middle-aged adults as well. Where are teenagers getting the money for these expensive vehicles and all the expensive adornments? The money has to come from jobs most teens, not having good grades, haven't earned the right to have, or from stupid parents.

5. If a teenager gets a ticket for speeding, aggressive driving, running a red light or stop sign, or any other dangerous form of maneuvering, his or her license should be taken away for at least a year. At the end of the year, it should be his or her responsibility to convince the parent(s) that he or she has learned his or her lesson, and will, henceforth, drive safely.

6. The law should completely revoke the license of any teen convicted of a DUI (driving under the influence), as well as requiring attending another driver education course.

7. The law should revoke the license of any teen convicted of aggressive driving. I also believe that police are lax in enforcing aggressive driving statutes. Police should be aggressive in enforcing aggressive driving standards!

8. Any teen known to be using or abusing drugs or alcohol should not be permitted near a car by his parents.

Do You Want Your Teen Killed?

I'm certain no parent wants his or her child to die, but why do most of you disregard everything just discussed? If you feel my tirade sounded like I was attacking parents, you are right! I don't want your child to die, I don't want my children to die, I don't want any child to die, and I don't want innocent bystanders to die. But that is exactly what happens when most teenagers are behind the wheels of cars. Only we parents can stop this slaughter. Won't you please listen?

15

Existential Attitudes: Our Deepest Beliefs

Our deepest beliefs are called our attitudes. Our two most important attitudes consist of how we view ourselves and how we view other people. These fundamental attitudes are established in our earliest years and subsequently determine the general way we function throughout the rest of our lives.

In this chapter we'll look at some of the insights great thinkers had about these attitudes, and what happens when negative attitudes develop early in life. In the following chapter we'll discuss what can be done to help teenagers who have developed negative attitudes to change these attitudes into more positive ones.

ATTITUDES ACCORDING TO
SOME GREAT THINKERS

Sigmund Freud, around the turn of the twentieth century, wrote that our personalities are established within the first six years of our lives. However, he believed that it is within the first three years that our two basic attitudes about ourselves and about authority figures are locked in. Once locked in, these two most important components of our personalities will affect our patterns of behavior for the rest of our lives. Fortunately, we know that attitudes can be changed later in life, but as one grows older changes become increasingly difficult. While Freud's theories mostly focus on other events during the following three years, ages three to six, his notions about the earlier development of these two basic attitudes are of particular importance in this book. Freud was quite vague, even though he wrote twenty-four volumes on his theory, about what precisely it is that parents do to facilitate establishing two healthy or positive attitudes. He was equally unclear about what they do wrong to establish negative attitudes.

Freud's disciple Alfred Adler reconceptualized these attitudes into what he called "feelings of inferiority and superiority." Again, he, too, was vague about precisely what parents should or should not do. According to Adler, if one has a good attitude about himself (or herself) then to him superiority means he will strive toward self-mastery, or superiority over his own personal emotional growth and personal abilities. If a child is made to feel inferior, then his quest for the rest of his life will be for superiority over other people.

One can look at a few historical figures and perhaps see some validity in Adler's point of view. For example, my readings of historical figures indicate that people such as Hitler, Stalin, and Richard Nixon each had deep feelings of inferiority and indeed devoted their entire lives attempting to be superior over others.

A more contemporary writer, Al Bandura, uses the term *self-efficacy*. This is the belief or attitude about one's ability to master or overcome whatever is necessary in life, that is, one's environment. Low self-efficacy is a lack of belief in oneself, while high self-efficacy is a sense of self-assurance that one can take care of business. He, too, indicates that these attitudes are established early in life.

TRANSACTIONAL ANALYSIS

Perhaps the easiest way to understand these concepts lies in the more reader-friendly terms used by the transactional analyst writers who were popular during the 1970s. Noted writers include Eric Berne, the founder of TA (Transactional Analysis), Thomas Harris, and Claude Steiner. Their descriptors for the two fundamental attitudes are I'm OK–You're OK. They call these attitudes our existential positions. *Existential* means our beliefs or meaning for existing or being alive. According to TA, these attitudes, once established, determine all our behavior and acts for the rest of our lives. All our interactions and behaviors with other people, which they call the "games" that we play, will constantly affirm these two basic attitudes toward ourselves and others. To the transactional analysts, once our attitudes are established in childhood, the rest of our lives follow a plan or script that perpetuates, reinforces, reaffirms, and bolsters these two beliefs. To the TA writers, little that happens in life occurs by accident. We set up our own social situations so that the outcome of our interactions with other people continuously reaffirms how we basically feel about ourselves and others.

The four basic attitude combinations or existential positions are:

1. I'm OK–You're OK (+ +)
2. I'm Not OK–You're OK (− +)
3. I'm OK–You're Not OK (+ −)
4. I'm Not OK–You're Not OK (− −)

How Existential Attitudes Are Established

Again, the TA people point to early childhood and how a child is treated. But, here too they aren't any clearer than Freud or Adler. To help us I'll borrow from a fairly closely related school of psychology called humanism or Rogerian psychology, named after its founder, Carl Rogers.

According to the humanists, Not OK attitudes are established by abuse, neglect, excessive punishment, conditional love (being loved only for performance), and lack of unconditional love (the lack of being loved just as you are or as a person, without having to perform). Any combination of sustained maltreatment by our parents can lock in a negative attitude about ourselves or others.

Once you understand this fundamental concept, then you'll make sense of much of a teenager's needs and behavior.

I'm Not OK–You're OK

In the I'm Not OK–You're OK existential attitude, the individual has a global belief that she is worthless and that she does not measure up when compared to other people. She sees others as better, more attractive, more capable, and more physically adept. The ongoing emotional state that can result from such a negative self-image is depression. This means that anyone with this attitude will spend most of her life battling ongoing feelings of sadness and worthlessness.

The family conditions that foster this attitude include neglect, all forms of abuse, and aloof or cold parents. Lewinsohn's research also shows that these individuals have a low rate of social reinforcement—affection and nurturance—and a high rate of negative events—being yelled at, disappointed, or punished.

The resulting cognitive or thinking pattern, according to psychologist Martin Seligman, has three dimensions that will perpetuate ongoing depression: (1) when something goes wrong, she blames herself, (2) she not only blames herself for failing at something, but she sees herself as totally worthless, and (3) she believes things will never get any better, which means the future always looks bleak. For example, if a teenage boy asks a girl out and she says, "I'd love to go but I'm busy. Perhaps some other time." The Not OK youth interprets this to mean: (1) It's my fault because I stuttered when I asked her, (2) I'm ugly, clumsy, and stupid. No one would ever want to go out with me, and (3) It's always going to be this way. No girl will ever go out with me. This thinking pattern maintains the sense of worthlessness and the depression.

Devin

Devin was one of the most remarkable sixteen-year-olds I have ever met. He came to therapy completely of his own accord. He had no insurance and his parents refused to help pay for the sessions. He told me he'd pay from his own savings. Even though he didn't ask, I insisted on a substantially reduced fee.

Depression was Devin's constant companion. Sometimes the pain was intolerable. At its worst, he couldn't sleep, he couldn't eat, his energy was almost nonexistent, and he'd hide in his bed until he absolutely had something that required his attention. He constantly felt anxious and nervous. He often couldn't control continuous episodes of crying. Many times he wished he could die. Devin lived a lonely, monastic life. He worked, attended classes, studied, read, and went for long, lonely walks. He had no one to talk to.

Devin was in his first year at an excellent university. He had to take a medical leave in his first semester after collapsing from exhaustion. He came to me at the suggestion of one of his professors. Devin was terrified that he'd never graduate from college.

His parents owned a small grocery store where Devin had worked since he was nine years old. He described arduous working conditions, such as scrubbing floors, carrying heavy cartons, cleaning, waiting on customers, and working long hours after school and on weekends. He was required to work every Saturday and every other Sunday. He was paid a minimum wage by his father. His parents literally never bought anything for him. This included no gifts for birthdays or Christmas. Everything he had, including his clothing and school supplies, were purchased from his earnings. Only shelter and food were provided. This was hard for him to understand since his parents had sufficient funds; they weren't poor.

Devin could not remember ever being hugged or kissed or told, "I love you." To his parents, he was a nonentity.

Devin, being a straight A student, had earned a full scholarship for college. But he needed help for room and board, which his parents denied him. His father flat-out told him, "No, because you don't have what it takes!" He continued working and struggled with a full course load at a very demanding university until he finally collapsed.

Being a very shy and retiring young man, he had never been on a date. When he didn't go to the high school prom, he asked the prettiest girl in the class if she had gone. She said, "No!" When he asked why, she angrily replied, "Because you didn't ask me!" This left him dumbfounded. He saw himself as unattractive and of little worth. He was neither. He was a handsome young man with a remarkable intelligence.

Devin's profile included no reinforcement, no love, no affection, no recognition, no indication of his worth, and neglect, and in addition, Devin was used as slave labor by his father. Are conditions ever more clear for a youngster to develop a Not OK attitude and spend most of his life in an ongoing state of depression? Devin remained a patient for a very long time. If ever I believed in someone, it was Devin. He is now a practicing physician.

Other pathological patterns can unfold. Problems with anxiety can be a life-long pattern when a child believes he's Not OK. Anxiety usually involves a fear that something bad will occur in the near or distant future. For a child with a long history of poor treatment, dread of the future is actually rather realistic.

Eating disorders are frequent for teenage girls. If a teenager deeply feels Not OK about herself, she may take extraordinary measures to at least be physically attractive to compensate for her Not OKness. Sadly drugs can also be a source of momentary soothing for a heart filled with despair and pain.

I'm OK—You're Not OK

The I'm OK–You're Not OK attitude is actually not what it initially seems to be because underneath the person really doesn't feel OK about himself. The overt, manifested, or surface behaviors include being hypercritical of others, sarcasm, frequent anger, finding fault with everything, and demandingness. In *DSM-IV* terms this describes a paranoid personality disorder.

Depression is often concurrent with the anger. Individuals like this aren't very likeable, and others stay away from them. They don't get invited to parties, and they don't maintain friendships. The loneliness they then experience periodically leads to episodes of deep depression. The family conditions that underlie this include parents who are frequently angry, have frequent arguments and fights within the family, commit mental abuse, and deliver constant criticism. Parents role model the very pattern of behavior a teenager may adopt.

Donny

When Donny, age sixteen, first came to see me he was very depressed after his girlfriend of two years ended their relationship. Because his depression was so profound it masked his true underlying personality. Gradually as the depression lifted, Donny's personality emerged. He began describing his girlfriend as "stupid." The word *stupid* was fast becoming a major part of his vocabulary. Soon everyone was "stupid," such as the other kids, the teachers, and his parents. He hated school, sports, parties, hot weather, cold weather, and on and on. Donny eventually admitted that he had slapped his girlfriend twice. Both incidents were over something very trivial. Loss of temper was very frequent for him.

It was evident that Donny learned his attitude and modeled his behavior after his father. His dad screamed constantly, at anything and anyone; in traffic the screaming was at other drivers, at home it was at his wife or at Donny. If a box of cereal wouldn't open easily, his dad would become enraged, screaming and tearing the box open, often spilling its contents all over the kitchen.

I tried to get Donny to work on his anger and negativism, but, once his depression and pain subsided, so did his motivation to get help, and he didn't want to continue in therapy. Without help, I believe Donny was condemned to a life of failed relationships.

I'm Not OK—You're Not OK

I'm Not OK–You're Not OK is extreme and is the profile of the broken and defeated adolescent. This is the child whose spirit is destroyed. When teaching my graduate counseling students, I describe the most telltale behaviors in teenagers that signify this mental state and for which they should be alert. This is the teenager who keeps his hands in his pockets, is constantly alone, walks close to the walls as if not wanting to be noticed, fails most of his classes, is frequently truant and spends the day aimlessly walking the streets, and manifests almost no interest in anything. In short this is a broken child.

This is the teenager that is heading for serious trouble. He doesn't like himself, and he hates the world. Actually hurting himself or someone else is a strong probability. Suicide, drugs, delinquency, aggression, and vandalism are very likely. If this type of teenager engages in such acts he'll probably do it alone, simply because he doesn't have friends.

The constellation of parental treatment often consists of severe neglect, severe abuse—especially mental abuse—profound absence of love and affection, extremely narcissistic or selfish parents, and possible parental substance abuse.

Ann

At fourteen, Ann was already a broken spirit. She was referred by the police after breaking windows and destroying school property late one evening. She was frequently truant and failing everything. School meant nothing to her. She would have sex with any boy, and when she did, she was like a robot that couldn't care less. For her, sex was not seeking affection; it was an act of anger just to show that she didn't care what she did. She smoked, and, whenever she could obtain alcohol, she'd drink heavily.

Both her parents were alcoholics. Both had frequent affairs. The only affection she got was when Dad fondled her. Her parents lived as if she didn't exist. Drinking, sex, and watching television were all they cared about.

I couldn't help Ann. I referred her to a female colleague who was a warm and caring person. She too failed. At fifteen Ann killed herself in a graveyard, using a gun she had kept buried there for several years for this very purpose.

I'm OK–You're OK

The healthiest existential attitude involves a teenager who feels good about herself and feels a sense of joy about other people and, in general, the world. What must parents know and do to have a teenager that feels this way? A lot!

A student once asked me the difference between knowledge and wisdom. I replied that knowledge was an accumulation of information and wisdom was how we apply it. We will cover in the remainder of this book what you need to know to establish an I'm OK–You're OK attitude in our teens. The wisdom for parents, as Jean-Luc Picard says, is to "Make it so" or put the information into action. Your job, therefore, is to gather the information and then to put it into action.

16 Love: The Desperate Need of Teenagers

Teenagers want to be independent and free. But, as Eric Fromm wrote, our greatest contradiction in life is, in order to be independent and free we must feel that we belong. We must feel deeply loved, profoundly accepted, and firmly secure before we are able to venture out on our own. Only a teenager who has been loved will be prepared for a healthy adult life.

THE KEY TO THE I'M OK—YOU'RE OK (+ +) EXISTENTIAL ATTITUDES

To Abraham Maslow, being loved is not something we merely want, a desire to possess something or someone; instead, he sees being loved as a need, a necessity for life. Without love we will literally die. With insufficient love, physical growth can be impaired, emotional growth can be distorted, and spiritual growth can completely stop.

Rene Spitz taught us during World War II that an infant not given love in the form of touching, caressing, and cuddling literally will die. He named this condition "infantile marasmus." Harry Harlow, a significant figure in psychology's history, taught us that unloved infants, later in life, have difficulty in forming attachments with others: this can last an entire lifetime. Without love, physical growth can be markedly stunted, resulting in smaller body size, less than average height, lowered immune systems, and proneness to allergies.

Ashley Montague writes, "Show me a criminal and psychopath and I'll show you an unloved tragedy." Without love, as Freud and others have shown, a child does not learn to value herself or others. Without love a child feels unsafe, fright-

235

ened, and rejected. Without love, as Maslow, Carl Rogers, Eric Fromm, Freud, and many more have shown, a child is doomed to a lifetime of all types of emotional suffering, such as depression, anxiety, personality disorders, and bad relationships. If a child is ever to establish the existential foundations of I'm OK–You're OK, she must feel loved.

TWO TYPES OF LOVE

Children need two types of love—unconditional love and conditional love.

The humanists have taught us about a child's need for unconditional love. This is the type of love given freely, without a child having to perform or achieve anything in order to earn it. The only reason necessary to be loved is "because you are my child." Unconditional love typically begins at birth. A mother or father cuddling her newborn child and humming a soft tune is giving a form of sustenance that is equally as important as food, water, and air. As a child grows older he still need lots of hugs and kisses. He needs a great deal of a parent's time and an enormous quantity of nurturance.

When children become teenagers, they act as if hugging and kissing are taboo. My sons, ages sixteen and eighteen, are in this stage. In front of their friends, no hugs or kisses are permitted. But, it's still OK when no one's around. While teens don't allow expressions of love in public, they secretly crave them and often will permit parents to express affection in private. They need to come home after school and be greeted with the mere look of love in your eyes and the smile on your mouth. Every day of their lives they need to hear, "Hey son, did you have a good day? You know I love you and it's good to have you home." Parents often tell me, "Well she knows I love her even if I don't say it." Sorry, not so. Your teenager must hear it. You must say it and you must show it.

Melodie Beattie experienced one of the greatest nightmares that can befall anyone when she lost her twelve-year-old son in a skiing accident. In her book *Lessons of Love*, she writes about this tragedy and about her years in grief and recovery. One of the lessons she learned is the harsh reality that life is not fair and anything can happen. In only a moment everything you cherish can be ripped away. Do not let today slip past you. Let your child know today and every day that you deeply love him. Say it! Show it!

Go in the room where your teen is sitting. Silently look at her. Study her face, be aware of her vitality. What would you feel if this wonder of yours were suddenly taken from you? Try saying, "I love you so very much, always know that."

Maslow calls unconditional love *belonging*. A child must know where and to whom he belongs.

Conditional Love

Behaviorists place great emphasis on the second form of love, conditional love. They call it *contingency management*, which technically means giving social rein-forcement for appropriate behaviors. Humanists balk at this, claiming that it's destructive to healthy emotional development. The reality is that unconditional love is essential for developing healthy attitudes and for healthy emotional growth while conditional love is essential for teaching and motivating children to develop proper behaviors. Thus, both forms of expression of love are essential.

Conditional love occurs when you show your joy for a good test grade. It's praising your teenage son while he is working diligently on his science project. It's crying happy tears when he graduates from high school. Behaviorists know that without conditional love the young will quit trying. It gives them the moti-vation to give their "all" in their most important job—their education. And their education is essential for survival.

How long will Johnny come home with good test and homework grades if you don't show you care? He needs that smile, that praise, and those happy tears for his hard work. This is what motivates him to sustain his efforts for the long hours of sitting at a desk.

Abraham Maslow stated that unconditional love, the love of belonging, comes first, but after that comes what he calls "esteem." This is the love given as ap-preciation for performance. This is the love that acknowledges a young person's abilities, hard work, and sustained efforts. Maslow classified esteem as a higher level of need that occurs only after belonging has been met.

Your teenager needs both.

IT'S NOT TOO LATE

What if you feel that your life has been too hectic and fear that your teenager hasn't received sufficient love during her early life? Can any damage that may have occurred in the development of their existential attitudes be reversed? Yes!

In my career I've seen hardened gang members who were gun-toting, drug-dealing teens change dramatically when given the right kind of love. Why are they in a gang in the first place? Any tough gang member will tell you that to them their gang is their main source of love. It's their family. Each gang member will do anything for the love of any other member of their gang family. To belong to a gang young initiates will do things such as take a severe beating from the entire gang or go out and kill a rival gang member. How ironic that they will commit acts of hate to earn love from their peers.

Many parents feel that it is difficult to give love to a teenager who is behaving in obnoxious, rude, and abusive ways. This is the hallmark of the oppositional/defiant teen. Indeed, it is difficult to be affectionate to a teen who behaves this way, but you've learned how to control this behavior in chapter 5. Once your teen is under control, it will be easier for you to realize that she is *still a child and that she needs your love.* When she becomes well behaved, you'll find it easier to express your true feelings.

I've been a practicing therapist for over thirty years. At one time in my career I directed an adolescent home. Rarely, in that home or during my career, have I seen a teen who did not respond to genuine love. We must set boundaries when their behavior is obnoxious, but then our work is not complete until they feel loved.

Cults are another "family" for some troubled teens. Mystery usually enshrouds our understanding of cults. We're told how cults brainwash teens and how teens have to be reprogrammed in order to get them out. Cult leaders know a secret for enlisting teenagers. Only those teens who feel inadequately loved and cared for make good candidates for cult enlistment. The cult scouts are skilled in detecting needy teens. All the cult member needs to do is offer teens what they want, which is a sense of belonging and feeling loved. Cults offer a superficial atmosphere of love and caring. You and I would readily see through this veneer, but a love-starved teen doesn't. Once in the cult, a teen will do anything to retain the group's love. What that "anything" is depends on the philosophy of the cult, but usually that means bringing in money and new members. Psychologist Leon Festinger taught us that once committed to something, a person must modify his thinking or belief patterns to justify his decision. Therefore, a suggestible teenager will adopt the cult's belief system to justify being committed to the group and doing whatever behaviors he is asked.

Rhonda

When I first met Rhonda's father, he looked quite defeated. He stated that he'd been depressed for over a year. His daughter, now eighteen, had run off with a young man to join a cult religious group in another state. At the time Rhonda was pregnant by the young man she ran off with.

Her father and mother repeatedly wrote her, begging her to give up the cult, get rid of the young man, and give up the baby for adoption. They wrote that they would do anything for her if only she would get her life in order. Her return letters were rare. Her father read everything he could about cults. He was in the process of hiring a deprogrammer to kidnap her and re-brainwash her, hoping to get her back to being the healthy young lady he thought he had always known. On the surface and according to her parents, they were a well-functioning, upper-middle-class family. They believed Rhonda was deeply loved and had been given everything she wanted. I drew different conclusions.

I judged Mom and Dad to be extremely materialistic and very self-absorbed. Appearances meant everything to them. Rhonda went to the finest private schools. She wore the best clothing. She drove an expensive car. Her father worked enormous hours overseeing his several business ventures. Her mother spent most of her time at "the club," shopping, or getting her hair done. She and Rhonda rarely spent time together. Occasional shopping for Rhonda's clothes seemed to be the only time they did spend with each other. However, on these trips, mother controlled Rhonda's apparel choices.

I saw Rhonda as receiving mostly conditional love. Expressions of unconditional love seemed to be rare. Rhonda had to be a showpiece for her parents. She had to be perfect. I suspected that Rhonda felt Not OK about herself, and I bet that she probably experienced depressions, emptiness, and feelings of inadequacy—all resulting from an almost exclusive diet of conditional love.

I advised her parents to call off the abduction and completely change their approach. I explained to them the importance of unconditional love. I suggested they change the content of their letters. The letters should consist of "we deeply love you, always have, always will, and will accept you just as you are with no strings attached."

After several of these letters, Rhonda began to reply more frequently. The tone of her letters began to change. She began writing that she missed her parents. Eventually phone calls began to be exchanged. I instructed her parents to make no demands on her, merely to be good listeners to her concerns and problems but offer no solutions. They were to repeat how much they loved her and missed her. They requested that she and her boyfriend visit, and that they would love to see their "grandchild." The pattern of these letter exchanges continued for several more months.

Finally, Rhonda's father came in alone for a session. Rhonda had begun to write about how unhappy she was and how her relationship with her boyfriend was becoming increasingly strained. During this session, Rhonda's father openly cried. He knew she was opening up and expressing her true thoughts and feelings. I urged him to remain nonjudgmental and to continue to reassure her of his and her mother's deepest love.

Eventually, Rhonda visited her parents with her boyfriend and the baby. Her parents were instructed to be fully accepting and to freely express the depth of their love for her. Several more visits were made with Rhonda and her boyfriend returning to the cult after each visit. After a year, Rhonda asked to move back home with the baby but not with her boyfriend. Her parents agreed but, as I instructed, with only one provision, that she either get a job or go to school. Rhonda stated that that was exactly what she wanted.

Rhonda quit the cult and returned home with the baby. She began attending a nearby university. After several months she requested her own apartment near the school. Her parents consented. Rhonda's mother and father shifted their love to a form of total unconditional grace, which means *we love you no matter what*. This unconditional love dramatically changed the family's relationships. I eventually began seeing Rhonda as a patient. Overcoming her poor self-image and her episodes of depression took considerable work, but over time, she made considerable progress. She began to feel OK about herself and OK about her parents.

This case shows that what psychologists once thought were irreversible deeply entrenched attitudes can indeed be changed later in life. Granted there are some teenagers who are beyond redemption, but usually they are the products of the most severely negative childhood conditions, such as severe abuse and neglect. Most teenagers really want to feel loved. If parents are willing to change, so can their teenager.

Rhonda's mother truly loved her, but she had to learn to show it and to say it. When Rhonda was visiting, her mother would walk up to her, hug her, and gently say, "I love you so much, sweetheart."

I'M OK–YOU'RE OK

When a teenager lives in a truly loving environment his existential positions can become I'm OK–You're OK. We can better understand these two fundamental attitudes as:

I'm OK +	*You're OK +*
I have: God's Love	I can: Love God
Parental Love	Love My Parents
Other Adult's Love	Love Other Adults
Peer Love	Love My Peers

These two basic attitudes can henceforth form your teenager's basic personality and his outlook for the rest of his life. Once these attitudes are firmly entrenched it is doubtful that severe behavioral and emotional problems will ever develop.

RESPECT FOR PARENTS

Parents often feel that their teenager doesn't respect them. But notice if you will, the I'm OK position of parental love and the You're OK position of loving one's parents. Respect for parents is an important value that can best occur in a home environment where love is abundantly given to a teenager, and then the love will be returned in the form of respectful behavior. A teen who doesn't feel loved will not be able to act in a loving way toward authority figures.

You have learned how to control teen behaviors, but always remember if you want your teen to love and respect you, do the same for him.

References

Ackerman, D. (1994). *A natural history of love.* New York: Random House.

Alberti, R. E., and Emmons, M. L. (2001). *Your perfect right: Assertiveness and equality in your life and relationships.* (8th ed.) Atascedero, CA: Impact Publishers.

Alexander-Roberts, C. (1998). *ADHD and teens: A parents guide to making it through the tough years.* Dallas, TX: Taylor Publishing Company.

Amen, K. G., Paldi, J. H., and Thisted, R. A. (1993). Brain SPECT imaging. *Journal of the American Academy of Child and Adolescent Psychiatry,* 32, 1080–81.

American Psychiatric Association. (1994). *Diagnostic and statistical manual of mental disorders* (4th ed.). Washington, DC: APA.

American Psychological Association (2000). *Diagnostic and statistical manual of mental disorders, IV, revised text (DSM-IV, TR).* Washington, DC: American Psychiatric Association.

Anderson, P. (1981). *High in America: The incredible story behind the marijuana lobby and one man's effort to keep America stoned and out of jail.* New York: Viking.

Arnold, L. E., Kleykamp, K., Votolato, N., and Gibson, R. A. (1994). Potential link between dietary intake of fatty acids and behavior: Pilot exploration of serum lipids in attention deficity hyperactivity disorder. *Journal of Child and Adolescent Psychopharmacology,* 4, 171–82.

Asberg, M., Thoren, P., Trashman, C., Bertilsson, L., and Ringberger, V. (1976). Serotonin depression: A biochemical subgroup within the affective disorders. *Science,* 191, 478–80.

Baldessarini, R. J. (1985). *Chemotherapy in psychiatry: Principles and Practice.* Cambridge, MA: Harvard University Press.

Barkley, R. A. (1993). *ADHD—what do we know?* New York: A Guilford Press Video.

———. (1981). *Hyperactive children: A handbook for diagnosis and treatment.* New York: Guilford.

———. (1995). *Taking charge of ADHD: The complete authoritative guide for parents.* Omaha, NE: Boys Town Press.

Barlow, D. H., and Durand, V. M. (2001). *Abnormal psychology: An integrative approach.* Albany, NY: Brooks/Cole Publishing Company.

Beck, A. (1967). *Cognitive therapy and the emotional disorders.* New York: Meridian Books.

———. (1989). *Love is never enough: How couples can overcome misunderstandings, resolve conflicts, and solve problems.* San Francisco, CA: Harper Perennial.

243

Berstein, S., and Kaufman, M. (1960). A psychological analysis of apparent depression following Rauwolfian therapy. *Journal of Mt. Sinai Hospital, 27,* 525–30.

Birmaher, B., and Ryan, N. D. (1999). Neurobiological factors. In C.A. Essau and F. Petermann (Eds.), *Depressive disorders in children and adolescents: Epidemiology, risk factors and treatment* (pp. 287–318). Northvale, NJ: Jason Aronson, Inc.

Breggin, P. (2001). *The antidepressant fact book: What your doctor won't tell you about Prozac, Zoloft, Paxil, Celexa, and Luvox.* Cambridge, MA: Perseus Publishing.

————. (2002). *The Ritalin fact book: What your doctor won't tell you about ADHD stimulant drugs.* Cambridge, MA: Perseus Publishing.

————. (1991). *Toxic Psychiatry: Why therapy, empathy, and love must replace the drugs, electroshock, and biochemical theories of the "new psychiatry."* New York: St. Martin's.

————, and Cohen, D. (1999). *Your drug may be your problem: How and why to stop taking psychiatric drugs.* Cambridge, MA: Perseus Publishing.

Breggin, Peter R. (1998). *Talking back to Ritalin: What doctors aren't telling you about stimulants for children.* Maine: Common Coverage Press.

Castellanos, F. X., Giedd, J. N., Eckburg, P., Marsh, W. L., et al. (1994). Quantitative morphology of the caudate nucleus in attention deficit hyperactivity disorder. *American Journal of Psychiatry, 151,* 1791–96.

DeGrandpre, R. J. (1999). *Ritalin nation: Rapid fire, culture and the transformation of human consciousness.* New York: Norton.

Duman, R., Heninger, G., and Nestler, E. (1997). A molecular theory of depression. *Archives of General Psychiatry, 54,* 597–606.

DuPaul, G. J. (1998). A paper presented at the Convention of the American Psychological Association, San Francisco, CA.

Ellis, A. (1962). *Reason and emotion in psychotherapy.* New York: Lyle Stuart.

Eysenck, H. J. (1952). The effects of psychotherapy: An evaluation. *Journal of Consulting Psychology, 16,* 319–24.

Flick, G.L. (2000). *How to reach & teach teenagers with ADHD.* West Nyack, NY: The Center for Applied Research in Education.

Giedd, J. N., Castellanos, F. X., Casey, B. J., Kozuch, P., et al. (1994). Quantitative morphology of the corpus callosum in attention deficit hyperactivity disorder. *American Journal of Psychiatry, 151,* 665–69.

Greenblatt, J. M., Huffman, L. C., and Reiss, A. L. (1994). Folic acid in neurodevelopment and child psychiatry. *Progress in NeuroPsychopharmacology and Biological Psychiatry, 18,* 647–60.

Gunther, J. J. (1963). *Death be not proud.* San Francisco, CA: Harper Perennial Classics.

Heilman, K. M., Voeller, K. K., and Nadeau, S. E. (1991).

Hibbeln, J. (1998). Fish consumption and major depression. *The Lancet,* 1213.

Hofstatter, L., and Girgis, M. (1980). Psychiatric depression: The common therapeutic principle. *Southern Medical Journal, 73,* 870–72.

Jakubowski, P., and Lange, A. (1978). *The assertive option: Your rights and responsibilities.* Ottawa, Canada: Research Press.

Kenedy, D. M. (2002). *The ADHD Autism connection: A step toward more accurate diagnosis and effective treatment.* Colorado Springs, CO: Waterbrook Press.

Lahat, E., Avital, E., Barr, J., Berkovitch, M., et al. (1995). BAEP studies in children with attention deficit disorder. *Developmental Medicine and Child Neurology*, 37, 119–23.

Levy, F. (1991). The dopamine theory of attention deficit hyperactivity disorder. *Australian and New Zealand Journal of Psychiatry*, 2, 277–83.

Lewinsohn, P. M., and Rosenbaum, M. (1987). Recall of parental behavior by acute depressives, remitted depressives and nondepressives. *Journal of Personality and Social Psychology*, 52 (3), 611–19.

Maxmen, J. S., and Ward, N. G. (1993). *Psychotropic drugs fast facts* (2nd ed.). New York: Norton.

Mischel, W. (1977). *Personality and assessment.* New York: Wiley.

Moore, Thomas. (1992). *Care of the soul.* New York: HarperCollins.

Mosby, Inc. (2004). *2004 drug guide.* St. Louis, MO: Elsevier.

Murphy, K. (1997, August 25). Why Johnny can't sit still. *Business Week*, 194E4.

Nasrallah, H., et al. (1986). Cortical atrophy in young adults with a history of hyperactivity in childhood. *Psychiatry Research*, 17, 241–46.

National Institute of Health (1998). *Summation report.* The ADHD Consensus Conference, Bethesda, MD.

Oliver, M. (1999). *History of philosophy: Great thinkers from 600 B.C. to the present day.* New York: Barnes & Noble.

O'Meara, K. P. (2003). *A prescription for violence.* Insight On the News, January, 4.

Papolos, D., and Papolos, J. (2002). *The Bipolar child: The definitive and reassuring guide to childhood's most misunderstood disorder.* New York: Broadway Books.

Peale, N. V. (1952). *The power of positive thinking.* New York: Prentice Hall.

Peck, S. (1983). *The road less traveled: A new psychology of love, traditional values, and spiritual growth.* New York: Vintage/Ebury.

Physicians Desk Reference. (2000). New Jersey: Medical Economics Co., Inc.

Rosemond, J. K. (2201). *New parent power.* Kansas City, MO: Andrews McMeel.

Stein, D. B. (1990). *Controlling the difficult adolescent: The REST program (the Real Economy System for Teens).* Lanham, MD: University Press of America.

———. (1999). *Ritalin is not the answer: A drug-free, practical program for children diagnosed with ADD or ADHD.* San Francisco, CA: Jossey-Bass.

———, and Baldwin, S. (2000). Toward an operational definition of disease, in psychology and psychiatry: Implications for diagnosis and treatment. *International Journal of Risk and Safety in Medicine*, August, 65–99.

Sulser. F. (1976). From presynaptic neurone to the receptor and the nucleus. In D. Healy (1996). *The psychopharmacologists, vol. 3* (pp. 239–58). London: Chapman & Hall.

Swanson, J. M. (1998). *The biological basis for ADHD.* A paper presented at the Consensus conference of the National Institute for Health, Bethesda, MD.

Thoreau, H. D. (1854). *Walden: Life in the woods.* Boston: Tichnor & Fields.

Valenstein, E. (1998). *Blaming the brain: The truth about drugs and mental health.* New York: The Free Press.

Valentine, M. R. (1987). *How to deal with discipline problems in the schools: A practical Guide.* Dubuque, IA: Kendall/Hunt.

Willmer, P. (1995). Dopamine mechanisms in depression. In F.E. Bloom and D.J. Kupper (Eds.), *Psychopharmacology: The fourth generation* (pp. 921–31). New York: Raven.

Witters, W., Venturelli, P., and Hanson, G. (1992). *Drugs and society* (3rd ed.). Boston: Jones & Bartlett.

Woititiz, J. (1983). *Adult children of alcoholics.* Deerfield Beach, FL: Health Communications, Inc.

Yurgen-Todd, D. (1998, July 18). Teenage Brains are different. *The Associated Press.*

Zametkin, A. J., et al. (1993). Cerebral glucose metabolism in adults with hyperactivity of childhood onset. *New England Journal of Medicine, 323,* 1361–66.

Zametkin, A. J., Liebenauenauer, L. L., Gitzgerald, G. A., and King, A. C. (1993b). Brain metabolism in teenagers with attention deficit hyperactivity disorder. *Archives of General Psychiatry, 50,* 330–40.

Zeller, E., Barsky, J., Fouts, J., Kircheimer, W., and Van Orden, L. (1952). Influence of isonicotinic acid hydrazide (INH) an 1-isonicotinzl-2 isopropyl hydrazyde (IIH) on bacterial and mammalian enzymes. *Experientia, 8,* 349–50.

Zimbardo, P. G. (1977). *Shyness, what it is, what to do about it.* Maine: Addison Wesley.

———, and Radl, S. (1981). *The shy child.* New York: McGraw-Hill.

Index

About the Author

Dr. David B. Stein is professor of psychology at Longwood University, a state college in central Virginia. He teaches Abnormal Psychology, Abnormal Child Psychology, Applied Behavior Analysis (Behavior Modification), Psychopharmacology, Psychology and Law, The Psychology of Terrorism and Homeland Security, and, of course, Introduction to Psychology. He has an extensive list of research publications and professional presentations. He is a best-selling author, and his books include: *Ritalin Is Not the Answer: A Drug-Free, Practical Program, for Children Diagnosed with ADD or ADHD; The Ritalin Is Not the Answer Action Guide: An Interactive Companion to the Bestselling Drug-Free ADD/ADHD Parenting Program; Unraveling the ADD/ADHD Fiasco: A Guide for Successful Parenting; and Controlling the Difficult Adolescent: The REST Program (Real Economy Program for Teens).*

Affectionately called Dr. Dave, he has won numerous honors and awards for his thirty years of devoted work in offering drug-free treatment and parenting alternatives for the most difficult and out-of control-children and teens. He has been listed in *Who's Who Among America's Teachers* for many years; he is a diplomate, he was awarded the 2001 outstanding teacher and scholar at Longwood; and his research on ADD/ADHD treatment was selected as one of the top ten for media coverage at the 1998 American Psychological Association convention. His book *Ritalin Is Not the Answer* was endorsed as required reading by all parents, educators, and doctors at the 2001 Ritalin Litigation Conference in New York. Increasingly, pediatricians and family physicians, especially since his work was featured in the 2001 text *Advances in Medicine*, are prescribing his books as an alternative to drugs, and as they report, with excellent success. When asked to describe himself, he readily states, "My most important position is being dad to three wonderful children."

He is also a criminologist and is a credentialed, ongoing consultant to the Virginia State Police. His duties include criminal profiling, crisis and hostage negotiations, critical incident responding, crime scene investigations, and threat assessment. He has written numerous criminal justice and police journal articles and book chapters, and made numerous presentations.

Dr. Stein is a member of John Rosemond's Affirmative Parenting team. He now answers reader's questions at the Affirmative Parenting website (www.rosemond.com), and he is a featured writer for John's magazine *Traditional Parent*. He is a highly sought after public speaker. Information about him, his speaking schedule, and how to arrange speaking engagements may now be made from his website: www.theparentacademy.com.